Writing War, Writing Lives

War affects life writing and lives affect war writing. The traditional forms of life writing – memoir, biography, letters and diaries – buckle under the strain of war. War writing has fewer traditional forms but exists at a similar extreme. The eight chapters in this book, written by leading and up-and-coming scholars in the field, illuminate the creative innovations, improvisations, and implosions which happen when the demands of writing war and writing lives collide. Central to all is the question of authenticity: how can wars and lives be known and who can speak of them with authority? This volume has a generous chronological and generic range, beginning in the early 1800s and stretching to twenty-first-century texts, and covering letters, diaries, fiction, 'fakeries', poetry, biography, testimony, songs, objects and digital media. The mix of authors is similarly varied: Thomas Hardy, W. H. Auden and Elizabeth Bowen rub shoulders with Yousif M. Qasmiyeh (a contemporary Palestinian poet), Farah Baker (a Gazan teenager) and the writers behind the pen names Araki Yasusada and Jiri Kajanë. This book was originally published as a special issue of *Textual Practice.*

Kate McLoughlin is an Associate Professor of English Literature at the University of Oxford, UK.

Lara Feigel is a Senior Lecturer in English Literature at King's College, London, UK.

Nancy Martin is a doctoral student in English Literature at the University of Oxford, UK.

Writing War, Writing Lives

Edited by
Kate McLoughlin, Lara Feigel and Nancy Martin

Routledge
Taylor & Francis Group
LONDON AND NEW YORK

First published 2017
by Routledge

2 Park Square, Milton Park, Abingdon, Oxfordshire OX14 4RN
711 Third Avenue, New York, NY 10017

Routledge is an imprint of the Taylor & Francis Group, an informa business

First issued in paperback 2018

British Library Cataloguing in Publication Data
A catalogue record for this book is available from the British Library

ISBN: 978-1-138-69368-5 (hbk)
ISBN: 978-0-367-02399-7 (pbk)

Typeset in AdobeGaramondPro
by diacriTech, Chennai

Publisher's Note
The publisher accepts responsibility for any inconsistencies that may have arisen during the conversion of this book from journal articles to book chapters, namely the possible inclusion of journal terminology.

Contents

Citation Information

The chapters in this book were originally published in the *Textual Practice*, volume 29, issue 7 (December 2015). When citing this material, please use the original page numbering for each article, as follows:

Introduction
Writing war, writing lives
Kate McLoughlin, Lara Feigel and Nancy Martin
Textual Practice, volume 29, issue 7 (December 2015) pp. 1219–1223

Chapter 1
Missing letters: reading the interstices in archival correspondence from the Napoleonic Wars and in Thomas Hardy's The Trumpet-Major
Kate McLoughlin
Textual Practice, volume 29, issue 7 (December 2015) pp. 1225–1244

Chapter 2
'And all because it is war!': First World War diaries, authenticity and combatant identity
Nancy Martin
Textual Practice, volume 29, issue 7 (December 2015) pp. 1245–1263

Chapter 3
Reframing life/war 'writing': objects, letters and songs of Indian soldiers, 1914–1918
Santanu Das
Textual Practice, volume 29, issue 7 (December 2015) pp. 1265–1287

Chapter 4
'The only diary I have kept': visionary witnessing in the second world war short story
Lara Feigel
Textual Practice, volume 29, issue 7 (December 2015) pp. 1289–1309

Chapter 5
Representing Nazi crimes in post-Second World War life writing
Victoria Stewart
Textual Practice, volume 29, issue 7 (December 2015) pp. 1311–1330

Chapter 6
Statelessness and the poetry of the borderline: André Green, W.H. Auden and Yousif M. Qasmiyeh
Lyndsey Stonebridge
Textual Practice, volume 29, issue 7 (December 2015) pp. 1331–1354

Chapter 7
'Paper is patient': tweets from the '#AnneFrank of Palestine'
Hope Wolf
Textual Practice, volume 29, issue 7 (December 2015) pp. 1355–1374

Chapter 8
Inventing the eyewitness: Araki Yasusada and Jiri Kajanë
Sue Vice
Textual Practice, volume 29, issue 7 (December 2015) pp. 1375–1394

Notes on Contributors

Santanu Das is a Reader in English Literature at King's College London, UK.

Lara Feigel is a Senior Lecturer in English Literature at King's College, London, UK.

Nancy Martin is a doctoral student in English Literature at the University of Oxford, UK.

Kate McLoughlin is an Associate Professor of English Literature at the University of Oxford, UK.

Victoria Stewart is a Reader in Modern and Contemporary Literature at the University of Leicester, UK.

Lyndsey Stonebridge is a Professor of Modern Literature and History at the University of East Anglia.

Sue Vice is a Professor in the School of English, University of Sheffield, UK.

Hope Wolf is a Lecturer in British Modernist Literature at the University of Sussex, UK.

Kate McLoughlin[a], Lara Feigel[b] and Nancy Martin[a]

Introduction

Writing war, writing lives

War affects life writing and lives affect war writing. In the eight articles in this volume, we see forms of life writing breaking their boundaries under the pressure of war. The ways in which this pressure is exerted are many and various. War has a massive impact on the individual (it can force a person into a new role, insist on new beginnings, efface identity, expose the body to violence); imposes certain narratives (military narratives, national narratives, protest narratives and personal narratives, among them); creates a demand for new life stories (military leaders, rank-and-file soldiers, combatants and non-combatants come into being), not least through the impulse to memorialise; produces tales that individuals need to tell (often cathartically); and creates an impetus to understand (on the part of both combatant and civilian). In such circumstances, standard forms of life writing (diary/journal, memoir, autobiography, biography) buckle. War writing has fewer (if any) standard forms, but as the traditional modes of life writing are manipulated, stretched, broken and eschewed, the telling of war that occurs simultaneously undergoes similar treatment.

The concept around which the eight articles in the volume cluster is authenticity. As Laura Marcus has noted, the '"referential", external dimension' of verification in relation to life writing has been largely superseded by '"internal" concepts of veracity', as evidenced by the '"authenticity" of the person', 'coherence concepts of truth', 'fictionality as a higher order of truth' and '"style" as the act of an individual and as revelation and authentication of that individual'.[1] A similar movement can be seen with regard to war writing, with the credibility of the war writer, earned through first-hand witnessing or demonstrated via the autopsy tropes, at a premium.[2] As the writing of lives enters the context of war, the need to achieve, or at least to evince, authorial authenticity and credibility is redoubled. In consequence, genre is warped and epistemology made patchy. Demonstrating this, the articles assembled here have a generous chronological and generic range, beginning in the early 1800s and stretching to twenty-first-century texts, and covering letters, diaries, fiction, 'fakeries', poetry, biography, testimony, songs, objects and digital media. They are arranged in chronological order of conflict – with one exception (discussed below) – allowing both a sense of historical succession to inform the intersecting generic and thematic strands and a sense of historical specificity to complicate them.

In 'Missing Letters: Reading the Interstices in Archival Correspondence from the Napoleonic Wars and in Thomas Hardy's *The Trumpet-Major*', Kate McLoughlin explores the textual effects of the wartime letter which is keenly expected but never written. From May 1806 to November 1808, Lieutenant Edward Teasdale, a member of the British forces fighting the French in Jamaica, sent letters to his mother in Yorkshire, begging her to write back to him. With recourse to these letters, now in the archive of the National Army Museum, London, McLoughlin notes the special value attached to personal correspondence during military service and illuminates the textual traces formed by the desire of and hope for letters. She then analyses the phenomenon of expected, but unwritten, letters in Hardy's novel *The Trumpet-Major*, published in 1880 but set contemporaneously with the Teasdale archive. Reading the interstices – the places where letters *should* be but fail to be – McLoughlin suggests that missing correspondence (whether expected by or from those on military service) summons into existence 'phantom-narratives' comprising 'suspended activity, waiting, introspection [and] stasis'. Here the generic crisis caused in life-writing by mass, industrialised, global warfare begins to make itself known, as large seams of experience prove resistant to available means of representation. But by exploiting phantom-narratives, Hardy introduces a distinctive epistemological texture to the novel which possesses a 'felt' authenticity unamenable to standard means of verification.

One hundred years after the Napoleonic Wars, the First World War was marked by a similar sense of the inadequacy of discursive resources. Nancy Martin's '"And all because it is war!": First World War Diaries, Authenticity and Combatant Identity' moves from the unwritten to the hitherto unexamined and unpublished. Analysing war diaries written by British soldiers during the First World War, her article explores how the decision to enlist in the military was articulated to the private self with reference to public representations of heroic masculinity or 'manliness': a first phase of self-redefinition. In a second phase, soldier diary-writers, now accustomed to life on the Western Front, turned to *things* – body parts, muddy breeches, milk, jam and mail – to express their new daily existence. A third phase involved re-casting soldierly identity as one of passive endurance, rather than heroic action. In defining and describing these phases, Martin reveals how war writing – in the form of recording the quotidian realities of combat service – *becomes* life writing, an arduous, ongoing process of self-reauthentication.

Martin's diary-writers grapple painfully to articulate their militarised selves, introducing to the private form of the diary an array of resources, from the motifs of public discourse to the description of everyday objects. Santanu Das's 'Reframing Life/War "Writing": Objects, Letters and Songs of Indian Soldiers, 1914–1918' goes a step further in arguing for a 'reconceptualisation' of the nature of life writing in the light of the experience of the more than one million men from undivided India who fought in the First World War. Largely non-literate, these men did not leave accounts in the standard forms of life writing – diaries, memoirs, autobiographies. If Martin's diary-writers *describe* mundane objects in an effort to express life in war, Das's sepoys tell their stories *through* objects – trench artefacts, dictated letters, and sound recordings, examples of which Das has recovered through intensive archival research. 'Life *writing*' and 'war *writing*' do not capture the forms of these stories, whose authenticity resides, as with Hardy's phantom-narratives, in their *feel*.

Moving to the next global conflict, Lara Feigel's article '"The Only Diary I Have Kept": Visionary Witnessing in the Second World War' continues the argument that the extreme experiences that comprise war put pressure on traditional forms of life writing. In the specifically surreal context of the London Blitz, writers such as Elizabeth Bowen, Henry Green, Rose Macaulay and William Sansom found the short story, which, by virtue of its very brevity is an apt generic vehicle for representing the strange or unseen, the perfect form in which to bear witness to the events they were participating in as firemen, ambulance drivers and ARP wardens. Conveying these events by means of an 'unrealistic realism', these writers turned the short story into 'a kind of war diary'. Re-thinking the 'visionary' short story as offering a particular kind of authenticity, Feigel illuminates the way in which genres not immediately associated with life writing become newly relevant forms of personal testimony in war.

In 'Representing Nazi Crimes in Post-Second World War Life Writing', Victoria Stewart continues the exploration of the pressure war exerts on genre. Stewart's article concerns postwar biographies of female Special Operations Executive agents – Jerrard Tickell's *Odette: The Story of a British Agent*; R. J. Minney's *Carve Her Name with Pride*; Jean Overton Fuller's *Madeleine*; and Elizabeth Nicholas's *Death Be Not Proud* – whose authors faced the challenge of missing or incomplete information about their subjects. Stewart characterises their responses to this challenge as 'fictionalizing' (in the case of Tickell and Minney) and 'fragmentizing' (in the case of Fuller and Nicholas) and illustrates how both techniques undermine the stability of biography as a genre. While such undermining may be inevitable in the project of representing lives, Stewart shows that the impulse to do so is at its height when life writing is also doing duty as war writing.

Lyndsey Stonebridge's 'Statelessness and the Poetry of the Borderline: André Green, W. H. Auden and Yousif M. Qasmiyeh' looks at the difficulties of form-finding from yet another angle. As Stonebridge notes, every conflict creates refugees, but the wars of the twentieth century produced population movements on an unprecedented scale. Traumatic testimony has long been the life writing genre of choice for those wanting to give voice to the dispossessed. But, Stonebridge asks, can such testimony really capture the complexity of this territorial violence? Taking the psychoanalyst André Green's notion of the 'borderline' as a starting point, Stonebridge explores the work of two poets of exile and displacement: W. H. Auden, who voluntarily departed from his native England as the storm-clouds of war gathered in 1939, and Yousif M. Qasmiyeh, a Palestinian poet now based in Oxford. In Stonebridge's words, both poets can be described as 'attending to the negative', to 'a state which is neither quite one thing nor another'. This is statelessness, and, in Stonebridge's analysis, both Auden and Qasmiyeh, rather than turning to traditional forms of life writing, instead exploit the capacity of poetry to give expression to this condition of life and of war.

The penultimate article, Hope Wolf's '"Paper is Patient": Tweets from the "#AnneFrank of Palestine"', turns to one of the most recent incarnations of life writing: the tweet. Farah Baker, a teenager living in Gaza who used Twitter to report the bombings she witnessed over the summer of 2014, has been controversially named the '#AnneFrank of Palestine'. Wolf discusses how Baker responded to the value placed upon authenticity and immediacy in war reporting in her tweets, while simultaneously exploiting the medium's capacity to rally support and express solidarity. She also traces the extent to which the digital meme can meet the challenge of reconciling the need for expressions of commonality with the recognition of complexity. As is the case with the analogue paper diary, the ability of users of social media to manipulate form is limited, but the limitations can prove – and do, in Baker's case – to be a creative stimulus. Wolf's article reveals inventiveness and resourcefulness in the use of digital media that maintain the (counter-)tradition of genre-defiance already encountered.

We have placed the final article – Sue Vice's 'Inventing the Eyewitness: Araki Yasusada and Jiri Kajanë' – out of chronological order of conflict, since it addresses the satiric end-point of the various generic developments which occur when war puts life writing forms under extreme pressure. Vice analyses the work of two writers who have been presented as if they were eyewitnesses to war and historical calamity: the poetry of Araki Yasusada about the atomic bombing of Hiroshima, and the short stories of Jiri Kajanë about the last years of Enver Hoxha's Cold War-era dictatorship. Neither writer actually existed; rather, their work was composed by those named as their translators. Vice shows how, in each case, the eagerness with which the work was received under its false attribution reveals the high market value accorded to testimonial works, a valorisation that persists despite (as the preceding articles demonstrate) the faltering of such forms in the face of war. The cultural capital of life writing, that is, is imported into a genre – war writing – that struggles to bear it, even as the 'translators' question and satirise this process and the authentication that it purports to confer.

In bringing together war writing and life writing, we hope to illuminate the boundaries and intersections of both. Amid an array of discoveries, the strongest emerging theme is that armed conflict challenges any attempts of life writers to purport to the factual. Under the impact of war, the fictionalising, form-breaking, rebellious tendencies of writing lives are released in a way that is creatively productive andauthenticity is re-thought. In response, a matching critical imaginativeness is called for.

[a] *University of Oxford*
[b] *King's College*

Disclosure statement

No potential conflict of interest was reported by the authors.

Notes

1 Marcus, Laura, *Auto/Biographical Discourses: Criticism, Theory, Practice* (Manchester: Manchester University Press, 1994), p. 261.

2 See, further, McLoughlin, Kate, *Authoring War: The Literary Representation of War from the Iliad to Iraq* (Cambridge: Cambridge University Pres, 2011), ch. 1 'Credentials'.

Kate McLoughlin

Missing letters: reading the interstices in archival correspondence from the Napoleonic Wars and in Thomas Hardy's *The Trumpet-Major*

An epistolary cache held in London's National Army Museum is notable for letters which are expected but not written. Lieutenant Edward Teasdale, deployed to Jamaica in 1807 as part of the British forces fighting the French in the Napoleonic Wars, wrote home repeatedly to his mother in Yorkshire, pleading with her to correspond with him. But he only ever received one letter from her. The lack of letters nonetheless produces a palpable sense of desire, hope and expectation. The same phenomenon is also evident in Thomas Hardy's novel *The Trumpet-Major*, published in 1880 but set during the Napoleonic Wars. Reading the interstices – the places where letters *should* be but fail to be – reveals the importance of 'phantom-narratives' in life writing and war writing. Phantom-narratives not only reveal otherwise unarticulated hopes and desires but also vary the epistemological texture of the novel.

'We rather expected a letter from Bob before this,' comments Bob Loveday's father in Thomas Hardy's *The Trumpet-Major* (1880) to a sailor who has brought news from Bob's ship (p. 331).[1] Along with the characters, the reader has also been expecting a letter from Bob, primed by the pattern of news-delivery in the novel and the narratological pressures exerted by his absence. The epistemological significance of letters (real and fictional) is well established: the letter troubles the boundaries between public and private,[2] between 'the utilitarian and the aesthetic aspects of writing',[3] between spontaneity and staginess, between self-construction and self-revelation. The history of letters has been claimed as the 'history of the post-Enlightenment subject',[4] particularly the female subject,[5] though the association between the letter and the self demands caution: as Mary Favret has pointed out, the 'transition from private expression to public property' at the end of the eighteenth century removed the letter from its 'fiction of individualism' and 'complicated its "feminine" identity'.[6] When a letter forms part of a series, these considerations are joined by others: dialogism, intersubjectivity, the notion of a discursive sphere. This article concerns a series of letters, or an 'epistolarium',[7] held in the National Army Museum in London. Dating from 14 May 1806 to an unknown day in 1809, this series shares the Napoleonic Wars setting of *The Trumpet-Major*. As is often the case, only one side of the correspondence remains in the archive. In such situations, the other side is very often inferred (and inference is a major interpretative mode in epistolary reading). But the epistolarium in this case comprises a set of letters in which, somewhat unusually,[8] only one side is extant because only one side was ever written. In this article, I engage in interstitial reading: reading (in) the gaps. My aim is to build upon scholarly thinking about epistolarity[9] to consider the epistemological significance of the missing letter (noting the implications for conceptualising authenticity): not the letter written but undelivered, about which Thomas Karshan, in particular, has written so illuminatingly,[10] but the letter desired and expected yet never composed and so never received. In the later part of the piece, I turn to *The Trumpet-Major* to suggest how this significance is exploited in fiction. The epistolarium and Hardy's novel form a natural pair of subjects for comparison not only because they both relate to the Napoleonic Wars, but also because both evince powerful 'phantom-narratives' arising from missing letters. Considered as phenomena of life writing, phantom-narratives reveal unspoken desires and preoccupations which may be impervious to authentication by corroborative evidence or rhetorical analysis but which nonetheless feel real. As phenomena of war writing, they expose the heightened anxieties produced when individual and collective fates in an armed conflict are unknown. In both cases, they add a complicating epistemological layer.

The epistolarium in question is a set of ten letters and two other documents.[11] Five of the letters ('letters A–E')[12] were sent by Edward Teasdale, a lieutenant in the 54th (West Norfolk) Regiment of Foot on military service in Jamaica during the Napoleonic Wars, to his mother, Mrs. Jane Teasdale of Darlington, Durham. Three further letters ('letters F, G and H') were sent to Mrs. Teasdale from Captain Robert Frederick of the 54th Foot Regiment. Another letter ('letter I') was sent to Mrs. Teasdale by a representative of Greenwood & Cox, the regiment's London agents, and the final letter ('letter J') was sent to her by Major W. J. Currey of the 54th. The two other documents are a notarised copy of Teasdale's will and a final statement of his financial accounts. Extracts from letters A-F and J[13] can be found in the appendix at the end of this article and the reader is recommended to peruse them before continuing.

*

This is a reticent epistolarium. Aside from a reference to the large drops of perspiration on the backs of his hands in letter C, Teasdale conveys nothing sensory of the environment in which he finds himself.[14] (Materially, the letters themselves are more eloquent, creased by folding, featuring the remains of red wax seals and postmarks and, in one case (letter C), substantiating by the large paper size Teasdale's apology 'I could get no Letter Paper her'.) Nor is there any description of garrison life or of any fighting he may have been engaged in. (On its arrival in Jamaica, the 54th's duties were 'diversified by the suppression of a mutiny in one of the West Indian Regiments': this is not remarked.)[15] No fellow-soldiers are mentioned by name. Teasdale makes his failure to be forthcoming explicit in letter C ('You must not expect that I shall write a great deal about the country and curiosities. they may be curious when you see them but hardly worth recounting') and letter D ('You cannot expect that I can have much to inform you concerning myself'). This lack of desire to import information is, *prima facie*, surprising. As Favret rightly points out, 'war correspondence constructs the distance between the warriors and their loved ones as an epistemological gap'.[16] A letter home is an opportunity to reduce that gap, to bring war home by conveying some of its realities to civilian family members. Teasdale does not take advantage of the opportunity. Instead, his letters evince three marked, inter-related preoccupations. These are the health risks posed by the Jamaican climate, his own family back home in England and letter-writing itself.

In the conditions of war – carrying out dangerous duties in an alien environment – it is scarcely surprising that soldiers' thoughts turn to family and home. 'Write to me! Write to me!! Write to me!' begged 1st Lieutenant Leopold Wolf of the Imperial and Royal Austro-Hungarian artillery in a letter from the Eastern Front to his fiancée Christl Lang at the beginning of 1916.[17] Discussing the First World War, Christa Hämmerle notes that letter-writers tend 'to orient themselves towards the normality of the pre-war period':[18] letters are a bolt-hole of familiarity. Teasdale's concern in letter D that 'many changes may have happened' while he has been away perfectly expresses a widespread, transhistorical concern. (The British Field Service Post Card via which troops in the First World War conveyed terse and highly regulated statements of news by deleting alternatives, included the option:

I have received no letter from you

{lately

{for a long time

– indicating that desire for mail was as important a message as the set of options including 'I am quite well' / 'I have been admitted into hospital'.)[19] By the time of the Second World War, it was taken for granted that, in the words of the Director General of the Post Office, 'fresh and frequent news from home was necessary for the soldier's comfort'.[20] General Montgomery ordered mail deliveries to begin in France on D-Day itself,[21] and, writing in 1944, the directors of the Mass Observation project noted the view that demoralising letters from home 'lost Germany the last war'.[22] As Jenny Hartley argues, reinforcing Hämmerle's point, letters allow a 'long-distance mothering role' to be performed, as women reproduce 'dailiness' for their soldier offspring, so creating 'parallel lives for those away from home'.[23] In his letters, Teasdale shows signs of yearning for such 'dailiness', inquiring after the neighbours (letter C) and his tenants (letter D). Liz Stanley adds the observation that letters are 'strongly metonymic of the *particular* writer, being a kind of proxy for them':[24] they bear a mother's hand in the form of her script and her touch in her contact with the paper. As Jacques Derrida writes in *The Post Card*: 'I touch you by sending you whatever, even if it is nothing, even if it is without the slightest interest.'[25] The sentiment illuminates Teasdale's remarks in letters C and D that his mother should not expect him to write much about himself or his new environment. Why, then, write? Because the sending of the news that there is no news is still a 'touch'. In Teasdale's view – prospectively endorsing Derrida – lack of content ('if all you wish to tell me about your selves will not make up a Letter' (letter C)) is an inadequate excuse for not writing, for not sending a reciprocal 'touch'. Teasdale's touch is evident in the grubby, blotted materiality of his own letters, whose signal presence renders the absence of similar objects from his mother's hands all the more poignant.

But Teasdale's obsession with receiving letters seems to be something more than a reaching for the familiar from an alien environment. He does not just want diverting news from home, he wants detailed information about his family, even unto his sixteenth cousin (letter D). He wants to know where his paternal great-grandfather lived and what he was (letter B). He wants to know whether another relative had any children (letter B) (perhaps viewing himself as a possible heir). He has discovered that a William Teasdale has died in Jamaica; he wonders if they can be related (letter C). If this is reducing the 'epistemological gap' between himself and his family, it is not in terms of bringing war home but of bringing home to war. Teasdale must know exactly who his family is and how he fits into it. Partly, this must reflect his desire for a 'touch': if news is lacking, factual information will do. But another possible explanation for his intense preoccupation with family lies in another of his three main subjects: the lethal Jamaican climate.

The risks to non-natives' health posed by the hot and humid conditions in Jamaica were very real. 'In carrying on the war in the West Indies, the hostile sword is merciful,' wrote Edmund Burke, 'the country in which we engage is the dreadful enemy'.[26] As Alan Bewell notes, soldiers and sailors were 'the people most likely to occupy the epidemiological contact zones opened up by colonial expansion' and so 'the ones most affected by colonial disease'.[27] Teasdale's regiment, the 54th Norfolk, lost 50 out of 78 officers and 469 out of 518 rank-and-file to 'climate' in the five years from 1807 to 1812:[28] an 87% mortality rate. Unsurprisingly, then, Teasdale often contemplates his own death: when he does so, he requests both news and information from home. Nothing comes. His desperate wish for familial data then translates into a preoccupation with the non-appearance of letters: from his siblings, but above all from his mother. In the absence of any replies to respond to, he focuses instead upon his third main subject – the practicalities of letter-writing – prescribing contents and length (letters B–D), speculating about delivery times and arrangements (letters A–D), repeating his address (letter D), explaining the large paper size (letter C) and directing the carriers to take especial care (letter B). When he reflects on not having heard from his mother, he expresses incredulity at the idea that his letters might not have reached her (letters C and D), and at a couple of points (letters C and D) seems to assume that she cannot have directed hers to him clearly enough. The unwritten letters form a vacuum in the epistolarium, sucking in attention and inducing in Teasdale a thematic stasis: until his mother writes to him, he can only write about the fact that she has not written to him. The eventual appearance of a letter from her galvanises him into chattiness (letter E); this letter is signed off with renewed affection.

There is not enough archival evidence to explain why Teasdale received only one letter from his mother in two years:[29] hypotheses might range from the possibility that she did indeed feel she had nothing to say to him to the possibility that she did write but the letters were lost between Darlington and her son's regiment.[30] But, for present purposes, the precise reason for her silence matters less than its effect. The impact of the unwritten and unreceived letter depends upon the conventional perception of correspondence as dialogic. Scholars of epistolarity such as Clare Brant, Rebecca Earle, Susan M. Fitzmaurice, Patricia Meyer Spacks, Margaretta Jolly and Liz Stanley have explored the implications of bivocal, dialectical letter-exchange, constructing correspondences as micro-canons representative of relational discourse and consensual 'truth'.[31] In 'Notes on the Image of the Undelivered Letter', Thomas Karshan emphasises the habit in modern culture, derived from Wittgenstein's ideas of communication through language (and resonating with Habermas's notions of rational communication), of conceptualising language 'as a message sent from a definite addresser to addressee'.[32] The undelivered message or letter therefore figures, in Karshan's analysis, 'resistance to the message-picture of language'.[33] Subverting the linguistic model of the definite message, the undelivered letter also stands for such indirect and indirectly communicated phenomena as 'nonsense, dream, nightmare, childhood, desire, incest, grief, obscurity, doubt, failure', all of which populate the realm of art.[34] The undelivered letter ruptures dialogue, fractures the discursive sphere, undermines efficient message-exchange.

The unwritten letter could also be said to do all of these things. But, crucially, it also strikes at the very inception of communication: message-creation. The letter unreceived because unwritten figures there being nothing to say. Indeed, it is not only that there is nothing to say: even the saying of nothing – the very trivial or phatic ('You cannot expect that I can have much to inform you concerning myself') – has been eschewed. No touch or trace has been vouchsafed. But as Teasdale's reaction to the lack of letters from his mother shows, the effect of silence is not neutral. It produces a curious stasis in the recipient (who is also, simultaneously, a non-recipient), a textual waiting, an obsession with reply. In their fervour to elicit response, his letters become dominated by the interrogative mood; indeed his very last (written) words to his mother are in the form of a question, asking whom a Yorkshire acquaintance has married. Denied dialogue, his letters also turn inward, focusing upon the task of writing, becoming meta-letters (note in this regard his insistence on the importance of being able to speak and write English well in letters C and E). His disappointment and frustration are palpable. Even stronger is the sense of his desire. This is the desire which, as Shari Benstock argues, constitutes the 'link between the postal system and psychoanalysis',[35] a link forged from expectation and from satisfaction denied and deferred. In the context of war, this desire becomes unusually charged because, for both the soldier on service and his loved ones waiting at home, the missing letter is a *memento mori.* Teasdale desires letters in order to forestall death: they are both signs of life and a distraction from ubiquitous reminders of mortality. As a micro-genre of war writing, the missing letter is a death-haunted interstice in which it is possible simultaneously to hope for the best and fear the worst.

Now, the significance of the unwritten letter is of a different epistemological quality to the externally verifiable narrative in life writing and war writing. Letters that are present, whether in actuality or in fiction, construct a narrative of *prima facie* authenticity that can be validated empirically, on the basis of corroborative evidence or even by rhetorical analysis. An absence of expected letters, by contrast, proposes a phantom-narrative that at best can only be gauged by inference. The phenomenon complicates the notion of authenticity since the matter of such phantom-narratives – hopes, desires and expectations – *feels* real. The unwritten letter induces a heartfelt response, in other words. As a feature of life writing, the phantom-narrative is a guide to what might otherwise be unspoken aspirations and yearnings. As a feature of war writing, it testifies both to the distressing unknowability of an armed conflict's outcome and to the particular agony that is an individual's uncertain fate. Used as a device in fiction, the missing letter deploys all the power of the phantom-narrative. In the rest of this article, I explore the ways the psychical and textual consequences of the unwritten letter are exploited by Thomas Hardy in *The Trumpet-Major*, which, though published in 1880, is set in the period of the Napoleonic Wars and which sends a character, Bob Loveday, to fight, as Edward Teasdale did, in the West Indies. This time, the letters are expected, not *by* but *from*, a soldier on active service, revealing a symmetry between hopes and desires in wartime at home and in the field.

The most famous undelivered letter in Hardy's oeuvre is the note thrust under Angel Clare's door by Tess Durbeyfield, informing him that Alec Durbeyfield raped her years before. The next day, Angel's demeanour to her is unchanged, prompting in Tess a frenzy of speculation – 'Could it be that her doubts were childish? that he forgave her; that he loved her for what she was, just as she was, and smiled at her disquiet as at a foolish nightmare? Had he really received her note?'[36] – which both mirrors and intensifies the narrative uncertainty also created. Tess later notices the 'faint white margin of the envelope' under the carpet, and herself experiences a 'feeling of faintness',[37] the white paper and her complexion figuring the uncommunicability of what she wished to impart (the sheet appears to be blank), the phantom-narrative of how things might have been different. Similar spectral narratives are also connected with unwritten letters in *The Trumpet-Major.*

The significance of the missing letters in *The Trumpet-Major* depends on the patterns of news-delivery established early in the novel. As Earle notes, letters were a source of news long before the existence of newspapers.[38] In fact, the two forms overlapped, as eighteenth-century newspapers published private correspondence from the front, with the effect, in Favret's words, of 'producing the [Revolutionary and Napoleonic] war in the guise of a serialized epistolary fiction'.[39] In *The Trumpet-Major,* newspapers and letters receive particular attention. Only 'one solitary newspaper', 'more than a fortnight old', reaches Overcombe (p. 94). Received by old Squire Derriman, it is read to him by Anne, and then passed on to Anne's mother, who acts to the villagers as 'letter-writer and reader, and general translator from the printing [*sic*] tongue' (p. 94):

> It was not without satisfaction that she stood at her door of an evening, newspaper in hand, with three or four cottagers standing round, and poured down their open throats any paragraph that she might choose to select from the stirring ones of the period. When she had done with the sheet Mrs. Garland passed it on to the miller, the miller to the grinder, and the grinder to the grinder's boy, in whose hands it became subdivided into half pages, quarter pages, and irregular triangles, and ended its career as a paper cap, a flagon bung, or a wrapper for his bread and cheese. (p. 94)

This is news – and textuality – as sustenance and as material object associated with consumption, recycled until it is exhausted.

Like the newspaper, in Overcombe a letter is an event (and here there is a potential difference from the Teasdale case: there is no evidence on which to hypothesise a communal reception of either the letters he sent to Darlington or those he craved in Jamaica). In the novel, at least six letters arrive. Bob writes a letter to Anne from his ship – 'short, but as much as she could expect in the circumstances' (p. 318) – its brevity reflecting its author's own ephemeral affections. John writes a letter to Bob to inquire if his affection for Anne is genuine; the confirmatory reply 'crackle[s] warningly in his waistcoat pocket' as he lays his hand upon it, its monitory presence reducing him to 'dumbness and gloom' (p. 351). Bob and John send one more letter each to the other, and there are also the 'letters' of old Squire Derriman – 'NW' and 'NE' (p. 252) – which he notes on a piece of paper and entrusts to Anne for safe-keeping and which later go astray. These are, by and large, metonymic letters, standing in for their authors. Two other letters in the novel have somewhat greater figurative significance: a letter from Bob to his father, the miller, containing news of his return, and a letter from Anne to John in which she confesses to having misjudged him.

When Miller Loveday is informed that a letter has been lying at the post-office for him for three days, the authorial voice comments, 'A letter at this time was such an event for hamleteers, even of the miller's respectable standing, that Loveday thenceforward was thrown into a fit of distraction' (p. 150). The thought of the unopened letter makes him unable to 'sleep a wink' (p. 151), he is described as 'anxiously waiting' for it (p. 156) and its arrival – even before the news it contains is known – becomes news itself: 'It had already been noised abroad that miller Loveday had received a letter [. . .] Letters were matters of public moment, and everybody in the parish had an interest in the reading of those rare documents' (p. 158). The prospect of the contents becoming known increases the momentum of the novel's narrative progress, and this proleptic impetus is reinforced by the miller receiving a foreshadowing of the letter: 'I now call to mind that there was a letter in the candle three days ago this very night – a large red one' (p. 149). A spark in a candle, according to Roger Ebbatson, 'was thought to indicate that the person to whom it pointed was about to receive a letter'.[40] A sudden flare, a coming letter is both eye-catching and potentially dangerous: this 'red' letter, with its news that Bob is coming home to be married – potentially a 'red-letter day'[41] – does indeed provoke consternation in Anne: 'The blood swept impetuously up her face [. . .] and as suddenly went away again, leaving her rather paler than before' (p. 156). The sudden flush mirrors the red spark in the candle, and the ensuing pallor is reminiscent of Tess's complexion when she discovers that her note to Angel has gone astray. The letter, that is, connotes life (redness, heat, sexual activity); its absence death (etiolation). The next letter in the novel is written from Anne to John, after she discovers his true motivation for sending away Matilda Johnson. The reader's attention is directed towards this letter as a material object: Anne holds it, 'sealed', in her hand (p. 235), Bob 'dislike[s] the sight of it' (p. 235) and it rests on the mantelpiece in view of the household. John reports reading it 'fifty times a day' (p. 270) and 'kisse[s] the writing' (p. 277). Highly visible, the letter is even more apparent when it goes missing. The fact of its having been sent is of differing importance to Anne and the miller, the former regretting the encouragement it will give to John, the latter wishing to ensure he receives it. Its departure intensifies, and figures, the narrative conflict.

Present letters therefore perform significant figurative and narratological work in the novel, but even more significant are two which Bob fails to write. How, it might be asked, can an unwritten letter be known about? As in the Teasdale epistolarium, the absent texts are marked by the desire and expectations of the would-be recipients. The first instance arises when Bob unexpectedly leaves to join the *Victory* under Captain Hardy. The lack of a letter from him is evident in Anne's appetite for news, which John tries to satisfy with articles from the newspaper ('not a word about the *Victory*' (p. 327)); in the efforts of the household to glean information; in the circulation of rumours; and in the painful omission of the names of the ordinary seamen in the death-lists. Then, the non-arrival of a letter from Bob is compounded by the arrival of other letters:

> [L]etters from survivors began to appear in the public prints which John so regularly brought to Anne; but though he watched the mails with unceasing vigilance there was never a letter from Bob. It sometimes crossed John's mind that his brother might still be alive and well, and that in his wish to abide by his expressed intention of giving up Anne and home life he was deliberately lax in writing. If so, Bob was carrying out the idea too thoughtlessly by half, as could be seen by watching the effects of suspense upon the fair face of the victim, and the anxiety of the rest of the family. (p. 329)

Not-receiving a letter is evident on Anne's face; though 'fair' might suggest beauty, it also denotes lightness of complexion. In Anne's 'fair face' animation – life – is suspended. In this waiting, letter-less period, her 'favourite reading' is the office for the Burial of the Dead at Sea (p. 329). News of Bob finally arrives, not by letter, but by word-of-mouth (Anne is afforded no touch or trace of him): he is alive and well but, crushingly for Anne, courting another woman. John's reaction to her anguish is to curse his brother's omission: 'Why didn't he come home; or if he couldn't get leave why didn't he write? 'Tis scandalous of him to serve a woman like that!' (p. 333) This posits a – forever unwritten – narrative trajectory, a trajectory in which a letter would have shaped the lives of Anne and John differently. The unwritten letter therefore figures lost possibilities, a haunting what-might-have-been.

Still no letter arrives from Bob, though now his movements are 'pretty accurately registered in the papers' (p. 340). John continues to bring these papers to Anne, but she no longer reads them. In this section of the narrative, no letter is lacking (even though no letter arrives) because none is expected. The phenomenon of the missing letter is only revived when John writes his letter to Bob to ask for a clarification: was his 'verbal renunciation' of Anne on the quay 'only a momentary ebullition of friendship, which it would be cruel to take literally' or had it 'passed from a hasty resolve to a standing purpose'? (p. 341). In John's mind, the written will elucidate the verbal, the letter will determine the literal:

> John waited anxiously for the answer, but no answer came; and the silence seemed even more significant than a letter of assurance could have been of his absolution from further support to a claim which Bob himself had so clearly renounced. Thus it happened that paternal pressure, brotherly indifference, and his own released impulse operated in one delightful direction, and the trumpet-major once more approached Anne as in the old time. (p. 341)

It is not only that the silence 'seems' to be significant. It *is* significant, so rendered by expectations established by the narrative, by references to the non-arrival of any letter, by the emotions induced in the characters and by the lack of certainty. In the absence of any word from Bob, Anne directs her affections to John; she now reinforces the lack of a letter by refusing even to listen to news from the papers:

> 'The shipping news is very full and long to-day, though the print is rather small.'
>
> 'I take no further interest in the shipping news,' she replied with cold dignity. (p. 351)

Lifelessness is marked again in the adjective 'cold'. It is ironic that, at this point, a letter has in fact arrived, and John knows that his brother still desires Anne. 'O, if it had but come a little sooner!' (p. 352): John's lament to himself again marks that the missing letter has established a phantom-narrative which now runs in parallel with the 'true' plot.

As Roger Ebbatson remarks, the 'keynote' of *The Trumpet-Major* is 'absence'.[42] Ebbatson lists among the missing Anne's dead father, Squire Derriman's fortune, Bob and John Loveday (at various junctures) and even Napoleon, 'expected every moment, like Godot, but destined never to appear'.[43] He might also have mentioned the two letters which Bob never writes, whose absence is as strongly felt as that of the brooding Napoleon and on which are founded an intense sense of what might have been. While the undelivered letter signifies that communication has been aborted, the unwritten letter suggests that it was never conceived. In its place is vacuum – suspended activity, waiting, introspection, stasis – but also more poignant abstractions such as desire, hope and fear. These phenomena are of a different epistemological order to those life and war narratives that can be independently verified, but the difficulties in authenticating them do not diminish their importance. Paradoxically, the unwritten letter summons into being a strength of feeling, which is particularly intense in the uncertainty surrounding lives in war.

University of Oxford

Disclosure statement

No potential conflict of interest was reported by the author.

Notes

1 Thomas Hardy, *The Trumpet-Major*, ed. Roger Ebbatson (Harmondsworth: Penguin, 1987). Page-numbers are given in the text.
2 See Rebecca Earle, 'Introduction: Letters, Writers and the Historian', in Rebecca Earle (ed.), *Epistolary Selves: Letters and Letter-Writers, 1600–1945* (Aldershot: Ashgate, 1999), pp. 1–12, 4.
3 Margaretta Jolly and Liz Stanley, 'Letters as/Not a Genre', *Life Writing*, 2.2 (2005), pp. 91–118, 92.
4 Clare Brant, 'Dueling by Sword and Pen: The Vauxhall Affray of 1773', *Prose Studies: History, Theory, Criticism*, 19.2 (1996), pp. 160–72, 160.
5 Carolyn Steedman, for example, maps the development of an 'interiorised, private self' articulated in 'the practice of women writing – novels, autobiographies, diaries, letters' ('A Woman Writing A Letter', in Rebecca Earle (ed.), *Epistolary Selves: Letters and Letter-Writers, 1600–1945* (Aldershot: Ashgate, 1999), pp. 111–33, 118).
6 Mary A. Favret, *Romantic Correspondence: Women, Politics and the Fiction of Letters* (Cambridge: Cambridge University Press, 1993), p. 13.
7 Liz Stanley defines the epistolarium as 'the 'entirety of someone's epistolary endeavour' ('The Epistolarium: On Theorizing Letters and Correspondence', *Auto/Biography*, 12.3 (2004), pp. 201–35, 204. In the present case, I am using it to signify the extant entirety.
8 Cf. Richard Steele's unanswered letters to his wife and the unilateral correspondences of Dorothy Osborne and Margaret Cavendish, analysed in Susan M. Fitzmaurice's *The Familiar Letter in Early Modern English* (Amsterdam: John Benjamins, 2002).
9 Janet Altman defines 'epistolarity' as 'the use of the letter's formal properties to create meaning' (*Epistolarity: Approaches to a Form* (Columbus: Ohio State University Press, 1982), p. 4).
10 Thomas Karshan, 'Notes on the Image of the Undelivered Letter', *Critical Quarterly*, 53.2 (2011), pp. 12–29, discussed further later.
11 2011-08-34, National Army Museum, London, UK. I am grateful to the staff of the Templer Study Centre for their assistance and for permission to quote from the Teasdale epistolarium.

12 2011-08-34-1–5.
13 Letters G, H and I (2011-08-34-6–8) are omitted as they contain only administrative detail.
14 Cf. Earle's claim that letters are 'concrete historical artefacts strongly rooted in particular cultures' and 'display the signs of the distinct environments in which they were conceived' (Earle, *Epistolary Selves*, 2).
15 Great Britain Adjutant-General's Office, *Records of the 54th West Norfolk Regiment* (1881) (London: Bastian Books, 2008), p. 36.
16 Favret, 'War Correspondence: Reading Romantic War', *Prose Studies: History, Theory, Criticism*, 19.2 (1996), pp. 173–85, 175.
17 Qtd in Christa Hämmerle, '"You Let a Weeping Woman Call You Home?": Private Correspondences During the First World War in Austria and Germany', in Rebecca Earle (ed.), *Epistolary Selves: Letters and Letter-Writers, 1600–1945* (Aldershot: Ashgate, 1999), pp. 152–82, 159.
18 Ibid., p. 165.
19 Qtd in Paul Fussell, *The Great War and Modern Memory* (Oxford: Oxford University Press, 1977), p. 184.
20 Sir Thomas Gardiner, *An Account of the Post Office During the Second World War* (Post Office Archive Post 56/63, qtd in Jenny Hartley, '"Letters are *Everywhere* These Days": Mothers and Letters in the Second World War', in Rebecca Earle (ed.), *Epistolary Selves: Letters and Letter-Writers, 1600–1945* (Aldershot: Ashgate, 1999), pp. 183–95, 181.
21 Ibid., p. 182.
22 *The Journey Home: A Report Prepared by Mass-Observation for the Advertising Service Guild* (London: John Murray, 1944), p. 23.
23 Hartley, 'Letters are *Everywhere* These Days', p. 187.
24 Stanley, 'The Epistolarium', p. 212.
25 Jacques Derrida, *The Post Card: From Socrates to Freud and Beyond*, trans. Alan Bass (Chicago, IL: The University of Chicago Press, 1987), p. 79.
26 Edmund Burke, *The Writings and Speeches of Edmund Burke* vol. 9/9, ed. Paul Langford (Oxford: The Clarendon Press, 1991), p. 273.
27 Alan Bewell, *Romanticism and Colonial Disease* (Baltimore, MD: The Johns Hopkins University Press, 1999), p. 69.
28 Great Britain Adjutant-General's Office, *Records of the 54th West Norfolk Regiment*, 37.
29 The epistolarium was donated to the National Army Museum in 2011 by one of Teasdale's descendants.
30 That Jane Teasdale could and did write letters is confirmed by Teasdale's reference in letter E to the letter which he received from her and Currey's reference in letter J to a letter sent by her to Captain Frederick (ironically the last remark in the epistolarium). As Susan E. Whyman notes, by 1800 'all ranks of society' were participating in 'a vibrant culture of letters' (*The Pen and the People: English Letter Writers 1660–1800* (Oxford: Oxford University Press), p. 5).
31 Clare Brant, 'Dueling by Sword and Pen', p. 160; Earle, 'Introduction', p. 5; Fitzmaurice, *The Familiar Letter in Early Modern English*, p. 28, 29; Patricia Meyer Spacks, 'Forgotten Genres', *Modern Language Studies*, 18 (1988),

pp. 47–56, 56; Margaretta Jolly and Liz Stanley, 'Letters as/Not a Genre', p. 91; Stanley, 'The Epistolarium', p. 203.

32 Karshan, 'Notes', p. 12, 13.
33 Ibid., p. 14.
34 Ibid., p. 15.
35 Shari Benstock, 'The Letter of the Law: "La Carte Postale" in "Finnegans Wake"', *Philological Quarterly*, 63.2 (Spring 1984), pp. 163–84, 172.
36 Hardy, *Tess of the D'Urbevilles*, ed. Juliet Grindle and Simon Gatrell (Oxford: The Clarendon Press, 1983), p. 297.
37 Ibid., p. 299.
38 Earle, 'Introduction', p. 4.
39 Favret, 'War Correspondence', p. 173.
40 Hardy, *The Trumpet-Major*, p. 388 n80.
41 The expression 'red-letter day', deriving from the practice of marking saints' days and festivals in the calendar and referring to 'any significant, memorable, or happy day', dates from 1811 ('red-letter day, n.,' C2a, *Oxford English Dictionary*, 3rd ed. online, accessed 10 July 2014).
42 Roger Ebbatson, 'Introduction', Thomas Hardy, *The Trumpet-Major*, pp. 13–39, 28.
43 Ibid., p. 28.
44 The letters are transcribed with original spellings and punctuation. Abbreviations are silently expanded.

Appendix[44]

Letter A (28-08-34-1)

Colchester Barracks Essex
May 14th 1806

Dear Mother,

I have just time before the Post goes out to inform you that my Regiment has recieved orders to march for embarkation, for the West Indies. – I am extremely pleasernt in this Regiment – and don't mind much about going there, if I should never come back, I leave it with you to dispose of what property I have left. but if you can send me by return of post or a day or two later ten pounds to lay in articles proper for the climate, I should be much obliged to you, if it is not convenient I do not press it. We march on Monday week and if a Letter does not catch me here it will at Tilbury Port where we embark. I know I have been extremely troublesome but I hope it will not be long. – after I get to Jamaica I shall certainly write to you I am now settled in a way of life and you may depend I shall not leave it. – I am afraid if I let this post <illegible> there will not be time to get a Letter from you, it is night and I have to send it a mile and a half 'tis to no purpose beginning to inform you of anything, for if I was I should never end.

Give my best Love to all my Brothers and sisters and believe me ever your affectionate son

Edward Teasdale Ensign
54th Regiment Foot
Direct
if we should
by its being un

Letter B [**28-08-34-2**]

Willerby, Motherbank Portsmouth
January 1th 1807

Dear Mother

I write to you, from on board the Willerby, laying at the Motherbank, Portsmouth: and expect to sail tomorrow for Jamaica, as the Wind is now fair – The whole of that part of the Regiment which is now in England go in three ships; and have no doubt of a pleasant voyage when once we get clear of the Channell. We are extremely well accommodated on board, and shall be very pleasant. – I am, also, pretty well provided in those things which are necessary for that climate. I shall, certainly, write on our landing at Kingston; but there is no reason why you should not, in the meanwhile, write to me, for you may depend upon it, I shall get it safe in Jamaica. And when you write, have the goodness to tell me a little more of the family; my poor cousins may be all dead from anything I know. By the bye, where did my great Grandfather Teasdale live, and what was he? Has Gentleman Teasdale of Blackwell any children? and that poor, poor half Brother of mine, that lives in Cockerton, what has become of him? You should write a long letter to me, to amuse me; – if you think it worth the while. Besides you must excuse me, if ever I return to Darlington and do not know some of my relatives; for you never put me in mind of them, and some of them are so insignificant they are very liable to go out of my head. Now that I am talking of forgeting ones relations I puts me in mind of a notion I sometimes have, that my Brother Thomas is not exactly pleased with the way I am going on. However as my own Judgment does not condemn me, it cannot be helped. I only hope he may have occasion to change his oppinion. For after all, I am really desirous of being in the good graces of my relations, though I may not allways have gone the right way to work. – You may see by this last phrase, that tho' I am liable to forget some of my relations, I have not forgot how I used to talk at Cockerton.

[. . .] your most
affectionate son
Edward Teasdale Ensign
54th Regiment

Please to take care of this Lettter

Letter C [28-08-34-3]
Dear Mother,

I expected to have heard from you, long before this time; as I wrote to you when on board the Transport at Portsmouth in December last, and cannot but suppose you recieved my Letter. I there informed you that we were ordered direct for Jamaica and any Letter directed to me there would arrive safe: however I have received none. Indeed I think I have some reason to complain of the few letters I receive, and they have been, lately, astonishingly short, even when I did not write for remittances – If all you wish to tell me about your selves will not make up a Letter, tell me something about your neighbours. – I suppose my Sisters eldest Boys are fine fellows by this time. Pray make them speak and write correctly; that is, correct English; it will be of as much value as any thing the Schoolmaster can teach them.

What house in Darlington do you inhabit? I hope you enjoy yourself – live comfortably. – From the known diligence of my Brothers and Sisters I have no doubt their pecuniary affairs go on swimmingly – Oh, I had allmost forgot to tell you something! I saw, about a fort'night ago, in a Paper that is published in this Island; an account of the death of a Mr. William Teasdale. I never suposed there was any person of our name in this Island.

As the place where he lived is near thirty miles from our quarters I have had no opportunity to make enquiry about his family perhaps I may know something about him by the next Letter I write.

You must not expect that I shall write a great deal about the country and curiosities. they may be curious when you see them but hardly worth recounting –

Everyone knows how hot it is in the West Indies, and you feel such a languor and lassitude which you do not in the hottest day in England. I'll give you an instance of the relaxation occasioned by the heat, which I do not recolect observing in England – when sitting quietly in the shade I have often taken notice of the large drops of perspiration on the back of my hands – [. . .]

We have been very healthy, having only lost 23 men in six months; there is one comfort; that when we are nearly all dead, they will order us home again!

I am dear Mother
your affectionate Son
Edward Teasdale
Ensign 54th Regiment

Stoney Hill
Jamaica
August 10th 1807
I could get no Letter Paper here

Letter D [**28-08-34-4**]
Dear Mother,

This letter will be the fourth I have written to you without having recieved any from you in return. It is almost impossible they can have not arrived; and if yours had only been directed for Jamaica I should undoubtedly have received them; unless they were sent by the last November Packet which unfortunately has been taken. – I am extremely anxious to hear from my family, for it is almost eighteen months since I have had a Letter from you and many changes may have happened in that time. You cannot expect that I can have much to inform you concerning myself. I have had pretty good health since I arrived in the Island, which is the chief thing people look to here, as being the most likely to lose. – I am not in the least want of money, which you may think somewhat strange remembering how rapacious I was a short time ago. Yet I sometimes have a desire to know how my own affairs <tear> in England are going on; I mean my very large estate; who are the tenants, and what are the Rents: – I pray you write me a very long letter, giveing me news of every person you think I can be interested in even to my 16th cousin; let one of my brothers or sisters devote the whole of a Sunday, when I know they have little else to do, in relating the news of the place, to divert for an hour a brother who is removed from them many, many miles.

Edward Teasdale
Ensign 54 Regiment
Mind to direct precisely after this manner. ————
Ens. Teasdale
54th Ret
Stony=hill
Jamaica

I don't think, after all, I should have treated you with so short a Letter, had it not been for an Officer of ours going to Kingston early in the morning and I having not longer <illegible> to write; mind you that I cannot send to Kingston every day.

Letter E [28-08-34-5]

Jamaica September 10th 1808

Dear Mother,

I have to acknowledge the Receipt of your Letter of the 1st of April last; and I am extremely happy to find that amidst the number of those whose deaths you have mentioned I have not to lament any of my immediate Relations. – Your list of Deaths certainly makes a very formidable appearance on Paper but it has small effect on the mind when the loss of one is almost forgot before your attention is called to that of another. – We do this business much quicker here; for a man must have had a very good character in his Company if he is particularly remembered a week after his Death. You must not think from that, tho' we are very sickly; for my Regiment has 'till lately been extremely healthy, and we have only lost two Officers since we came into the Island; and in my Opinion neither of them died by the fever of the country.

The flank companies about a fortnight ago were marched down from Stony-hill to Kingston (I am a Lieutenant in the Light Comp^{y}) and since that time we have become rather sickly.

We marched down 200 strong and upon an average have lost a man a Day; but we buried two yesterday and there is one dead allready to day – this is the suckly season – we shall be better by and by.

[. . .] I am happy to hear my Brother has become so highly polished; I am certain you must all think with me, that it is not aginst the morals of any man to be polite and easy in every situation.

But no man can be called a Gentleman who does not speak and write his own language correctly. Do you know, I sometimes <torn> was he not already permanently settled, that a commission in the Army would not be a bad thing if you had the interest to procure it. – But I suggest that only cursorily – you see I have a very high idea of my own profession – I see from the number of young rogues, there is no danger of the family becoming extinct, I desire you will give my love to all and every one of them [. . .]

I am, dear Mother your affectionate Son Edward Teasdale

Lieutenant 54 Regiment

I believe you need not to pay the postage, and I by <some?> of your will write soon. – I hope you have plentiful crops – live comfortably – live respectably – tell me who Mr Harrison of the North York married. – I saw him at Portsmouth.

Letter F [28-08-34-6]

Stoney Hill, Jamaica, 19: November 1808

Madam.

It is with the deepest regret that I have to announce to you the death of your Son, whose dissolution took place on the morning of the 15th November, after a few days confinement, he fell a victim to the disease of this Climate.

He was attacked whilst stationed at Up-Park Camp, from whence he was moved to a comfortable Lodging housed in Kingston & was in the course of four days from the very great skill and attention of a Medical Gentleman in a convalescent State, unfortunately he considered himself stronger than he really was & removed to this place. – The Journey was too much for him, he relapsed, & tho' nothing was left undone, the disease proved of so malignant a nature (being the confirmed Yellow Fever) that it baffled every endeavour of the Medical Gentleman, & he expired on the third day after his arrival.

Most truly do I condole with you Madam on the loss of this amiable young Man, but it must be a great consolation to you to know, that in the circle in which he moved he was most highly respected and deservedly Beloved.

His remains were entered with Military honors, he was regretted by all, but by those who knew him best, by those his loss was most surely felt. –

[...]

A short time previous to his death he made a Will, a Copy of which I send you, the original shall be taken particular care of untill a safe opportunity offers of forwarding it to you. –

Having now performed the last, but truly painful Office due to my brother Officer & friend,

I remain
Madam

Your most Obedient Honorable Servant

Robert: Frederick

Major & Capt. 54th Regiment

PS I shall be happy to give you Madam, any further information you may require. –

Letter J [**28-08-34-12**]
Madam

I have the honor to enclose a statement of the effects and <illegible> of the late Lieutenant Teasdale 54th Regiment, which has been examined by a board of Officers, and found correct. [. . .]

I cannot deny myself the satisfaction of confessing what I am convinced must be grateful to your feelings; that your son, the late Lieutenant Teasdale, was universally esteemed and respected by all his brother Officers, who sincerely lamented his loss.

Major Frederick has communicated to me, your letter to him of the 12 Inst last.
W. J. Currey
Major 54th Regiment

Nancy Martin

'And all because it is war!': First World War diaries, authenticity and combatant identity[1]

In this article, I examine the complexities of men's personal identification with the image of soldier as represented primarily on the pages of combatant diaries. The diary, as a private, self-reflexive form, allows for an examination of what Michael Roper has rightly highlighted as a consistently neglected area of First World War scholarship: 'the behaviour and emotional dispositions of individual men' as they attempt to navigate the inherent contradictions and complexities of their new role as heroic soldier. As government worked to recode (and control) the wartime behaviour of its citizens, the diary often provided a rare venue through which the individual could reevaluate his newly militarised identity. As the diarists draw on martial metaphors and make allusions to ancient mythologies, they betray a desire rhetorically to authenticate the newly militarised, masculine self. Of course, as the civilian experiences industrialised combat, the language of traditional rhetoric often comes to seem inadequate – if not callous – in the face of the war's indiscriminate brutality. As a result, many attempt to present a more accurate, or 'authentic', picture of war and its horrors. Traditional rhetoric is replaced by graphic depictions of broken and fragmented *things* – a change in style that signifies a change in self-perception.

In his autobiographical 1930 novel, *A Generation Missing*, Carroll Carstairs outlines the basic trajectory of the civilian recruit's war story:[2]

> In the beginning war is adventure. Then comes war-weariness, a period of adjustment. You stick it or give up. The third phase is an acceptance, a resignation, and a surrender to faith. The brave man is the man who gets through to the third phase.[3]

This passage, void of what Samuel Hynes calls 'the capitalized nouns of the high tradition', signifies a fundamental change in combatant conceptions of war, masculinity, and heroics.[4] While Carstairs' Irish Guardsman is speaking of war in general, what he is ultimately describing is his own First World War story, a story that would be mirrored on the pages of countless British combatant diaries, letters, and novels. Indeed, after hearing the Guardsman's brief account of war, the narrator states: 'he echoed my subconscious. He put into words what I had felt and was groping for'.[5] In stark contrast to the rhetoric used to describe the idealised hero of 1914–15, a hero of 'wonderful coolness and daring' according to *The Daily Telegraph*, here the successful soldier is presented in a more passive form.[6] His manhood is proven not though shows of strength or valour, but through a patient and resigned *endurance* of the war's trauma and suffering. In other words, bravery, the fundamental tenet of 'manly' virtue, has been redefined. This redefinition was perhaps an inevitable outcome of the First World War's unprecedented destruction, as idealised conceptions of masculinity collapsed in the face of the war's violent and uncanny reality. Indeed, the young civilian recruit, long-trained in the language of heroics by schools, clubs, and religious institutions, would often find himself confined and rendered passive in trenches, deprived of autonomy; in essence, emasculated. He was therefore left to reconceptualise his image of the heroic soldier and, in turn, his conception of self. While the association between masculinity and military service was not new – the 'heroic soldier' has been the most enduring and powerful form of masculinity since the ancient Greeks – the connection was deepened and intensified in the midst of the anxious cultural climate of the early months of the war, as the nation placed the heroic soldier at the centre of its search for a renewed sense of national identity. As proudly declared by Reverend Alexander Irvine in a characteristically zealous sermon to the nation's newest recruits: '[The British soldier] is the incarnation of England that was, and is, and is to be!'[7]

This article hopes to make a contribution to recent work in endurance studies. Alexander Watson's 2008 text, *Enduring the Great War*, examines the motivations and coping mechanisms of German and British Soldiers, highlighting the importance of emotional support among men on the front. Focusing primarily on letters, Anthony Fletcher's recent study, *Life, Death and Growing Up on the Western Front* (2014), powerfully argues for the significance of home in men's ability to cope with the war's horrific realities. Other studies, in particular those focusing on shell shock, further challenge the concept of masculinity and its transformation; such texts include Peter Barham's *Forgotten Lunatics of the Great War* (2004), Michael Roper's *The Secret Battle: Emotional Survival in the Great War* (2009), and Jessica Meyer's *Men of War: Masculinity and the First World War in Britain* (2009).[8] Building on this scholarship, in this article I examine the complexities of men's personal identification with the image of soldier and the ways in which this image is both transformed and maintained on the frontline diary page. Focusing in particular on the writings of public school-educated officers, I first explore depictions made in the war's early months and then in the midst of its chaos.[9] In this context, the diary, as a private, self-reflexive form, allows for an examination of what Michael Roper has rightly highlighted as a consistently neglected area of First World War scholarship: 'the behaviour and emotional dispositions of individual men'[10] as they attempt to navigate the inherent contradictions and complexities of their new role as heroic soldier. As government worked to recode (and control) the wartime behaviour of its citizens, the diary provided a rare venue through which the individual could reevaluate his newly militarised identity. Men who had recently enlisted often turned to constructions of the soldier that were familiar to them, drawing on martial metaphors and alluding to ancient mythologies in order to rhetorically authenticate the newly militarised, masculine self. Once civilian men experience combat, however, the perception of authentication is fundamentally altered. After the devastating losses of the Somme, for example, the language of traditional rhetoric often came to seem inadequate – if not callous – in the face of the war's indiscriminate brutality. Many men attempt to present a more accurate, or authentic, picture. Idealised depictions of cavalry charges and metaphors of ancient crusades are often replaced by graphic and fragmented depictions of broken, unrecognisable *things* – body parts, shattered objects, dirt and mud.

This is not to suggest that classical allusions and glorified rhetoric disappeared on the Western Front; they did not. Some men continued to use the idealised language of the war's early months. Furthermore, this change in style was not always dramatic. Men document *both* positive and negative experiences. While at rest, away from the front, for example, some men describe their enjoyment of comfortable billets, beautiful undamaged fields, and new villages. In these moments the diary intertwines with travelogue. Additionally, while still in the trenches, men often describe their ingeniously constructed 'domestic' spaces. In other words, there are moments of calm, and indeed, enjoyment, in the midst of chaos.

However, while such diversity is important to note, the new, more fragmented and graphic, style undoubtedly dominates in the war's later years. This form was meant to capture, with immediacy, the unmediated experience of the war's realities. Beyond alterations on the page, this change in style signifies a change in self-perception in the writer. As the diary traces the complex ways in which war both effaces and shapes new conceptions of the self, war writing *becomes* life writing (and vice versa). The diarist then, in a sense, writes his newly militarised self into being. In the words of one such combatant writer, 'what I feel I like to record'.[11]

*

The First World War combatant diary occupies a complex place in the epistemology of testimony. As a genre, the diary defies the traditional structural forms of narrative. Focusing generally on the immediate present, it is serial, open-ended, often repetitive and contradictory. Diaries often display a reshaping and revising of an individual's experiences and perceptions, illustrating what Nussbaum describes as the constantly shifting self, or 'selves'.[12] In Suzanne L. Bunkers' words, the diary presents 'life as *process*, not *product*'.[13] Furthermore, the *form* of the war diary itself is multiple. While some men carry the more traditional, leather-bound volume, others use tiny pocket books (fitting in a breast pocket), or Field Service Notebooks – paper often being in short supply. Some men meticulously date every entry, even noting the weather and time of day, while others note the passage of time in major battles, or in the alteration between front and rest camp. Found pressed between the worn pages of some are treasured mementos from home: photographs, a lock of child's hair, flowers from the family garden. In others, there are sketches of weapons, open fields, destroyed buildings, and trenches. The length and form of the entries also vary widely; while some men carefully document even the most minute of details – from the mundane to the horrific – other entries appear perfunctory, citing only the fundamentals: 'in reserve trench. relieved at 10 pm by Wilts. sharp frost. some rain', writes F. S. Collings on 25 March 1915.[14] Such varying lengths and narrative styles undoubtedly reflect the equally varied function of the diary in the context of war. And yet, while such diversity demands caution when making generalisations, some broad conclusions can be drawn. The war diary is a site for both the documentation and navigation of a profoundly new, and often terrifying, reality. Through the act of writing, the individual imposes some level of control over this otherwise chaotic experience. The 'I' on the page – whatever the length or descriptive quality of the words that surround it – is an assertion of *the individual* in a culture of impersonal uniformity and mass movement. On the pages of these texts there is often oscillation between chaos and coherence, between fragmentation and unity, as men attempt to both maintain and redefine their masculine 'sense of self' in the midst of war's excitement, monotony, and trauma. In the succinct words of one new recruit, H. T. Clements, 'This seems a curious war, during the last four days everything in comfort. The next merde'.[15]

In an important article that examines masculinity and subjectivity as depicted by middle-class veteran writers, Michael Roper argues that there was a *postwar* reconceptualisation of 'manliness'. In Roper's words, 'beginning just after the war itself and continuing up to the final quarter of the century, there emerged among the British middle class a means of reflexively assessing the codes of "manliness"'.[16] While I agree that combatant writing of the 1920s and 1930s undoubtedly demonstrates a clear critical engagement with prewar masculine ideals, I would argue that this reconceptualisation in fact began long before the war's end. Its rhetorical roots can be traced on the diary pages and letters of front-line soldiers, as they, in the midst of the war's destruction, attempted to navigate the jarring disjunction between ideology and lived experience. Indeed, what is not overtly said, but rather implied, by Carstairs in the above passage is that the civilian recruit's understanding of himself *as a man* was changed in, and by, war. His redefinition of bravery, however unconscious, was reached though personal experience of the war's reality, a reality that made performance of idealised pre-war masculine scripts impossible.

That bravery was a crucial element in this process had been established by long-standing cultural, social and educational influences. The selective syllabus of the public schools, for example, often celebrated the steadfast soldier who fearlessly performed his imperial duties, while popular boys' literature presented its masculine heroes as physically dominant athletes, full of 'pluck' and prowess. While bravery in these histories and adventure stories had no single definition, it was generally used to refer to one who is capable of selfless and fearless *action*. In the context of early First World War propaganda, the term was similarly predicated on an image of war as active combat, wherein steadfast men charged an enemy they could see, thereby claiming the battlefield ground they had won. In recalling his excitement during Cavalry training in September of 1914, Arthur Hamilton Gibbs writes: 'it was with the spirit of crusaders that we galloped cross-country with slung lances, or charged in line upon an imaginary foe with yells that would demoralize him before our lance points should sink . . . '.[17] Gibbs' romantic illusion of war here illuminates a fundamental assumption held by many young men in 1914: the individual in war has power and control, each as essential to the brave soldier as his rifle or bayonet. In other words, his personal, outward displays of 'Courage' and 'Valour' are directly connected to what would presumably be clear victories in battle. After experiencing the realities of the Western Front, the writers of trench diaries were led to redefine bravery, and hence masculinity, and hence their selves.

In the analysis that follows, I will first provide a brief discussion of 'enlistment narratives', highlighting one man's early association with the image of the soldier hero. Contemporary literary scholarship has largely ignored depictions of men's individual reasons for enlisting, briefly citing the 'rush to the colours' and preferring to focus rather on the experience of the war's trauma and dissolution as depicted by a small selection of literary men (typically Siegfried Sassoon, Robert Graves, Wilfred Owen, etc.). And yet, these moments of early consideration are particularly significant. What typically occurs is an identification with a heroic, manly ideal of narrow contours, an ideal to which many men would attempt to conform not only in outward appearance and action, but also in their writing. Indeed, the 'soldier hero' is often a central trope of early war narratives; it provides the heroic register through which many men (in varying degrees) configure their letters, memoirs, and diaries. In the second section, I will turn to the Western Front, tracing some of the complex changes that occur in men's writing as they attempt to negotiate the form of their new role, amid the violence, excitement, and boredom of the trenches and rest camps. In the midst of this navigation, life writing and war writing intertwine.

1. 'I am Tommy Atkins!':[18] heroic masculinity, male identity and recruitment in First World War combatant diaries

The unpublished diary of one young recruit, W. T. Colyer, captures the experiences of many men in the early months of the war. An ex-public schoolboy from Merchant Taylors, he had rushed from his London office to Duke Street, Euston, where he joined the Artists' Rifles on 5 August 1914. His diary – which actually appears to be a complex, hybrid form of diary and memoir – recalls his initial thoughts the morning after war was declared:

> Would they invade us, I wondered. By George! If they should they'd find us a tougher nut to crack than they had expected.
>
> My bosom swelled and I clenched my fist. I wished to goodness I were in the Army now. What a fool I had been to ignore the circular ... If I had listened then, I might have been with the British Expeditionary Force just gone to France ... I wondered what they were doing now. Probably engaged in some terrific fight which we shall hear about tomorrow. [...]

> And then the impulse came, sending the blood tingling over all my body: why not join the Army now? A great and glorious suggestion. It might not be too late.[19]

The pride and excitement in this passage is palpable. Colyer's use of emotionally charged language – 'a great and glorious suggestion' – highlights his internalisation of the period's heroic rhetoric. Indeed 'Glory' was a staple of the high tradition – a staple that would famously be mocked by Wilfred Owen later in the war. That same evening he found himself in the crowded headquarters of the Artists' Rifles, surrounded by 'fellows obviously bound on the same mission'.[20] He describes his future fellow soldiers as having 'an eager light in their eyes which beckoned the ardent impelling force within'.[21] Colyer's elevated, if not bombastic, language reveals his romantic illusions not only about war, but about England. Conditioned by the imperialist values of the public school system, he believed wholeheartedly in both the justice of the British cause and the 'natural superiority of the British people'.[22] As such, he was eager to cast himself in the role of heroic soldier and to 'offer himself up on the ... altar of his country's honour, so to speak'.[23] The heroic model is explained by the fact that middle-class men like Colyer were educated through a selective syllabus, which focused on the Empire's past successes. This selective history was coupled with a celebration of the 'robust manly qualities' supposedly garnered though sport, as the two combined were thought to prepare England's future leaders for their imperial duties. As declared by a contributor to the extremely popular, *Boys Own Paper* in 1892:

> One thing is certain, and may as well be at once admitted, that as long as England wishes to maintain her supremacy and reputation as a great nation, our boys must be trained in those games which develop physical strength, endurance, skill and courage.[24]

Conditioned in many ways to view war as the greatest 'game' he could partake in, it is not surprising that Colyer was 'restless, excited, [and] eager to do something desperate for the cause of England'.[25] It is even less surprising that his writing depicts what he describes as a new and revitalised 'sense of self' after 'the great deed was done'.[26] Indeed, his elevated language reveals a desire to authenticate not only his patriotic enlistment, but also the 'proper' masculine identity it signifies and secures. Drawing a revealing comparison between enlistment and a marriage proposal, he writes: 'I went home throbbing with a new vitality, as (I imagine) a man might who had just plighted his troth to the girl he had loved at first sight'.[27] The simile is telling; it equates enlistment – a requirement of wartime masculinity – with an equally affirming 'manly' milestone:

marriage. Furthermore, the reference is clearly a sexual one; his '*throbbing* with a new vitality', suggests arousal at the thought of war. And of course he, like many others who had 'plighted their troth' to king and country in early 1914, was amply rewarded for performing the 'proper' masculine scripts:

> So home I went each evening, with my rifle on my shoulder. As I walked through the streets people looked admiringly at me, and I felt more than ever pleased with myself. Girls smiled at me, men looked at me with respect, the bus-drivers wished me luck and refused to take money for my fare, and everybody made way for me, as being on the King's business.[28]

While the army's severe shortage of accommodation and materials in the early months of the war meant that Colyer could not yet don the newly ordained symbol of militarised masculinity – the khaki uniform – his rifle, for the time being, was enough to mark him as a man.

Colyer's romantic illusions of war here reveal a fundamental assumption held by many: the war would provide countless opportunities for individual displays of courage and bravery; his image was of *active* combat, of exciting battles with clear and swift victories. Such excitement and enthusiasm – common, though certainly not universal in civilian recruits – often continued though training and transport to the front. Charles May, Captain of the 22nd Battalion of The Manchester Regiment, writes of his men's excitement for battle in November 1915: 'Promise [the men] a regular hell of a time in France and you can't please them better. Their keenness to go is marvellous and I trust will hold when they get there'.[29] In his diary on 21 February 1915, H. T. Clements, a Private, highlights a similarity between the officers and the ranks; he writes of his unit's growing enthusiasm as they march towards the front for the first time. After proudly relaying his excitement at his unit's being 'taken for regular troops', he assures the assumed reader – perhaps a future self – that 'the nearer we reached the firing line, the higher our spirits rose'.[30] Viewing the war as a test of their manhood, these men reflect excitement and a desire to authenticate the newly militarised, masculine self. In Colyer's words, 'We wanted to be up and doing things. We wanted to be real soldiers, not theatrical representations of them'.[31] Of course, neither Clements nor Colyer could imagine what their role as 'real' soldier would entail. Tales of glorious charges and personal victories were a feature of past wars, wars that has been romanticised through the selective syllabus of the public schools. The 475-mile Western Front would become a mire of trenches, an underground, primeval landscape, filled with rats, lice, and mud. In this dark, subterranean world, men's daily lives were spent largely in wait; it was 'months of boredom punctuated by moments of extreme terror'. I will turn now, in Part Two, to the Western Front, examining the complex changes that occurred in men's writing. It is here that the generic distinctions between war writing and life writing blur and collapse.

2. 'Goodbye to Galahad':[32] tracing the turn in language, as the idealised recruit becomes the 'old soldier'

It is necessary first to outline the changes in the form and style of men's wartime writing more generally. As these changes are rooted in men's experience of the war's trauma, it is important to note that, while gender operates in these texts, it is certainly not the only – or even the most dominant – aspect of combatant identity. Simply stated: in 1916, after the devastating losses of the Somme, men's writing on the front altered dramatically.[33] The extremity of violence, coupled with the sheer strangeness of trench battle, forced a change in style. Traditional heroic descriptions are often replaced by graphic depictions of broken, unrecognisable *things* – pieces of buildings, objects, and men. David Jones, in his Preface to *In Parenthesis* (1937), speaks to the nature and root of this change in style:

> This writing has to do with some things I saw, felt, & was part of. The period covered begins early in December 1915 and ends early in July 1916. The first date corresponds to my going to France. The latter roughly marks a change in the character of our lives in the Infantry on the West Front. From then onward things hardened into a more relentless, mechanical affair, took on a more sinister aspect ... In the earlier months there was a certain attractive amateurishness, and elbow-room for idiosyncrasy that connected with a less exacting past. The period of the individual rifle-man, of the 'old sweat' of the Boer campaign, the 'Bairnsfather' war, seemed to terminate with the Somme battle.[34]

As men like Jones experienced the realities of this 'relentless, mechanical affair', their frontline writing changes; life writing *becomes* war writing as sequential narrative is replaced by fragmented description of the speaker's gruesome surroundings. The language of traditional rhetoric is not merely abandoned, but bitterly mocked. 'But now I've said good-bye to Galahad', writes Siegfried Sassoon in November 1916.[35] This change is certainly not surprising. The war, as argued by Samuel Hynes, was a new reality, one characterised by brutal (and random) violence, futility, and monotony; this new reality required a new language. But beyond this, the change is not surprising because it fits within the confines of the war's grand narrative. The narrative of the naive and eager recruit who is broken and disillusioned by war is a fundamental aspect of popular collective memory. While recognising this, my interest here lies in the implications this change had for the self-perceptions of *individual* men, and further, how this change is represented, navigated, and contained in their private writings.

As it becomes clear that modern, mechanised war is characterised by annihilation – of things, of landscape, of men – all that is left is to describe things simply *as they are*. In a letter written on 31 October 1916, after he had spent just two months at the front, civilian officer, Coningsby Dawson writes,

> We advance over the old battlefields – everything is blasted. If you start digging, you turn up what's left of something human ... Here I sit in an old sweater and muddy breeches, the very reverse picture of your picture of a soldier ... Our chief interest is to inquire whether milk, jam and mail have come up from the wagon-lines; it seems a fairy-tale that there are places where milk and jam can be had for the buying. See how simple we become.[36]

This passage is empty of the idealised abstractions of his early (pre-experience) letters, which speak of 'heroic crusades' and 'the greatness and glory of war'. In other words, life writing has here transitioned into war writing. Descriptive rather than narrative, the passage provides a simple, emotionless listing of what he experiences daily: blasted battlefields, body parts, muddy breeches, want of milk, jam, and mail from home – each fragmented item seems to form an equal part of the general chaos of his surroundings. The simply worded description offers a way of fixing, or giving some sense of order to, a fragmented reality. This dramatic change in language, in turn, implies an equally dramatic change in self-perception. Dawson's comment that he is 'the very reverse picture of [his family's] picture of a soldier' is telling. It signifies his now intimate understanding of the jarring distance between ideology and lived experience. His family, safe on the home front, are unaware of the war's realities. Their 'picture of a soldier', in Dawson's view, remains one of abstract heroic and noble action. As Dawson sits, sedentary in his muddy breeches and old sweater, he is a 'reversed soldier', the virtual opposite of what he had once imagined. Here, the act of writing about one's authentic experience of war appears to bring about a more 'authentic' understanding of self – 'how simple we become'.

Dawson's reference to the 'simple' things that are of 'chief interest' to soldiering men too is significant. Men's frontline diaries make near constant reference to such small desires – the pleasure of a warm meal, dry socks, and a day's relief from the rain. Indeed brief entries that reference *only* these pleasures are common. 'Machine-gun instruction 9 am to 12.30 pm. Rations good, four and a half loaves between ten men with cheese and jam per day',[37] serves as the entire entry for 31 March 1916 in the diary of Harry Drinkwater. On Sunday, 13 June 1915, Private F. S Collings succinctly writes: 'Resting in field. Fine'.[38] These brief entries, focusing on the attainment – or desperate want – of simple necessities, also subtly signify the transition from new, civilian recruit to experienced soldier. The 'chief interest' of these men is no longer to prove themselves as 'soldier heroes', but is, rather, for simple, everyday comforts: milk, jam, and mail. In Drinkwater's words: 'By now I am a regular old soldier and have just collared a couple of the engineers' candles'.[39] The attainment of life's most basic needs here allows for the maintenance of one's sense of self. When men are warm, fed, and have news from home, they feel not simply comfortable, but stable and whole.

Of course, maintenance of the 'coherent self' in war was, for many, a constant internal battle. Once idealised young recruits, like Colyer, Dawson, and Drinkwater, experienced the realities of trench warfare – both terrifying and monotonous – their perception of themselves as soldiers was fundamentally altered, along with their needs and desires. This is the period of 'adjustment' referred to by Carstairs in the article's opening passage; it marks the recruit's initiation in war, and subsequent transition from naive and inexperienced civilian to *experienced* (and knowing) soldier. H. T. Clements subtly contemplates this change in his diary on 20 April 1915. After reminding himself of his first reaction to the trenches – citing the page this falls on for future comparative reference, he writes: ' . . . (page 64) we thought it was something wonderful. Now it seems quite a commonplace thing wandering in front of the trenches'.[40]

In his important study of the 'transformation of personality in war', Eric Leed rightly argues that 'war experience is nothing if not a transgression of categories'.[41] On the Western Front, 'distinctions that were central to orderly thought, communicable experience, and normal human relations' were often shattered.[42] In Dawson's words: 'It seems as though war does to the individual what it does to the landscape it attacks – obliterates everything personal and characteristic'.[43] Indeed, the man who had gone to war imagining great cavalry charges and swung lances would find himself cooped up in an underground cesspool, surrounded by death, with no enemy in sight. Often hidden only a few hundred yards away, the 'Boche' was generally visible only in the form of the bullets and mortar shells that breached the parapet. In this context, personal triumph over the 'barbarous hun' becomes impossible; '[one] cannot tell if our fire has any effect'.[44] In this form of warfare, machines dominated, and their unprecedented destructive power rendered men subservient, forcing them underground, while the landscape above them was annihilated. Indeed, the French and Belgian countryside, decimated by near-constant bombardment, quickly became a wasteland, a world where nothing was recognisable and where death and life were relentlessly churned together. A trench occupied by one unit was inevitably the site where others had died. Death was ever-present; both seen and unseen, it bombarded the senses. In a letter sent from the front, Wilfred Owen writes, 'I have not seen any dead, I have done worse. In the dank air I have perceived it, and in the darkness, felt'.[45] The near-constant presence of the dead made abundantly clear the nature of death in modern, mechanised war; it is random, indiscriminate, and incredibly undignified. In the face of this unpredictability, men are forced into a passive, unknowing position. Their fate is not determined by personal acts, but chance. Even a moment of action, of control – the throwing of a grenade – can be unexpectedly halted, and rendered irrelevant, by death. Men are therefore stripped of control of even their most basic instinctual desire to protect themselves. Both period and contemporary psychiatric assessment find the root of many men's eventual breakdown *here*, in the repeated suppression of one's most basic instinct: self-preservation.

This is also where the change in self-perception originates. As a mere cog in the war's great machine, the soldier must resignedly remain, against all instinct, in the underground world. His role, generally speaking, is passively to wait, amid falling bombs and surrounded by the dead. In their wartime diaries, combatants often vividly describe their experiences of both immovability and imprisonment. In his brief 1914 trench diary, one unnamed Sergeant Major writes: 'constant traffic rubs the sides of the trench into a smooth paste and the bottom becomes like a soft paste which turns into liquid mud, ankle deep ... It pours with rain ... they must dig themselves out of sight before daylight arrives otherwise the enemy in the trenches about 400 yards to our front would make short work of us'.[46] In such passages the walls of the trench figure simultaneously as a source of protection and confinement. Below the surface of No Man's Land, men are forced into a position of passivity. Often left lying prone in the face of bombardment, they are not active agents, but passive victims.

In his diary, W. T. Colyer narrates his first experience of trench warfare in a description that is representative of the war's confinement. After describing an uneventful first patrol, he writes:

> I was just dozing off when I was suddenly brought to life again by a very distinct 'boom' from behind the German lines, followed by a peculiar sighing sound. I hold my breath. Some monstrous thing which I could not see, came whirring ... high over the trench ...

> The day's shelling had commenced ... to say I was in a 'howling funk' would be to overstate the case, yet I did not feel nearly as plucky as when on the patrol. There was such a difference between advancing [ ] with one's rifle tightly grasped and a definite object in view, and lying passively in an ice-cold swamp in the dawn ...
>
> As I lay on my side my weight sank into the swampy ground, so that the mud came over the top of my waterproof sheet, and I was literally lying in a mud bath. I was absolutely fed up with the whole business. I simply counted off the hours before it would be dark and I should get out of it ... [47]

This passage, written by the same recruit who had once imagined 'adventuring forth to do battle' for the 'glorious empire',[48] makes clear the jarring disjunction between ideology and *lived* experience. Here Colyer describes the forced passivity of the trenches in vivid detail. In the face of monstrous bombardment, he can only wait, covered in mud, 'holding his breath'. Far from the imagined figure of stoic, definitive action, he is here rendered passive, a figure to be acted upon. It was through repeated experience of this confinement and forced passivity – wherein death was ever present – that the young, civilian recruit became the 'old soldier'.

In reflecting this complex transition, his frontline writing subtly (and often resignedly) adopts the language of endurance. In the words of one such 'old soldier': 'war is indiscriminately awful, but still we who are left carry on ... Tomorrow is to be another big strafe'.[49] Phrases like 'Carry on' and 'Stick it' commonly recur in men's frontline writing. This was particularly the case after 1916 – once the thousands of ex-public school recruits had experienced modern war. These phrases highlight the redefinition of masculinity that occurred in trench warfare. While models of Victorian and Edwardian 'manliness' had certainly emphasised self-control, *endurance* is more complex.[50] As argued by Jessica Meyer, in her historical study, *Men of War*: 'Men who endured were those who controlled their emotions not only in the moment of fear and stress but also when confronted with the on-going horrors of warfare'.[51] It is here, in the language of endurance that surfaces in men's wartime diaries, that we find the root of men's 'post-war reassessment of manly ideals'.[52] Charles May speaks of the necessity to endure as he describes the terror of patrols, where one must 'crawl on [his] stomach over noisy jam tins' and 'wiggle through grass. All the while your body seems bigger than an elephant's' as you obsess 'that every Fritz in the line has seen you'. And yet, even after denying the value of such terrifying duties, he writes: 'You hate it at the time but endure it'.[53] Describing an attack on the Somme, W. T. Colyer similarly writes that he 'must appear calm and cheerful, whatever [he] may feel like'. Later, after confessing to his diary that he 'can't stand this torture much longer', he dutifully reminds himself that 'the fact is [he] must push forward'. This is the language of passive resignation. Endurance has become the hallmark of the soldier. His bravery and courage, in this context, is not of the idealised, and literary, 'heroic' kind – exemplified by the pre-experience pages of Colyer's Diary. It is, rather, a gritty and painful commitment, a dogged perseverance. In Harry Drinkwater's words: '[It] is a long time to face such an ordeal of one's own free will – it was a cold courage, and well done'.[54]

As endurance replaces idealised acts of bravery, *fear*, in turn, is readily admitted on the diary page. Words and phrases like 'windy', 'wind up', 'nervy', and 'nerves' recur constantly – new words for a new reality, each signalling a fundamental change in conceptions of both war and heroics. While *nerve*, for example, refers to a pre-war conception of bravery – the brave soldier has 'nerve and daring' – 'nerves' are something different; nerves require control. In this context, control refers to a form of *internal* struggle that must be overcome, a form that contrasts starkly from the personal (largely *physical*) victories once imagined by the new recruit. When Harry Drinkwater refers to his being 'in a somewhat nervy condition', after dodging 'shells and rifle grenades' 'all through the night',[55] he is referring directly to his need to the *control* his fear. Such simple word changes on the pages of combatant diaries illuminate not only the writer's integration into the war's 'culture' – adopting its language – but also his redefinition of heroics. Indeed, fear, now recognised as the universal reaction to war's chaos, is readily admitted. H. T. Clements', for example, writes: 'I rather had the wind up [. . .]. Crouching down in the mud . . . it is a terrible sensation – [it is] no wonder that men go mad'.[56] As men experience the mechanised front, fear no longer negates bravery, but is, rather, fundamental to its redefinition: the brave man overcomes his constant fear and 'carries on'. In his diary, Colyer provides a lengthy and careful assessment of fear and its fundamental role in war:

> Fear!
>
> That strange and unpleasant emotion, universally shared in greater or less degree by all exposed to the immediate possibility of a violent death: what an influence it had, what a part it played, in men lives in the trenches! And yet how rarely in war books is anything written about fear. Inspiring accounts of bravery, triumphant records of heroic deeds, exist in plenty, yet nothing about fear . . . For the fact is, of course, that bravery and fear are inseparably bound up with each other. Unless a man feels fear he can never be

> brave: bravery being nothing more or less than the successful control of fear.[57]

While the successful soldier must control his fear, he is able to both admit and examine it on the pages of his diary. In such instances, the diary can function as a tool. In rehearsing moments of intense anxiety, fear can be mitigated and a greater understanding of self, of one's capabilities and needs under immense strain, can be traced on the page. R. W. Wilson, for example, a member of the Royal Engineers, writes of his overcoming of fear: '[I] felt nervous at being in open at first, but soon realized it had to be faced. (Starting saying now "be strong and of good courage" and then leaving it at that)'.[58] In a lengthy passage documenting the day's terrifying charge, J. S. Gatley poignantly describes his mastering of fear before breaching the parapet in Gallipoli:

> 3 minutes to go and I whisper a short prayer and feel quite calm now, and many farewells and promises are made to inform each others wives or Mothers in case anything happens. One minute to go and an order to get ready and the whistle goes, we scramble up and over the top.[59]

Harry Drinkwater, the commanding officer of men like Gatley, writes with pride of men's mastering of such potentially overwhelming fear. For Harry, it is *here* that glory lies – a glory redefined. Speaking directly to the change in his – and many other men's – perception of war and heroics, he writes:

> It will be always a matter of joy to remember how the fellows, all thoroughly well-shaken, jumped out from the different places of cover and got to business with their rifles . . . [This] was not war as understood in the literal sense, before the trenches came into being. As war was understood – where, with bayonet and rifle one side goes for the other. [. . .]. Each individual man could, if he had wished, have sunk into some shell-hole and away from danger, but he did not do so, he took his place in line and awaited the oncoming Germans. There was no outward glory attached to it, it was all done in the dark and done so readily it passed unnoticed.[60]

This passage, written on 4 June 1916, presents Harry as the 'old soldier'. Having gotten 'through to the third phase' of war, as outlined by Carstairs' in the article's opening passage, 'he is the brave man'. His diary, like that of Colyer, Clements, McKerrow, and May, traces his experience (and navigation) of the war's chaos, from adventuring recruit to experienced, and knowing, soldier. As we have seen, the soldier's altered conception of self is both expressed and developed on the diary page. The diary, in this context, serves as a site for documentation, but also for declaration, edification, and examination of the self at war. Indeed, the combatant diarist, in a sense, *writes* his newly militarised self into being. As men's experience of the war's realities brings about the subtle redefinition of courage and cowardice, fear and bravery, the combatant diary, on the whole, suggests that the authentic experience of war has brought about a process of re-authenticating the self.

University of Oxford

Funding

This research was supported by the Social Sciences and Humanities Research Council of Canada.

Disclosure statement

No potential conflict of interest was reported by the author.

Notes

1 The diaries and private papers referenced in this article, including those of 2nd Lieutenant H. T. Clements, Captain C. K. McKerrow, R. W. Wilson, Captain W. T. Colyer, Captain D. H. Pegler, J. S Gatley, and F. S. Collings, are housed in the Documents and Sound Section of the Imperial War Museum, London. My sincere thanks are given to both the IWM and the copyright holders for permission to quote from these private, remarkable papers. The title citation, 'And all because it is war!' is taken from the published diary of Charles May: *To Fight Alongside Friends: The First World War Diaries of Charlie May*, ed. Gerry Harrison (London: Harper Collins, 2014), p. 8.
2 Carroll Chevalier Carstairs, an American art dealer, served (and was severely wounded) in the British Army's Grenadier Guards.
3 Carroll Carstairs, *A Generation Missing* (London: William Heinemann, 1930), p. 164.
4 Samuel Hynes, *A War Imagined* (New York: Macmillan, 1990), p. 116.
5 Carstairs, *A Generation Missing*, p. 164.
6 Anonymous, 'British Army at the Battle of Mons', *The Daily Telegraph* (26 August 1914), p. 7.
7 Dr Alexander Irvine, *God and Tommy Atkins* (London: Hutchinson, 1918), p. 125. Irvine travelled to military camps throughout England to deliver sermons to new recruits. The book is a compilation of these sermons.

8 Alexander Watson, *Enduring the Great War* (Cambridge: Cambridge University Press, 2008); Anthony Fletcher, *Life, Death and Growing Up on the Western Front* (New Haven, CT: Yale University Press, 2014); Peter Barham, *Forgotten Lunatics of the Great War* (New Haven, CT: Yale University Press, 2004); Michael Roper, *The Secret Battle: Emotional Survival in the Great War* (Manchester: Manchester University Press, 2009); Jessica Meyer, *Men of War: Masculinity and the First World War in Britain* (New York: Palgrave Macmillan, 2009).

9 Due to the confines of space, the article necessarily draws on a limited number of primary texts. The inclusion of further corroborative material, including any post-war writing by these men, will have to remain for a future, extended study.

10 Michael Roper, 'Between Manliness and Masculinity: the "War Generation" and the Psychology of Fear in Britain, 1914–1950', *Journal of British Studies*, 44.2 (2005), p. 345.

11 May, *To Fight Alongside Friends*, p. 128.

12 Felicity A. Nussbaum, 'Toward Conceptualizing Diary', in James Olney (ed.), *Studies in Autobiography* (New York: Oxford University Press, 1988), p. 135.

13 Suzanne L. Bunkers, 'Reading and Interpreting Unpublished Diaries by Nineteenth-Century Women', *AutoBiography Studies*, 2.2 (1986), pp. 15–17.

14 F. S. Collings, Pocket Diary, 25 March 1915, Imperial War Museum, Documents. 7113.

15 H. T. Clements, War Diary, 23 March 1915, Imperial War Museum, Documents. 3413. The Oxford English Dictionary defines 'Merde' as a French exclamation for 'shit'; it is generally used as a mild, humorous substitute.

16 Michael Roper, 'Between Manliness and Masculinity', p. 345.

17 Arthur Hamilton Gibbs, *A Grey Wave* (London: Hutchinson, 1920), p. 20.

18 Irvine, *God and Tommy Atkins*, p. 125.

19 W. T. Colyer, War Diary, Imperial War Museum, Documents. 7256, pp. 314–15. It should be noted that Colyer's War diary is in fact part diary and part memoir in form. Colyer appears to have copied his war experiences from his diaries into 3 bound, handwritten books, in which he has occasionally added retrospective comments. Additionally, large sections of the texts are unnumbered and are without specific dating.

20 Ibid., p. 322.

21 Ibid., pp. 322–3.

22 It should be noted here that Colyer's elevated language is also likely tied to his desire (whether conscious or not) for posterity. Later in the diaries, for example, he directly addresses the implied reader. Furthermore, the cultural context of his retrospection may have also coloured his description. The citation is taken from Peter Simkins' book, *Kitchener's Army: the Raising of the New Armies, 1914–1916* (Manchester: Manchester University Press, 2007), p. 168.

23 Colyer, Diary, p. 322.

24 Quoted by John Springhill, 'Building character in the British Boy', in J. A. Mangan and J. Walvin (eds), *Manliness and Morality: Middle-class*

Masculinity in Britain and America 1800–1940 (Manchester: Manchester University Press, 1987), p. 67.

25 Ibid., p. 315.
26 Ibid., p. 323.
27 Ibid.
28 Ibid., p. 330.
29 May, *To Fight Alongside Friends*, p. 2.
30 H. T. Clements, War Diary, 21 February 1915, Imperial War Museum, Documents. 3413.
31 Colyer, Diary, p. 331.
32 The complete phrase, 'But now I've said good-bye to Galahad', is taken from Siegfried Sassoon's 1916 sonnet, 'The Poet as Hero' (line 9). The term 'Old Soldier' is used by many combatant writers (see for example, Graves', *Goodbye to All That*, p. 224). The title, highlighting experience, also subtly implies a change is self-perception, especially when self-employed.
33 Samuel Hynes makes a similar point in the fourth chapter of *A War Imagined*, entitled 'Running Down'. It should also be noted that 1916, while a rough approximation, is what most scholars cite as the war's turning point, primarily as a result of the Somme.
34 David Jones, 'Preface', *In Parenthesis* (London: Faber and Faber, [1937] 1963), p. ix.
35 Siegfried Sassoon, 'The Poet as Hero', in Rupert Hart-Davis (ed.), *The War Poems* (London: Faber and Faber, [1916] 1983), p. 61.
36 Coningsby Dawson, *Khaki Courage*, ed. W. J. Dawson (London: John Lane/ The Bodley Head, 1917), pp. 96–7.
37 Harry Drinkwater, *Harry's War: The Great War Diary of Harry Drinkwater*, ed. Jon Cooksey and David Griffiths (London: Ebury Press, 2013), p. 62.
38 Collings, Pocket Diary, 13 June 1915.
39 Drinkwater, Diary, p. 59.
40 Clements, Diary, 20 April 1915. (typed transcription p. 17).
41 Eric Leed, *No Man's Land: Combat and Identity in World War One* (Cambridge: Cambridge University Press, 1979), p. 21.
42 Ibid.
43 Dawson, *Khaki Courage*, letter, 5 February 1917.
44 Unnamed solider, War diary, Imperial War Museum, misc. 229, item 3269.
45 Wilfred Owen, *Wilfred Owen: Collected Letters*, ed. Harold Owen and John Bull (London and Oxford: Oxford University Press), p. 429.
46 Unnamed soldier, War diary, Imperial War Museum, misc. 229, item 3269.
47 Colyer, Diary, p. 430–3.
48 Ibid., pp. 361–2.
49 Pegler, War diary, 15 September 1916, Imperial War Museum, Documents. 4357
50 The famous war psychologist W. H. R. Rivers saw the public school as having successfully taught the young officer 'to repress, not only expressions of fear, but also of emotion itself' (cited by Showalter, *The Female Malady*, p. 175).

51 Jessica Meyer, *Men of War: Masculinity and the First World War in Britain* (New York: Palgrave Macmillan, 2009), p. 143.
52 Roper, 'Between Manliness and Masculinity', p. 345.
53 May, *To Fight Alongside Friends*, pp. 134–5.
54 Drinkwater diary, p. 131.
55 Ibid., 90.
56 Clements, Diary, 30 May 1916, 3 June 1916.
57 Colyer, Diary, Chapter entitled 'Fear', p. 245.
58 R. W. Wilson, War Diary, 1 July 1917, Imperial War Museum, Documents. 7066 (typed transcription, p. 1).
59 J. S. Gatley, War Diary, 4 June 1915, Imperial War Museum, Documents. 15727.
60 Drinkwater, Diary, pp. 95–6.

Santanu Das

Reframing life/war 'writing': objects, letters and songs of Indian soldiers, 1914–1918

Undivided India (India, Pakistan, Bangladesh and Burma) contributed to the First World War more than one million men, including combatants and non-combatants, who fought in places as far-flung as France, Gallipoli, Mesopotamia, East Africa, Egypt, Palestine and Central Asia. But these peasant-warriors have largely been deleted from the annals of 'Great War and modern memory' which till recently had remained Eurocentric. But how do we write the lives of men who were largely non-literate and did not leave us with the super-abundance of diaries, memoirs, poems and journals? Based on intensive archival research, this article unearths a variety of material sources – trench artefacts, mutilated letters and sound-recordings – not only to recover the sensuous world of the Indian sepoys but to ask for a reconceptualisation of the nature of life-writing with its hitherto textual bias. The article at once challenges the colour of war memory and conventional ways of reading – and writing – lives in times of war.

A tremulous yet incantatory voice – interrupted by awkward silences and sharp intakes of breath – crackles from an old phonograph record as the needle scratches against the disc. The speaker refers to himself in the third person, as he narrates his life story in Punjabi, with the voice rising and pausing and rising again till it reaches, and almost spits out, the final word at the end of each line:

> There was a man who would have butter back in India
>
> He would also have two *sers* of milk.
>
> He served for the British.
>
> He joined the European War.
>
> He was captured by the Germans.
>
> He wants to go back to India.
>
> If he goes back to India then he will get that same food.
>
> Three years have already passed.
>
> There's no news as to when there will be peace.
>
> Only if he goes back to India will he get that food.
>
> If he stays here for two more years then he will die.
>
> By God's grace, if they declare peace then we'll go back.[1]

This is the story of Mall Singh, an Indian prisoner of war in the 'Half-moon Camp' at Wünsdorf outside Berlin. The recording was made on 11 December, 1916. He was forced to stand in front of a phonograph machine held before him by his German captors and instructed to speak. More than the 'warm scribe my hand'[2] – lurking behind the manuscript, souvenir or artefact – this bleak voice-recording touches us on that fragile spot where categories collapse. A voice calls out from the phonograph, strains itself in the act of recording: the trepidation, the timbre, the laboured enunciation, the slight breathlessness seem to bridge the gap between technological reproduction and lived experience. Listening to it now, the body and emotion of the speaker seem insurgent, filling in, flowing out, authenticating an encounter with a disembodied voice from 100 years ago.[3] The effect is powerful and uncanny: we are in the presence of the 'real', in whatever way we may define the term.

What is the relation between the sensory (here the sonorous), the testimonial and the 'authentic'? Or, to put the question another way, what is it to listen or to view or even to touch rather than to read in the act of recovering past lives and bodies? 'To listen is *tender l'oreille* – literally, to stretch the ear – an expression that evokes a singular mobility, among the sensory apparatuses, of the pinna of the ear – it is an intensification, a curiosity or an anxiety' notes Jean-Luc Nancy.[4] Exploring the relationship 'between a sense (that one listens to) and a truth (that one understands)', Nancy comments on the age-old hierarchy of the senses, with the visual privileged over the aural, in their relation to the 'conceptual' and yet, the hierarchies shift as we consider questions of contact, trace and affect. Sound and touch, clinging more to the body than vision, pertain to the domain of the intimate; 'visual presence', Nancy notes, can pale before 'acoustic penetration'.[5] But the question that surely must also be asked, in our context, is whether Mall Singh's voice penetrates us because of the way it sounds, or because of the poignant story it tells, or because, in some undefinable way, Mall Singh is *present* in it. The borders are porous; 'sense' and 'truth' (to use Nancy's terms) are fused and often confused in the affect of 'hearing', as it joins 'listening' and 'understanding' (and hence the importance of 'translation', inter-sensorial and linguistic).

What is being said can disturb the pinna as much as the voice. Mall Singh's was among the 2677 audio recordings made by the Royal Prussian Phonographic Commission between 29 December 1915 and 19 December 1918, using the First World War prisoners (POWs) held in Germany.[6] They included a large number of colonial prisoners, including Singh. I shall come back to these men and the recordings later in the article, but for the moment, let us examine the voice-testimony at hand. Desolate, homesick and hungry, Mall Singh distils all the pain and longing into the images of *ghee* (butter) and the two *sers* [a form of measurement] of milk. Home is remembered as taste; but the image conjures into being, beyond memory and desire, the socio-economic conditions of the society he comes from: the agricultural–martial world of colonial Punjab (today divided between India and Pakistan).

Mall Singh's voice is not just a fresh and tantalising source but opens us new ways of 'reading' – and writing – life in times of war: it confronts us with the role of the sensuous, the material and the intimate; it forces us to the weave together a narrative of fugitive fragments, the flotsam, jetsam and lagan of life wrecked by war; it points to the importance of relicts as zones of contact between warm life and historical violence, sacral sites where testimony is born. The wavering of the voice, the blood and bullet-holes on trench artefacts, the creases and crinkliness of trench-letters are in many ways the hand-prints and face-prints of war in the act of writing its own violent life – its peculiar mode of communication – as it slices through human lives and reduces them to piece-meal narratives. What I am arguing for is a mode of reading that goes merely beyond 'reading' – a more active engagement with the material, the aural and the haptic; to *sense* life, as it were, while being alert to the traces of violence; to how, in a fragmentary, tentative, hesitant way, a narrative is built up; to be alive to the role of affect in the relicts and the 'reader'.

Forms and genres are informed by their own histories and hierarchies. Are the different kinds of source material, belonging to different media, to be given equal value? Does materiality invest testimony with the aura of authenticity and if so, what is the relation between affect and the politics of 'combat gnosticism'?[7] Here I shall examine some of these issues with relation to a specific community – the Indian soldiers who served in the Western Front between October 1914 and December 1915. While I have written elsewhere about the small but powerful body of Indian war literature – poems, memoirs and the war novel *Across the Black Waters* by Mulk Raj Anand – here my focus is on fugitive fragments which impinge on our senses and thought.[8] If life-writing involves, as Hermione Lee notes, both 'making up' and 'making over' a 'quasi-fictional story-like shape', with the 'need for accuracy' pulling against it,[9] a project like this one is even more precarious and ramshackle, tipping over to the world of 'make-do' with its assemblage of half-known sonic, textual and material fragments. Such a mode of engagement, as I seek to demonstrate, challenges our notions *both* of life-writing and war-writing, raising questions about agency, posthumous presence and reception. In the colonial context, they take on, as I shall argue, even more vital intensities of meaning. I shall first provide a brief background about these men and then go on to examine three different kinds of testimonies: objects, letters and songs.

Indian soldiers on the Western front

The nineteenth century saw the extensive militarisation of the agricultural and dairy farming communities of the Punjab through the construction of the idea of 'martial races' and the system of rewards of fertile 'canal colonies' for military service. In the post-Mutiny years, the British colonial army had decided that certain ethnic groups – such as Sikhs, Punjabi Mussalmans, Pathans, Gurkhas, Dogras, Jats – were 'naturally' more war-like than others and thereby restricted the recruiting pool of India's vast military to a narrow strip of land along the northern and north-western part of the country, particularly the Punjab. In return, these men – traditionally farmers and dairy-producers – were given agricultural lands. Locking land-grants onto military service was the perverse genius of the British colonial administration that propelled hundreds of thousands of young men, such as Mall Singh, to join the British army and venture into the wide unknown.

The production of ghee and milk back home depended – literally – on their service abroad.[10]

The military-agricultural nexus shaped the texture of everyday life and its narratives; army cantonments sprang up in the heart of rural Punjab. For this community, soldiering was a profession; their life stories became war stories as they grew up in the army and travelled, like their fathers and forefathers, to places such as Cyprus, Egypt, Somalia and China for various 'small' wars – though few knew for whom or what they were fighting, except for those 11 rupees at the end of the month. In 1914, undivided India (comprising today's India, Pakistan, Bangladesh and Burma) had the largest voluntary army in the world. And of all the colonies in the British, French and German empires, it contributed the highest number of men to the war. Between August 1914 and December 1919, it sent overseas over a million men, including 622,224 soldiers and 474,789 non-combatants, who sailed to France, East Africa, Mesopotamia, Salonika, Palestine, Suez, Gallipoli, Aden and the Persian Gulf.[11] They were the twin conscripts of colonialism and modernity for it was the conjunction of cheap labour-markets and modern modes of transportation that facilitated their mobilisation. Of them, some 140,000 were sent to France and Flanders where they served between October 1914 and December 1915, when the Indian infantry was withdrawn and sent to Mesopotamia.

The Indians were among the almost four million colonial troops (from French, German and British colonies) who served in the war.[12] Yet, these men were also the most 'silent' of communities – their experiences have remained largely 'incommunicable' not just because of their traumatic nature but, more immediately, because they did not know how to read or write. The erasure of four million lives from the annals of the 'Great war and modern memory' because of their non-literacy – the absence of written testimonies – also exposes the crippling inadequacy of terms such as 'war-*writing*' and 'life-*writing*', with their textual elitist bias. Indeed, to focus narrowly on the scripted and the literary would leave out the experiences of the majority of soldiers across the world even today and indeed through history (Britain had its first literate army only in the Boer War) and reduce their life stories to the ventriloquism of a select literate cognoscenti. In a context where the colonial soldiers did not leave us with an abundance of diaries, journals, poems and memoirs, it is necessary to go beyond the textual to other forms of evidence – the material, the visual and the aural – and establish a dialogue between them. Mall Singh's voice-recording is not just a fresh source but puts pressure on the very scope and definition of 'war-*writing*' and 'life-*writing*' and underlines the absolute need to 'expand the frame' – both in terms of source material and methodology.

Touching things

In the centre of Kolkata, the former capital of British India, stands the Cenotaph-like memorial (Figure 1) to the soldiers killed in the First World War. Surrounded by statues of the leaders of the Indian nationalist movement, the memorial – with its Latin dates and the statues of the English Tommies marked by their Saxon features and Western military uniform – is for the local people a relic of the Great European war. It is also symptomatic of the cultural amnesia that marks Indian metropolitan middle-class memory (except in the Punjab) about the country's own participation in the conflict.

Figure 1. First World War memorial in Calcutta. Copyright Santanu Das.

Yet memories exist silently, stubbornly, privately. The Flemish countryside continues to throw up traces of its Indian past. A couple of years back, a body was exhumed and identified as that of a Gurkha sepoy when a new road was being built near the Irish cemetery outside Ypres; just last year, I visited a barn in the small village of Ouderdam which was used as a casualty-clearing station for the Indian sepoys.[13] Artefacts of the Indian sepoys can be found around the world. In Ypres, I came across *lotas* – brass water-mugs – with the names of sepoys inscribed on them (Figure 2), and on one of them, an etching of a peacock; in the recruiting village of Bondsi in present-day Haryana (part of colonial Punjab), a man turned up during an interview with a cigarette case his great-grandfather, serving in France, had received from Queen Mary in 1914 as a Christmas gift; in the Australian War Memorial, I chanced upon the diary of an Australian private where an Indian sepoy had signed his name in Gurmukhi, Hindi and English.[14]

A search through my own extended family in Kolkata revealed the war memento of Colonel Dr Manindranath Das (Figure 3): his uniform, whistle, razor, brandy bottle, tiffin-box and album, as well as the Military Cross he was awarded for tending to his men under perilous circumstances. Alongside it was also a German shell-case he had found and which had been locked up in the family wardrobe for nearly a century – almost a metaphor for the subterranean way the memory of the First World War functions in India. Das was one among several distinguished doctors

Figure 2. Lota or water vessel. Private collection. Copyright Dominique Faivre and Santanu Das.

Figure 3. 'Tiffin-box' used by Captain Dr M. N. Roy. Private collection. Copyright Santanu Das.

from the Indian Medical Services who served in Mesopotamia. But most moving of all the artefacts I have come across were those belonging to Jogen Nath Sen in a small archive in the former French colony of Chandernagore in West Bengal: a dog-tag (to identify the injured), a photograph of a young European woman, a 'Book of Friendship' possibly given by this lady (signed as 'Cis'), a small leather wallet and finally a pair of broken glasses, placed next to a photograph of Sen wearing them. The label said: 'Broken and bloodstained glasses belonging to J. N. Sen, Private, West Yorkshire Regiment ... he was the first Bengalee, a citizen of Chandernagore, to be killed in 1914-1918 War' (Figure 4).[15]

Why do these objects touch and move us? Like the crackling voice of Mall Singh, these artefacts have a precious, living quality for they are the archives of touch and intimacy. The inscribed *lota*, the rusty cigarette-box, the diary, the tunic, the tiffin-box, the whistle, the brandy bottle or the broken glasses evoke the body of the user or possessor, hand-prints and face-prints – quiescent but palpable. They not only congeal time but also conceal processes of care. Like its more famous European cousin, the pocket-watch on Edward Thomas's wrist, its hands perpetually fixed at 7.36 am as it recorded the time of its master's death, the broken and bloodied glasses of Sen had borne testimony to the final moments

Figure 4. Objects belonging to J. N. Sen. Copyright Chandernagore Museum and Santanu Das.

of his life. The fragility of the glasses intensifies their Ozymandias-like persistence, particularly when seen next to the photograph of Sen wearing them: the effect, like the voice of Mall Sigh, is uncanny. The poignant materiality of the objects results from a constant frisson between presence and loss: a constant reminder both of the sensuousness of the life they had known and of its absence. In his celebrated essay on museum culture, 'Resonance and Wonder' (1990), Stephen Greenblatt points out the 'resonance' that certain material objects of the past hold for us – the threadbare fabric of an old chair or a vase broken by Marcel Proust – not because of their aesthetic value but because 'of use, the imprint of the human body on the artefact'. More recently, he has suggested that historical anecdotes and vignettes provide for him the 'touch of the real', giving insights into 'the contact zone', the 'charmed space where the *genius literarius* could be conjured into existence'.[16] Similarly, Susan Stewart has noted how, in glass-cases in museums, 'the contagious magic of touch is replaced by the sympathetic magic of visual representation' and observes 'the constant play among deixis, tact, proximity and negation'.[17] Indeed, war-objects and life-objects are sensory palimpsests where multiple bodies, experiences and time-scales touch and rub against each other in a series of fantasised encounters. And yet, the most visceral of encounters are dependent on the surrounding information, on the power of narrative and context.

Consider, for example, the glasses of Jogen Sen. Our responses are largely determined by the information in the label: 'broken and bloodstained'. But that single label led me to a research-trail and the gradual unravelling of a remarkable life. Jogen Sen, son of a widowed mother, had come to the University of Leeds in 1910; by 1913, he had taken a degree in Engineering and was singing in the choir of the Mill Hill Unitarian Chapel; he volunteered in the opening months of the conflict in the Leeds Pals Battalion and was the only non-white member of the West Yorkshire regiment; he was gunned down on the night of 22 May, 1916, and his death as reported in *The Times* on 4 September 1916 as 'A Bengali Soldier's Death'. During an interview in 1988, Arthur Dalby, a Leeds Pals veteran, remembered his Indian comrade:

> We had a Hindu in our hut, called Jon Sen. He was the best educated man in the battalion and he spoke about seven languages but he was never allowed to be even a lance corporal because in those days they would never let a coloured fellow be over a white man, not in England, but he was the best educated.

More revelations followed in 2001, when a wartime letter surfaced, written by another Leeds Pals comrade. Private Burniston, just before his own death on July 1, 1916, wrote: 'I heard poor Jon Sen had been brought in killed. He was hit in the leg and neck by shrapnel and died almost immediately.'[18] In 2004, almost by accident, I had discovered the glasses of an unknown young man tucked away in a small, dark, dusty glass-cabinet in the Chandernagore archive; exactly ten years later, in 2014, I revisited the archive, armed with the story of his life and a film crew. This time, the glasses were no longer in the cabinet but had been taken out for us. They looked different from what I remembered, transformed undoubtedly by all that I knew now. I lifted with my naked hands Jogen Sen's glasses which looked uncannily like my own – the standard gold-rimmed glasses worn by the Bengali *bhadralok* ('gentlemen') over generations; the process was intimate and unsettling.

Letters

Two photographs from the Imperial War Museum archives accost each other with particular poignancy. The first image is a close-up of hands: a white hand – uniformed, confident and bureaucratic – grasps and guides the fingers of the 'coloured' hand to get a thumb impression. The caption says: 'An Indian, unable to write, is putting his thumb impression on the pay-book'[19] (Figure 5). Insurgent under this touch is not just the body of the participants but the weight of colonial history. This brisk, bureaucratic touch is answered in the second photograph by a more

Figure 5. 'An Indian, unable to write, is putting his thumb impression on the pay-book'. © Imperial War Museums.

lingering, tender moment. Here, a wounded (and semi-literate) sepoy dictates to a scribe or a fellow-sepoy a letter (Figure 6).[20] The violent traces of war are all too evident in his wheelchair-bound body; but the clunky

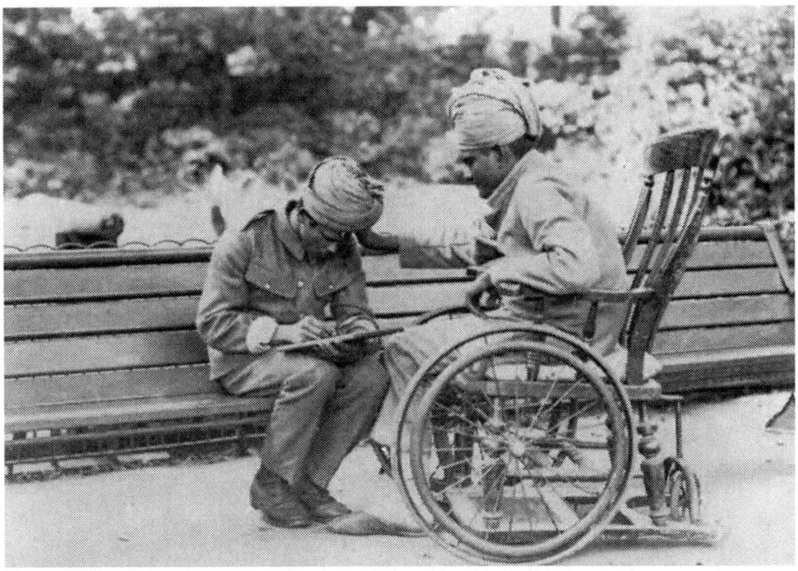

Figure 6. A wounded sepoy dictates a letter to a scribe or fellow-sepoy. © Imperial War Museums.

mechanism is offset as the sepoy leans across to touch the scribe or fellow-sepoy. As opposed to the impersonal rub of fingers in the first photograph, this is a gesture of gratitude, trust and intimacy: thank you for writing, the hand says, as the body fills in the gap left by language. It also provides insights into the collaborative and oral processes through which the letters – our main sources of information – were composed.

The most substantial yet tantalising sources remain the censored versions of these letters by the Indian troops. Between March and April 1915, the Indian soldiers from France were writing around 10,000 letters a week. What have survived are substantial extracts from the letters, as selected and translated by the colonial censors at the time to assess the 'morale' of the Indian troops. Their heavily mediated nature thus undermines their testimonial value but, as David Omissi notes in the introduction to his anthology *Indian Voices of the Great War: Soldiers' Letters, 1914-1918* (1991), 'The crucial issue is, surely, less what we cannot learn from these letters, than what we can learn from them.'[21]

However, given their multiple sites of textuality – mouth to hand, hand to print, Hindi, Gurmukhi, or Urdu to English, whole to part – these letters put pressure on the very concept of 'authenticity'. Are these letters private or public? How far can one generalise about Indian war experience on the basis of textual fragments? It is tempting to read these letters – incomplete, fragmentary, tantalising – as the sign of the necessarily partial knowledge we have of trench-life, the material trace of the impossibility of ever fully understanding trench experience. By early 1915, the soldiers realised that their letters were being read and censored, and they drew on elaborate codes to avoid censorship, as in the following letter written in April 1915, after the battle of Neuve Chapelle, advising against further recruitment: 'The black pepper which has come from India has all been finished, so now the red pepper is being used. But the red pepper is little used and the black more.'[22] The 'black pepper' refers to the Indian troops while the 'red pepper' refers to the English.

These letters are best read not as transparent envelopes of sepoy experience but as *palimpsests* where underneath accretions by different agencies, one can hear the echoes of the sepoy heart. Neither the transcript of trench experience nor just scribal embellishment, these letters are among the earliest examples we have of South Asian subaltern 'writing' - some of the earliest encounters between textual form and plebeian testimony. Life-writing here begins *as* war-writing; at the same time, these missives from France and Flanders bear testimony to a subaltern history of feeling. One can imagine the range of emotions – thrill, wonder, excitement, fear, terror, horror, homesickness, grief, envy, religious doubts – that the sepoy must have experienced as he encountered new lands, people, cultures. For centuries, he had been travelling as an imperial sentinel – in

Somalia, China, Malta, Egypt – but during the First World War, he wrote for the first time and the processes of colonial censorship paradoxically ensured that extracts from his letters survived. Sepoy letters thus have the distinction of being South Asia's first examples of life-writing from 'below'.

These letters open up a whole new world in First World War history and culture, and cover an extraordinary range of topics and emotions, from an initial sense of wonder at the modernity of France ('The country is very fine, well-watered and fertile . . . Each house is a sample of Paradise'), to comments on the people, their clothes and manners, or the occasional thrilling account of romance and sexual braggadocio ('The ladies are very nice and bestow their favours upon us freely'), to observations on issues such as gender, education and class distinctions. The letters are haunted by the images of the heart: 'My heart wishes to unburden itself,' 'My heart was day and night fixed on home,' 'My heart is sadly failing,' 'My heart is not at ease, for I can see no way of saving my life.' Perhaps because of the censors, or internal pressures of masculinity, honour and patriarchy, feelings are often not voiced directly; instead, they lead to a thickening of language as emotions such as horror, resignation or homesickness express themselves in images, metaphors and similes:

> The condition of affairs in the war is like leaves falling off a tree, and no empty space remains on the ground. . . . When we attacked the German trenches we used bayonet and the kukri, and the bullets flew about more thickly than drops of rain.[23] (Amar Singh Rawat (Garhwal Rifles) from Kitchener's Indian Hospital to Dayaram Jhapaliyal in Garhwal, 1 April, 1915)
>
> For God's sake don't come, don't come, don't come to this war in Europe. . . . Cannons, machine guns, rifles and bombs are going day and night, just like the rains in the month of Sawan. Those who have escaped so far are like the few grains left uncooked in a pot.[24] (Havildar Abdul Rahman (Punjabi Muslim) from France to Naik Rajwali Khan in Baluchistan, 20 May, 1915)
>
> As tired bullocks and bull buffaloes lie down in the month of Bhadon so lies the weary world. Our hearts are breaking, for a year has passed while we have stood to arms without a rest . . . Germany fights the world with ghastly might, harder to crush than well-soaked grain in the mill. For even wetted grain can be ground in time. . . . We have bound ourselves under the flag and we must give our bodies.[25] (from Santa Singh, hospital in Brighton, to his uncle in India, 18 August, 1915)

The images of 'dry forest in hot wind' or 'tired bullocks' or 'well-soaked grain' are not just communicative gestures or literary embellishments but repositories of feeling: although they have been transported thousands of miles, images from the agrarian world of the Punjab are used as the men try to make sense of themselves, the world and the war; their traditional cognitive and narrative processes are at once drawn upon and pushed to their limits. Realism is eschewed for the metaphoric, the fantastic, the mythical as they bear testimony to life as *felt*. Whether occurring at the level of experience or representation, these letters, freighted with images, similes and allusions, can be read as Indian *literature* of the trenches: these men may have been non-literate but being non-literate does not mean being non-literary.

The letters are often treated as linguistic bubbles on the dark sea of South Asian plebeian history but they are rooted in the extraordinarily vibrant oral culture of the Punjab. In *The Social Space of Language: Vernacular Culture in British Colonial Punjab* (2010), Farina Mir excavates the remarkably polyglot nature of 'literary formation' of the Punjab through its various sites of *oral* circulation: the recitation of qissas (stories), poetry competitions, the singing of *shabads* (devotional songs) or plays in village fairs and religious festivals.[26] Between 1884 and 1901, when the British army officer Richard Temple decided to collect folktales – the basis of his three-volume *Legends of the Punjab* – he hired 'bards' to *perform* these texts, showing the deep connections between orality and memory. What we see in the letters is the remarkable transition from a vibrant and robust oral culture to a textual culture of letter-writing: a whole generation of men who had grown up listening to stories now begin to draw on those structures as they start to narrate their own lives. This possibly explains why Mall Singh refers to himself in the third person, or begins the way he does: 'There was a man.'

Songs

However, of all the sources, the most haunting are the voice-recordings made in the German POW camps. Around a thousand Indian soldiers were taken prisoners on the Western Front and most of them were kept in the twin camps of Zossen and Wunsdorf, south of Berlin (Figure 7). At both these camps, the POWs were studied, photographed, sketched, and their voices recorded for purposes of academic research. Mall Singh's soulful lament, with which we began, was one of the over 300 South Asian recordings in this 2677-strong archive of audio recordings produced by the Royal Prussian Phonographic Commission between 29 December 1915 and 19 December 1918.[27]

Masterminded by the philologist Wilhelm Doegen, the Commission comprised thirty academics – including ethnologists, linguists and anthropologists – who toured thirty-one prison camps in Germany and made

Figure 7. Ram Singh, an Indian POW washes his feet before praying while a German guard watches him in the POW Wünsdorf camp. Copyright Museum Europäischer Kulturen, Berlin.

recordings in approximately 250 languages and dialects. A photograph from a contemporary publication shows Professor Heinrich Luders – a professor of the Oriental seminar in Berlin University, who became quite close to some of the POWs and was concerned about their welfare – interacting with a group of Gurkha sepoys and taking down notes on the language (Figure 8). Yet, the conditions under which many of the sound-recordings were made were harsh: another picture captures the very process. The person whose reading is being recorded is flanked on either side by a German official: a hand on the speaker's shoulders holds him firmly in place so that the voice is projected onto the phonograph funnel while the other hand of the officer holds a sheet of paper from which he is made to read out. A popular text the soldiers were often given to read was the 'Parable of the

Figure 8. Professor Heinrich Lüders from Berlin University with a group of Gurkha prisoners at the Wünsdorf camp from *Unsere Feinde* (Stuttgart, 1916).

Prodigal Son'. If Friday had his tongue cut out in Coetzee's *Foe*, these prisoners seem to have been muted in the very act of speaking, forced to read out from a text given to them by their captors. But Mall Singh, managing to bypass authoritarian control and communicating to us his plaintive message, seems to defy such formulation: *can* the subaltern then speak?

In her celebrated essay on subaltern speech (first published in 1988 and revised subsequently), Gayatri Chakravorty Spivak moves from her critique of the models of Western subjectivity to a note of 'passionate lament', as she tells us the story of Bhubaneswari Bhaduri, with its combination of revolutionary nationalism, suicide and the tragic failure of communication, and makes the controversial claim: 'The subaltern cannot speak.'[28] In this frisson – the over-articulate poignancy of the story brushing against the claim made in the concluding statement – lay the power of the essay, and its seemingly paradoxical nature. Has not Bhubaneswari Bhaduri spoken most powerfully through her dead, menstruating, bleeding body? Of the various responses this essay has spawned, Rajeshwari Sunderajan provides one of the most acute and corrective expositions:

> [Bhubaneswari] serves as the figural example of the subaltern who cannot – but in fact, does speak. 'Cannot' in this context signifies not speech's absence but its failure. . . . In other words and more generally, the locution 'Can the Subaltern speak' is an invitation to rethink the relation between the figural and the literal.[29]

The plangent materiality of the German POW sound-recordings seems to push this differential relation between the literal and the figural to a crisis-point. Here at long last, or so it seems, is the unmediated subaltern voice: archival recovery, the shellac recording, peasant consciousness and wartime captivity touch and blend, speaking to us powerfully across a century. Who was Mall Singh addressing, as he spoke into the funnel of the recording machine? 'By speaking', writes Spivak, 'I was obviously talking about a transaction between the speaker and the listener.'[30] Forced to address a recording machine rather than a responsive individual and locked at the site of failed communication – 'not speech's absence but its failure' – Mall Singh's voice has echoed through the corridors of First World War history for almost a century in its desperate attempt to find a listener. Mall Singh could not speak, even though he spoke so urgently; or, to push Spivak's formulation further, he seems to speak to us so urgently today precisely because he could not speak then.

Spivak's troubling question – 'With what voice-consciousness can the subaltern speak?' – becomes freshly resonant in the context of these extraordinary recordings.[31] Of the 2677 sound-recordings in the Archive, around 135 recordings seem to be that of South Asian prisoners. The languages used are Hindi, Urdu, Punjabi, Marathi, Nepalese, Khas, Gurkhali, Bengali and English. They range from minimal linguistic exercises such as the 1.09-minute recording of Karamar Ali reading out the letters of the Bengali alphabet to Bela Sigh describing his arrival in Marseilles to the 3.20-minute-long speech of Mohammed Hossin (Hussain) narrating the story of his capture by a German ship and of his life in the POW camp.[32] Can they be examined alongside the letters to understand more fully the intimate and affective history of these men? To uncover a subaltern history of emotions from so aggressive an ethnological and propagandist an archive is to stretch the practice of reading the colonial archive against the grain to its limit. Any reading has to be necessarily tentative and incomplete. But one wonders why any particular story was selected above others by these narrators? Of course it depended on what the sepoys remembered or wrote down but often these men chose parables and tales that echoed their own predicament. Thus, the story narrated by a sepoy of 'a parrot who died shivering with cold' gathers special poignancy when we realise that it was recorded in December 1916 in the Wünsdorf camp which had a mortality rate were as high as 18 per cent. Or consider the following audio recording:

> Swan and Heron became friends. Swan lived in his own homeland but Heron was staying in Swan's homeland away from his own homeland. Heron used to feel nostalgic about his own homeland. Swan asked him the reason for his unhappiness. Swan said to

> Heron: 'why are you unhappy and why don't you eat anything?' Heron replied that he has received news about his homeland and was therefore nostalgic. Swan thought that perhaps Heron's home was far better than Swan's homeland and that was why he was missing it. Swan concluded by saying that one's nation (vatan) is very dear to one, it may not be very good, but even then, one is desirous to return to one's own land.[33]

Is it at once an ingenuous plea to the outside world and a desperate form of life-narrative to articulate its own predicament?

An important clue is provided by the German scholar and linguist Heinrich Lüders who closely studied the Indian troops at Wünsdorf.[34] Lüders observed:

> Certainly, the majority did not have the confidence to tell a coherent story. Instead they preferred to sing a song, either alone or accompanied by others. ... Old verses are constantly altered, extended and copied until something utterly new emerges. The singer is at the same time always to a greater or lesser degree the poet, and people know that too; 'if I want to sing a song, I make one up', one of them admitted.[35]

Indeed, one such song was recorded on 6 June, 1916 – one of the most heart-breaking of testimonies in the whole pantheon of First World War life stories. All that is known about it is that it was sung by 'Jasbahadur Rai', a 23-year-old Gurkha sepoy from Sikkim/Darjeeling, and that it was a 'Gurkha song, own words'. Jasbahadur must have died shortly afterwards for his grave can be found outside the Zossen camp. In the final part of this article, it is to him that I would like to turn.

The song is recoded in two instalments; here is the first one:[36]

Nepali transcription	English translation
Sisai kholā badhi jyān āyo bagāyo bulbule	With the rising of the Sisai river, I came, carried in its bubbling flow
Na ḍuī jānu na basī āunu, man rūnchha durūrū	Neither can we fly away, nor can we arrive while staying put, the heart cries, sobbing
Hai suna suna, sun lāune didī, man rūnchha durūrū	Listen, oh listen, gold-wearing sister, the heart cries, sobbing
Pāniko bulbul, yo manko chulbul, bujhāūchhau katin din	The bubbling of water, the restlessness of this heart, how many days will it take to console yourself?

Nepali transcription	English translation
Hai suna suna, sun lāune kānchhī, bujhāūchhau katin din	Listen, oh listen, gold-wearing little one, how many days will it take to console yourself?
Dui paisa bache tabalmar sigret salkāula mārchisle	If I save two cents, I'll light a Tabalmar cigarette with matches
Hindustān pāri, ke rāmro pahāḍ, ghā̃saiko khaliyo	Across Hindustan, what beautiful hills, storage places for fodder
Baseko pirtī, chutāunam bhayo, man bā̃dha baliyo	The love we've had, we now have to break apart, bind your heart and be strong
Hai suna suna, sun lāune chari man bā̃dha baliyo	Listen, oh listen, gold-wearing birdie, bind your heart and be strong

Like Mall Singh's, the song is interrupted by awkward pauses and sharp intakes of breath. Yet there is a passionate intensity to the singing, a compulsive need to tell: the voice rises and falls, high-pitched, desolate, undeterred. Traumatised by his experience and perhaps haunted by the knowledge of his approaching death, Jasbahadur turns an ethnographical experiment into one of the most haunting examples of life-narrative.

In both metre and melody, Jasbahadur draws on a subgenre of Nepali song called *jheyru*, which was traditionally a feminine lament. The refrain 'Hai suna suna' ('Listen, oh listen', lines 3, 5, 9), Ancient Mariner-like, draws the listener into the song through an intricate sonic structure, combining alliteration (*suna suna sun laune*) with a pattern of repetition with variation centring around the addressee – 'didi' (elder sister), 'kanchi' (little girl), 'chari' (birdie). In the centre of this masculinist universe is its silent interlocutor – a little girl – anxious, weeping, disconsolate; the pain of separation is built into the very structure of narration. Water (*pani*) courses through the song, first entering as memory ('Sisai', a river in Nepal, and then the sea journey) but soon seeps into its every pore as bodily fluid ('cries, sobbing') before being translated back to water for purification of the dying body ('will you wash my body'): memory, metaphor and mourning are knitted together through onomatopoeia and rhyme ('paniko bulbul, ei monko chulbul': the bubbling of the water, the restlessness of the heart) as sound becomes the sense. Cigarettes and matchsticks rub against mountains and flowers, Belgium and Germany are brought together, the year of the war's eruption is remembered through sense perception. Jasbahadur is the First World War poet par excellence for he records history not as grand narrative or even cultural memory but as what Raymond Williams calls 'a structure of feeling', as in the poems of European soldier-poets. Blurring the boundaries between song, reportage, lament, j'accuse, prison-narrative and compulsive testimony, it is also the birth of life-writing as war-writing while a local Nepali genre – the *jheyru* – is called upon to bear lyric testimony to historical trauma.

In her inspired study *Body Parts: Essays on Life-Writing* (2010), Hermione Lee notes that the challenge for the biographer lies in the art of evocation rather than narration, in being able to touch life at several points rather than try to capture its complete arc. What life-writing does is to rescue from oblivion not the entire narrative but certain vital moments: 'bodily sensations and memories', 'moments of physical shock' or the 'left-over parts of a life'.[37] The method that Lee suggests is more like the art of the short story than that of the *bildungsroman* – an aesthetics of fugitive fragments. As signalled in her very title, there is an insistent harping on the body, the material, the senses:

> What makes biography so curious and endlessly absorbing is that through all the documents and the letters, the context and the witnesses, the conflicting opinions and the evidence of the work, we keep catching sight of a real body, a physical life: the young Dickens, bright-eyed and sprightly in a crimson velvet waistcoat, Rimbaud dust-covered and scrawny or Joyce with a black felt hat, thick glasses and a cigar.[38]

If Lee's vignettes are still largely from the realm of written – diaries, letters, novels – what these semi-literate sepoys force us to do is to go beyond the textual. What the *lota*, the blood-stained glasses, the cigarette-box, the scrawl on the diary, the mutilated letters, the hesitant, faltering voice of Mall Singh or the compulsive singing of Jasbahadur Rai evoke – when assembled, matched and made to bear pressure on each other – is not the completeness of one life, one story; instead, they help us to *sense* the life of a whole war-ravaged community whose 'body parts' – like scattered limbs of the Egyptian god Osiris or the Hindu goddess Kali – lie strewn all across the globe.

King's College London

Acknowledgements

I am grateful to the editors – Lara Feigel and Kate McLoughlin – for their invitation to contribute to this volume, their patience and their thoughtful comments which have helped to improve this piece. The article is part of a bigger book-project – *India, Empire and the First World War: Objects, Images, Words and Music*, to be published by Cambridge University

Press in 2017 and some of the research is showcased in the short YouTube video *From Bombay to the Western Front* (https://www.youtube.com/watch?v=6stybO5v7SY). This article shares some archival and research material with another recent article of mine – 'Indian Sepoy Experience in Europe, 1914-1918: Archive, Language and Feeling' in *Twentieth Century British History* (August, 2014), but the argument and focus of the present piece is different.

Disclosure statement

No potential conflict of interest was reported by the author.

Notes

1 Mall Singh, Voice-recording, Humboldt University Sound Archive, PK 619. Translation from Punjabi by Arshdeep Brar.
2 'The Fall of Hyperion', in *The Poems of John Keats*, ed. Miriam Allot (London: Longman, 1970), pp. 657–8.
3 See Gillian Beer's wonderful reading of Keats's hand in 'Four Bodies on the Beagle', in *Open Fields: Science in Cultural Encounter* (Oxford: Oxford University Press, 1999), p. 14, which has influenced my understanding of Mall Sing's voice.
4 Jean-Luc Nancy, *Listening* (New York: Fordham University Press, 2007), p. 5.
5 Nancy, *Listening*, pp. 2–3.
6 These archival sound recordings are still largely unknown. For the fullest record on the German POWS at Wünsdorf, see Ravi Ahuja, Heike Liebau, and Franziska Roy (eds), *'When the War Began, We Heard of Several Kings': South Asian Prisoners in World War I Germany* (Delhi: Social Science Press, 2011), particularly Britta Lange's essay on 'South Asian Soldiers and German Academics', pp. 149–86.
7 See James Campbell, 'Combat Gnosticism: The Ideology of First World War Criticism', *New Literary History*, 30 (1) (1999), pp. 203–15.
8 For a different approach, where I *do* draw upon published memoirs and literary texts, see my essay on 'Touching Semi-literate Lives', in Maria Dibattista and Emily Whitman (eds), *Modernism and Autobiography* (Cambridge: Cambridge University Press, 2014). Also see my article 'Indian Sepoy Experience in Europe, 1914–1918: Archive, Language and Feeling' in *Twentieth Century British History* (August 2014) which shares some archival material with the present article, but the focus and argument is different.
9 Lee, *Body Parts: Essays on Life-Writing* (London: Chatto, 2005), p. 28.
10 For military histories of India and the First World War, see David Omissi, *The Sepoy and the Raj, The Indian Army, 1860-1940* (London: Macmillan, 1994), Gordon Corrigan, *Sepoys in the Trenches: The Indian Corps on the Western*

Front 1914-1918 (Staplehurst, UK: Spellmount, 1999), and George Morton Jack, *The Indian Army on the Western Front: Indian Expeditionary Force to France and Belgium in the First World War* (Cambridge: Cambridge University Press, 2014); for socio-cultural history, see Santanu Das, *Indians on the Western Front 1914-1918* (Paris: Gallimard, 2014) and the chapters on the First World War in Rozina Visram, *Asians in Britain* (London: Pluto Press, 2002), and Gajendra Singh, *The Testimonies of the Indian Soldiers and the Two World Wars: Between Self and Sepoy* (London: Bloomsbury, 2014).

11 The above figures are from *Statistics of the Military Effort of the British Empire During the Great War, 1914-1920* (London: His Majesty's Stationery Office, 1920), p. 777 and reproduced in *India's Contribution to the Great War* (Calcutta: Superintendent Government Printing, India, 1923), p. 79.

12 For figures and context, see Santanu Das, *Race, Empire and First World War Writing* (Cambridge: Cambridge University Press, 2011), p. 4 (pp. 1–32).

13 Interview with Paul Jacob for the documentary *From Bombay to the Western Front: Indian Soldiers in the Great War* (https://www.youtube.com/watch?v=6stybO5v7SY).

14 Interview with collector Domique Faivre, France and villagers in Haryana for Radio 4 programme on 'Recruitment and Resistance', 15 October 2014 (http://www.bbc.co.uk/programmes/b04l0zq5); Charles Stinson, 'Diary', Australian War Memorial, Canberra, PR84/066.

15 J. N. Sen, Artefacts at the Dupleix Museum, Chundernagore, West Bengal. These archival finds as well as freshly discovered documents at Leeds have now inspired a BBC documentary on J. N. Sen (http://www.bbc.co.uk/news/uk-england-leeds-31761904).

16 Stephen Greenblatt, *Learning to Curse: Essays in Early Modern Culture* (New York: Routledge, 1990), p. 172 (pp. 161–83); 'Touch of the Real', *Representations*, No. 59 (Summer 1997), p. 29 (pp. 14–29).

17 Susan Stewart, *Poetry and the Fate of the Senses* (Chicago, IL: Chicago University Press, 2002), pp. 174–5.

18 All this information can be found on the web page dedicated to him under the Leeds Pals Battalion website (http://www.leeds-pals.com/soldiers/jogendra-sen), accessed 16 February 2015. In a happy and rare coincidence, I was speaking about Jon Sen and showing pictures of the glasses in a talk at Leeds when I was interrupted mid-sentence by a gentleman in the audience who told me that the subject of enquiry was mentioned just outside the lecture-hall in the Leeds Memorial! There has recently been a whole project on Jogen Sen by a group of scholars at Leeds, and BBC Yorkshire is doing a short documentary on him.

19 Imperial War Museum (henceforth abbreviated as IWM) Photograph Archives.

20 IWM Photograph Archives.

21 Omissi, *Indian Voices of the Great War: Soldiers' Letters, 1914-1918* (Basingstoke: Macmillan, 1991), p. 9. Also see Omissi, 'Europe Through Indian Eyes', *The English Historical Review*, 122 (496) (2007), pp. 371–396; Visram, *Asians in Britain* (London: Pluto, 2002), pp. 169–401.

22 Mausa Ram from Kitchener's Indian Hospital to Naik Dabi Shahai, April 1915, *Censor of Indian Mails 1914-1918*, British Library, India Office Records (abbreviated henceforth as IOR), L/MIL/5/825/2, 208.
23 IOR, L/MIL/5/825/2, 245.
24 IOR, L/MIL/5/825/3, 394.
25 IOR, L/MIL/5/825/5, 758.
26 Farina Mir, *The Social Space of Language: Vernacular Culture in British Colonial Punjab* (Berkeley: University of California Press, 2010), p. 17.
27 See Jürgen Mahrenholz, 'Ethnographic Audio Recordings' and Britta Lange, 'Academic Research on (Coloured) Prisoners of War', in Dominiek Dendooven and Piet Chielens (eds), *World War I: Five Continents in Flanders* (Ypres: Lannoo, 2008), pp. 153–65, and Britta Lange, 'South Asian Soldiers and German Academics', in *'When the War Began, We Heard of Several Kings': South Asian Prisoners in World War I Germany*, pp. 149–86.
28 This was first published as Spivak, 'Can the Subaltern Speak?', in Cary Nelson and Lawrence Grossberg (eds), *Marxism and the Interpretation of Culture* (London: Macmillan, 1988). My references are to its reprint in Rosalind Morris (ed.), *Can the Subaltern Speak? Reflections on the History of an Idea* (New York: Columbia University Press, 2010), abbreviated hereafter as *CSS*.
29 Rajeswari Sunderajan, 'Speaking of (Not) Hearing: Death and the Subaltern' in *CSS*, p. 112.
30 Gayatri Chakravorty Spivak, 'Subaltern Talk' in The Spivak Reader eds. Donna Laudry and Gerald Maclean (New York and London: Routledge, 1996), p. 289.
31 'Can the Subaltern Speak?' in *CSS*, p. 255.
32 Mohammed Hossin (Hussain), 'Story from the Gull', Lautarchiv, Humboldt University, PK1151.
33 Lautarchiv, Humboldt University, PK828.
34 See Lange, 'South Asian Soldiers and German Academics', p. 157.
35 Heinrich Lüders, 'Die Gurkhas', in Wilhelm Doegen (ed.), *Unter fremden Volkern. Eine neue Volkerkunde* (Berlin: Stollberg, 1925), p. 135 (pp. 126–39). I use the translation quoted in Lange, 'South Asian Soldiers'.
36 Jasbahadur Rai, recorded on 6 June 1916, Lautarchiv PK 307. I am very grateful to Anne Stirr for the translation.
37 Lee, *Body Parts*, p. 4.
38 Ibid., p. 3.

Lara Feigel

'The only diary I have kept': visionary witnessing in the second world war short story

This article explores the popularity of the short story in the Second World War, arguing that for writers including Elizabeth Bowen, Henry Green, Rose Macaulay and William Sansom the short story formed a kind of war diary, assuaging their need to witness authentically the history they were participating in as firemen, ambulance drivers or Air Raid Precautions (ARP) wardens. Focusing on stories set in London, the article suggests that the short story was unusually appropriate for representing the bombing war because both the short story and the bombing incident are structured around a single protracted moment or series of moments. So too, partly because of its temporality, which prevents the kind of extended rational analysis common in novels, the short story is conducive to representing the strange or unseen. In a war that saw the dismantling of the boundaries between ordinary and extraordinary, and living and dead, the short story came into its own as a form well-suited for what is here termed 'unrealistic realism' or what Elizabeth Bowen called 'lucid abnormality'. This is an aesthetic in which realist documentary narratives can be peopled with ghosts, making it possible for Bowen to describe her wartime ghost stories as 'the only diary I have kept'.

In the wake of the Second World War, the firefighting short story writer William Sansom described the genesis of his wartime short stories. During the early weeks of the Blitz, convinced that he would be dead in a week, he had decided to write an accurate account of his recent experiences. 'I thought, Hell I'll write down exactly what all this feels like'. In view of his impending death, he was not concerned with being publishable, only with being authentic in documenting the thoughts and feelings brought about by firefighting. 'The truth, the wish to tell it to myself and a few others, was plainly the kernel of the matter'.[1] He was a participant in an extraordinary moment and he wished to record as truthfully as possible the history that he was both witnessing and forging.

Sansom's desire to witness was shared by many on the Home Front in Britain during the Blitz and indeed by combatants and non-combatants in all theatres in the Second World War. Compiling his recent anthology of Second World War diaries, Richard Aldrich found that 'thousands of people who regarded their lives as unremarkable concluded that they had now become "witnesses to war"' and felt compelled to write a diary at this time. Typical of these is Anne Somerhausen, a Belgian woman who rushed to find pen and paper as she heard the first bombs dropped on Brussels. 'Somehow, shaken out of my sleep I knew . . . I must record all this for my children to read some day'. Looking back on his wartime diary, Oliver Harvey, the private secretary to Anthony Eden (then Leader of the House of Commons), observed that the value of his diary lay in 'its "hotness", in the immediate impression and atmosphere'.[2]

Those who were writers already felt the duty to observe and record even more strongly. The firefighting novelist Henry Yorke (who wrote novels under the pseudonym Henry Green) described the war as 'an absolute gift to the writer. Everything is breaking up. A seed can lodge and sprout in any crack or fissure'.[3] In the middle of the Blitz he announced that he was 'working, at writing like a beaver. What I'm doing is absolutely no good but it's the only thing to do'.[4] However somewhat surprisingly, relatively few of the writers who participated in the war as combatants or more commonly in the Civil Defence Services in London kept diaries. Committed diarists such as Evelyn Waugh (enlisted as a marine) or Virginia Woolf (largely at home in Sussex) continued to do so, others such as Graham Greene (working in the Ministry of Information by day and as an Air Raid Precautions (ARP) warden at night) and William Sansom kept diaries for a week or so at a time but these tended to be abandoned when the events of the war overtook them. Busyness alone does not account for this. Huge numbers of politicians and civil servants who were equally pressed for time managed to keep up wartime diaries, driven by the need to witness described by Sansom and Yorke. Instead, it would seem from Sansom's account of his short story writing that the function of diaries – Somerhausen's need to record for future generations, Harvey's need to make the most of his immediacy – could be fulfilled by fiction; that stories written to tell the truth could share the 'hotness' of Harvey's diary.

It is significant that in Sansom's case the fiction was short. During the Blitz, writing in the twenty-four hours of leave firemen were granted after their forty-eight hour shifts, both Sansom and Yorke wrote brief, autobiographical sketches, not yet ready to attempt to weave their experiences into a longer form. Similarly, the ARP warden novelists Elizabeth Bowen and Graham Greene were writing short stories and the ambulance-driving Rose Macaulay wrote an autobiographical short story in 1942 that constituted her only fictional writing of the war.

The popularity of the short story in the Second World War has received surprisingly little attention.[5] It was clearly partly the result of shortages of time and paper.[6] But perhaps there were formal qualities that made the short story unusually well-suited to document this particular war. In this article I will argue that the short story was a dominant literary form between 1939 and 1945 and will ask why this was the case. In the process I will contend that short stories in this period constituted a form of life-writing, specifically fulfilling the function of diaries. Though longer works of fiction and non-fiction were also written, I am suggesting that the particular compulsion to witness that I have noted in Sanson and others manifested itself in short story writing, and that this was the case because short stories were an appropriate form for witnessing the particular experience of being in London under the bombs.

The focus is on short stories set in London during the bombing war (primarily the Blitz but also the later periods of bombing) by writers who were involved in the Civil Defence services in some capacity, because bombed London is the most prevalent setting for war stories written at this time. It seems significant quite how high a proportion of these stories were autobiographical, told from the perspective of a character who shares the outward circumstances and even the first name of the author, blurring the boundary between fiction and reportage. Tellingly, even when the stories do not seem to be overtly autobiographical, the writers often testify that they are. At the end of the war Elizabeth Bowen described her wartime stories as only 'nominally "inventive"'. Instead they were 'the only diary I have kept': 'received impressions of happening things ... that stored themselves up and acquired force without being analysed or considered'.[7]

The suggestion that Bowen's peculiar wartime short fiction, populated as it is by demonic taxi drivers and feather-boa-clad ghosts, forms a kind of diary is both strange and fascinating. In describing the need to witness in a time of war, writers often talk about the need to pare down their language and restrain their plotting for the sake of authenticity. Kate McLoughlin has seen war writing throughout the centuries as characterised by a tendency towards 'underwriting'.[8] In the Second World War this was called for by Sansom, who stated that in questing for truth he eschewed 'tricks, affectation, calculation', and by John Lehmann, who found 'precocity' in any form 'abhorrent' as editor of the influential magazine *New Writing*, where many of these wartime stories were first published.[9] Yet for Bowen in this postscript to her wartime stories, any accurate portrait of the time was necessarily 'hallucinogenic' because she and her contemporaries had lived in an atmosphere of 'lucid abnormality' (p. 95). This hallucinogenic quality is, I will argue, also found in Sansom's stories, despite his avowal of the need for simplicity, and it is there too in stories by Green and Macaulay. It seems that in witnessing the war realistically and in creating stories that fulfilled the function of diaries, these writers did not confine themselves to the traditional tools of the realist fiction-writer. Exactly why this was and what they were doing instead will be the central questions propelling this article.

Moments

Arguably the short story was unusually appropriate for the Blitz because both the short story and the bombing incident are structured around a single moment or series of moments. In his 1947 study of *Westminster at War,* Sansom described how during the war in London under the 'urging drone' of the bombers and the patterns of the weaving searchlights, 'the moments became vivid and active'. These were 'hot, cold, sharp, slow moments of intense being; moments that then extended themselves into hours'.[10] This sense that the war created pockets of time in which past and future were eliminated is also manifest in Bowen's 1948 novel *The Heat of the Day,* where she describes the Blitz as a whole as a moment outside time, with Londoners 'afloat on the tideless, hypnotic, futureless to-day'.[11]

The suspended present was partly created by fear. Frightened that any day might be their last alive, people lived for the moment, eliminating all thoughts of past and future. In a diary entry in June 1940, fearing that England was about to be invaded, the civil servant Harold Nicolson observed that the probability of death did not fill him with despair because he was able 'almost entirely to dismiss from my thoughts any consideration of the future' and found it easier to forget the past than when the situation was 'less catastrophic'.[12] Time became synchronic (circular and subjective) rather than diachronic (linear and clock-driven). This may be true during any war or period of intense danger, but once the bombs started to fall nightly in September 1940 the timeless present became more specific to this particular war as the moments described by Sansom began.

For anyone working in the streets of London during a raid as a warden, ambulance driver or firefighter, the fall of a bomb was a moment suspended between anticipation and aftermath. Before, there was the dread of the planes, the fear that they would drop their load in this particular direction, that you might die within seconds from a direct hit or from the falling debris that would follow it. Afterwards there was the need to run from the blast, to survey the damage and to begin the arduous work of rescue or salvage. But first-hand accounts of the bombing repeatedly describe how, during the actual moment when the bomb fell, time stopped.

Graham Greene dramatised this in his 1943 novel *The Ministry of Fear* where the protagonist Arthur Rowe loses consciousness briefly when his room is hit. Awaking, he is unsure if it has been an instant or a much longer period of time. His head is singing; he feels as though he has been walking in his sleep. Space as well as time is unfamiliar. It is as though he is 'in a strange country without any maps to help him, trying to get his position by the stars'.[13] Time lengthens during the moment of the bombing both because of the physical effects of the blast and because of the possibility of death. In that instant of possible death there is the potential for the eternity that follows death. The moment of survival offers a reentry into time. And the sense that the bombs stopped time when they fell was given a kind of physical actuality when clocks nearby ceased to function, paralysed by the blast. In *The Heat of the Day* Bowen described London as a city of 'shock-stopped' clocks (p. 93).

The 'vivid and active' moments brought into being by a bomb could extend beyond the instant of the bombing and incorporate a whole night. Working as an ARP warden during the famous night known simply as 'the Wednesday' on 16 April 1941, Graham Greene found that time went very slowly during the minutes in which he was attending to the wounded victims of an explosion. The hour that had passed since the first bomb in their area seemed 'a long while' and time was all the more confusing because the light from the flares and fires was so intense that it appeared to be broad daylight.[14] Similarly, both Henry Yorke and Sansom found that time seemed to cease during the minutes or hours in which they were engulfed in smoke, attending to fires.

Because the war in London was experienced as a series of disconnected moments in which time stopped, the form of the diary, with its implication of a day by day diachronic continuum, became less appropriate than the more synchronic form of a short story. In the short story too, a moment is often highlighted. The short-story theorist Mary Rohrberger has argued that the short story, more than any other narrative structure, veers towards 'spatial form' and Bergsonian flux:

> synchronicity defines the short story's base. Analogy not only objectifies the moment in space by stopping the clock between ticks but also connects past and future by encompassing successive states, each of which follows and contains that which precedes it.[15]

Expressing similar ideas from a more practical perspective, Sansom described the story as nearer to the poem than the novel, usually concerned with 'one episode', 'blown up big or refined beneath the microscope'.[16]

It is telling that when the writers under discussion here did write diary entries, they tended to be shaped as short stories, expanding a particular moment rather than forming part of a more continuous narrative with a past and a future. This is the case for many of Sansom's diaries in the 'Fireman's Journal' he kept briefly in 1941. The entry for September 25 begins as a kind of wartime fairy story:

> It was a blue, moonlit night and the flames blazed orange. The house stood dark and detached in its own garden of trees and shrubbery walls. It was all dark up to the top two floors and there the bright fire suddenly began.[17]

It is also the case for Greene's one-off diary entry from 16 April, which begins at ten to nine with Greene and his lover Dorothy Glover sitting apprehensively waiting for the bombs before cutting to midnight, when Greene goes on duty as an ARP warden. This is all preparation for the protracted moment that dominates the diary entry, which begins at a quarter to two when after hours of waiting the flares come down right on top of him and then, 'without the warning of a whistle', there is a huge detonation and a shop window showers down on their helmets. As he goes from one injured figure to another, Greene finds that 'time went very slowly and I wanted to get out'. This particular blown up moment then expands to include the fall of another bomb. The window of his post blows in but he is not frightened because, caught in the present, he has 'ceased to believe in the possibility of surviving the night'. His diary entry ends, in the manner of many short stories at this time, with an anti-climactic aside. Rushing, wounded and underslept, to take a train to Oxford the next morning to give a talk, he goes into a chemist and asks for a packet of razor blades. 'Don't you know there's a war on?' he is asked by the furious chemist.[18]

Essentially, there is not a significant formal difference between this diary entry and the more autobiographical and realistic of the war stories, especially those written at the start of the Blitz by the two firefighting fiction writers, Green and Sansom. Green's 'Mr Jonas' and 'A Rescue' (both published in *New Writing* in 1941) and Sansom's 'The Wall' (published in *Horizon* in 1941) all depict single, realistic nights of firefighting from the perspective of a first-person fireman narrator who in Green's case is even referred to as 'Henry'. The question here is not whether diaries can or should be reclassified as short stories or short stories as diaries, but what these writers gained from assuaging their need to witness through short stories rather than diaries except, not insignificantly, economic remuneration. What was it about the short story form that made it peculiarly suitable for documenting the Blitz in London?

This is partly a question of visual description and imagery. Although Greene in his diary does compare the flares coming down, dribbling their flames, to 'great yellow peonies', Sansom and Green went much further in their stories in painting word pictures of the fire.[19] In 'Mr Jonas' three jets of water directed against a conflagration are compared to 'three high fountains which, through sunlight, would furl their flats in rainbows as they dispersed' but have instead 'played these up into a howling wind to be driven, to be shattered, dispersed', falling into 'a cloud of steam rose-coloured beneath'.[20]

The appropriateness of the short story lay also, as I have already suggested, in its temporality. The wartime stories are more insistent than Greene's diary entry in drawing attention to the protracted moments created by the bombing. Sansom's 1941 'The Wall' is structured around the anticipation and aftermath of one of these moments that occurs at about 3 am in the middle of a shift. Beforehand, the narrator and his colleagues are busy 'playing a fifty foot jet up the face of a tall city warehouse and thinking of nothing at all'. This is itself a state in which time is forgotten, in which one hour succeeds another as they continue to pour 'careless gallons' through the window, knowing the fire will fester for hours. Then suddenly the upper half of the five-storey building heaves towards them. It hangs there for a 'timeless second' before toppling down.[21] The majority of the story's four pages are given to anatomising this second.

During the course of the second, the narrator goes from thinking of nothing at all to thinking of 'everything in the world'. New eyes seem to open at the sides of his head so that he can see the 'hemispherical panorama' of the scene minutely. He assesses the empty alley at the side of the building, seeing every detail with unusual clarity, so that there is time within that second to wonder 'what in hell' is sold by 'Catto and Henley', whose sign swings over one of the shops (p. 109). He is aware that he could shout 'Drop it' and then run into the alley but he is held 'hypnotised, rubber boots cemented to the pavement' by the suspension of time itself, which seems to numb all initiative. Having described the alley,

Sansom goes on to describe every feature of the building, listing the number of windows on each floor and describing the fire which seems to bulge from the black-framework, 'like boiling jelly that expanded inside a thick black squared grill' (p. 110). At last the second draws to a close and the wall falls down on top of them. One of the narrator's colleagues is killed; he and two others are dug out, saved because they are framed by one of the window spaces he had seen bulging with boiling jelly.

This is more than the slowing of time described in Greene's diary entry. Like a diary entry, Sansom's story is insistent in its proliferation of ordinary realist detail: we know that this is the firemen's third job of the night, that the jet of water they are driving at the building is fifty foot long, that the City alleys are puddled with black water. But if this detail is amassed to enable authentic witnessing then what is being witnessed here is also the unreality of perception occasioned by the distortion of time. When the wall starts to fall on him, the narrator enters a hyper-aware state in which he believes that within the single second of a wall's fall he is able to read all the shop signs in the alley and to count and picture the forty windows on the building. The suggestion is partly that this is a moment of photographic precision. His mind is compared explicitly to a camera in which rapid photographs are taken in quick succession. But even allowing for the heightened perception enabled by danger, what is seen seems incredible in its detail.[22] Realist witnessing is pressed into the service of an apparently unrealistic experience in a way that is possible because this is fiction.

Lucid abnormality

Again and again, writers and critics in the 1940s expressed their sense that this war required a move beyond realism and even that the Blitz had actualised artistic modes that had previously seemed unrealistic: surrealism, the gothic, the visionary.[23] The sight of a house turned inside out or a tree with a top hat in it gave surrealism a strange actuality; the prevalence of death that brought the felt presence of yesterday's dead among today's living made the ghost story oddly realistic.[24]

For Sansom the oddness of the war in London was partly accounted for by the collision between ordinary life and war:

> It is true that under bombardment life in a city is physically more comfortable than in the field; but against this might be ranged a deeper mental discomfort, for the citizen lives still among familiar things, and over the threatened kitchen and the threatened shops

> there rests always the reminder of better days. These familiar places are much alienated and chilled in the shadow of war.

This strangeness within the familiar was more evident in London than in any of the European cities that were bombed, where the damaged tended to be more absolute, especially as the war progressed, and ordinary life became less possible. It is a strangeness dramatised in Sansom's story 'In the Morning', which opens with a fireman joining a team of firefighters pouring water into a burning shed, frustrated because as soon as one flame is extinguished another appears to take its place. Looking at his watch, the protagonist observes that it is 'extraordinary' that it is half-past nine in the morning. Only an hour earlier, he was lying 'on his own bed, in his own home, with the shape of his own wife shivering above him with a cup of tea'. For years in peace-time he awoke to his familiar room and wife so now 'for all real purposes' it is still to the old days of peace that he awakens. Yet some seconds later the war inevitably intrudes, an 'artificial' new experience 'superimposed upon an older, more real way of living'.[25]

This disconnection, the abnormality of a war that is superimposed onto familiar surroundings, is part of what is being witnessed in the war writing of this time. Sansom and Green in particular are interested in the strange mental state occasioned in the firefighter by the fires he fights: both the experience of the protracted moments and the heightening of the senses they bring about. Arriving at the fire in 'Mr Jonas', Green's narrator feels 'withdrawn into himself', as though he is in a region where the conditions are 'something between living and dying . . . betwixt coma and the giving up of living' (p. 84). In the midst of the fire, he becomes blinded by the smoke, which makes him feel that he is not a participant in the scene, 'that all this must have been imagined' (p. 86).

For Sansom this extreme sensory deprivation made the possibility of recording the war questionable. In an undated diary entry he worried that his experiences were 'too violent for the arts to transcribe; there will never be an adequate reportage to convey to posterity a living idea of the truth of such experience'. This was partly because it was 'through the senses we must first perceive things' and under the bombs the senses of the recording artist were dulled: 'he is blinded, deafened, numbed and dulled by the storm of noise and light sweeping around him'.[26]

This diary entry is revealing because it enacts precisely what it is describing as impossible. The suggestion here is that the violence of the war prevents accurate witnessing but in fact at the same time as announcing this Sansom is witnessing the sensation of being caught up in that violence, precisely by describing the sensation of being unable to describe it. Sansom does this more explicitly in his story, 'The Witnesses', a tale told from the perspective of a fireman's eyes. This is an account of an expanded moment in which a fireman, operating a hose, believes that he sees a smile of hatred in the face of the pump operator and panics that the operator is about to accelerate the water pressure and kill him. Initially he is paralysed by fear in 'a pause, a terrible imagined silence' as 'time freezes solid'. Then at the last minute he leaps up, flings his hose away from him and throws himself against the wall. The story ends with the eyes' uncertainty. They cannot know if this was merely a moment of fear at the sudden bright glare of the fire, transformed into a smile of hatred by the fireman's brain, 'the unreliable agent that informed us, the witnesses, his eyes'.[27]

What is being witnessed in Sansom's diary entry and story as well as in Green's 'Mr Jonas' is a sensory experience so overwhelming that it calls into question the possibility of witnessing. Certainly, it is an experience too odd to be caught by conventional reportage or realism. During the Second World War, several commentators pointed out that this war seemed to call for a form of unrealistic realism; that its truths could be captured best by a visionary mode of writing. In the spring of 1944 John Lehmann wrote an editorial essay in *New Writing and Daylight* arguing that the best books of the war (Greene's *The Ministry of Fear* and Green's *Caught*) combined realism with 'dreams, symbolism, poetic asides or internal monologues' which not only added interest but, crucially, added to the '*truth* of their pictures of the world'. Recalling the realism of the 1930s novel, he found that the war, with its 'violence, change and suffering' had rendered realism inadequate. History itself was now 'transparent and symbolic' and so there could be 'no true and complete picture of existence in which the unseen, what lies beyond our five senses and logical proof, does not play a part'.[28] Looking back, Lehmann found that Shakespeare had written in a similarly intense and incendiary age and that the prevalence of ghosts even in his more realistic plays was a testament to this.

Lehmann is not prescriptive about the textual form best placed to mix the realistic with the unseen but arguably it is the short story. Theories of short fiction have always identified the short story as less realistic than the novel. In 1995 Terry Eagleton suggested that whereas realism, the 'most common modal perspective of the novel', is primarily a 'cognitive form concerned to map the causal processes underlying events', the short story can 'yield us some single bizarre occurrence of epiphany or terror whose impact would merely be blunted by lengthy realist elaboration', incorporating the 'ineffable or unfathomable'.[29] Charles E. May has been one of many short fiction theorists to suggest that the short story tends to focus on mystery and the unfamiliar partly because of its origins in the oral myth and the romance. Here May draws on the ideas of Walter Benjamin who lamented in a 1936 essay on the Russian writer Nicolai Leskov that the rise of the novel had coincided with the dissemination of information (chiefly through the wide availability of news), sidelining the short story with its tendency to 'borrow from the miraculous'.[30] For May as for Eagleton the short story's ability to stray into the realm of the unfamiliar is related to the formal demands of the genre: 'what often has been termed the "artificial" patterning of the short story heightens intensity, thus creating the cryptic, elliptical nature of the genre'.[31]

According to Benjamin the storyteller writes more memorably than the novelist because in embracing mystery he 'forgoes psychological shading', allowing the reader or listener to integrate the story into his own experiences (p. 91). In an introduction to a collection of 'modern short stories' written in the same year as Benjamin's essay, Elizabeth Bowen unwittingly concurred with Benjamin in praising the short story for being 'an affair of reflexes, of immediate susceptibility, of associations not examined by reason', tending to 'heroic simplicity'. Like Benjamin, Bowen thought that some of the best short stories were issued from Russia. When it came to stories written in the English language, she favoured those from Ireland and America because in her view the Irish and Americans demonstrated a superior capacity to feel and represent involuntary amazement. For Bowen this was more possible in a culture where life was, or had been lately, 'physically exciting or uncertain'. She explained that the younger Irish writers had almost all carried arms while American civilisation kept the Americans nervously as armed men.[32]

If we accept Bowen's argument that violence is oddly conducive to the non-realist, mysterious short story then it is not surprising that the Second World War made short story writers of the English. Certainly, in a 1963 introduction to the work of William Sansom, Bowen praised just this quality in Sansom, whose first short stories were published at the time. Here Bowen wrote that though the short story appeared to represent reality it was not realistic: 'it relies on devices, foreshortenings, "effects"'. The narration necessarily involved an 'element of conjury', and Sansom was the 'evident master of this'. 'Where it comes to conveying hallucination, I know few if any who can approach him'.[33]

Bowen could be talking about her own short stories here, including those she had written before the war. What had changed for her and, in her analysis for Sansom, was that her own visionary, hallucinogenic method had become realistic. The daily life of Londoners had become the material of the Russian or Irish short story. Tellingly, Bowen's introduction to Sansom's stories resonates with her account of her wartime stories in the 1945 postscript. Here, in describing her stories as a diary, she suggests that this is partly because they had 'their own momentum' and so seemed 'flying particles of something enormous and inchoate that had been going on', sparks from an experience that was both her own and other people's at a time when 'the overcharged subconsciousnesses of everybody overflowed and merged' (p. 95). For Bowen this is in part the explanation for the 'rising tide of hallucination' and the 'lucid abnormality' observable in her stories. Everybody in London in the war, she says, had 'strange deep intense dreams' as well as daytime fantasies that compensated in part for the dessication of their lives by war (p. 96) As a result she did not find it surprising that stories in which she claimed to have invented nothing should be populated by ghosts. The ghosts like the hallucinations were a 'saving resort' enabling the people around them to survive spiritually at a time when the 'personal cry of the individual' was threatened:

> It is the 'I' that is sought – and retrieved at the cost of no little pain. And the ghosts . . . They are the certainties. The bodiless foolish wanton, the puritan other presence, the tipsy cook with her religion of English fare, the ruthless young soldier unheard of since 1916: hostile or not, they rally, they fill the vacuum for the uncertain 'I'. (p. 98)

Ghosts

We are now back where we started, with the question of how a ghost story can be a form of diary; how a ghost story, that is, can be a form of realism or even reportage. If the short story came into its own in the war then it seems to have been because the short story as a form mirrored the bombing war's tendency to create 'vivid and active' moments and because it was a genre well-placed to reflect the unreality of perception occasioned by this distortion of time. It is this unreality of perception that many wartime writers were concerned with witnessing and the inclusion of ghosts seems to have been one way to do this.

Bowen's postscript introduces the possibility of a kind of reportage of the (potentially collective) unconscious, suggesting that the ghost story can be the diary of the unconscious wartime self. Her statement that ghosts 'fill the vacuum for the uncertain "I"' is cryptic but seems to suggest that the individual, frightened by the occlusion of the self occasioned by the public nature of the war, takes refuge in a private relationship with the unseen. This would imply that people were more likely to be receptive to ghosts than they had been before the war. But if ghosts could be part of daily experience at this time then it was partly also because of the ubiquity of death. In *The Heat of the Day*, Bowen describes how during the Blitz 'the dead, from mortuaries, from under cataracts of rubble, made their anonymous presence – not as today's dead but as yesterday's living – felt through London' (p. 86). Unsure which of their acquaintances were dead and which alive, people found that 'the wall between the living and the dead thinned' (p. 87).

Arguably the presence of the dead as well as the presence of violence accounts for the rise of the short story at this time. According to Benjamin, 'death is the sanction of everything that the storyteller can tell'. In his view, the novel had replaced the short story by the early twentieth century partly because death had been 'pushed further and further out of the perceptual world of the living'. Where there used to be no house or room in which someone had not died, people now lived in rooms that had 'never been touched by death' (p. 94). This is a somewhat suspect generalisation given that when Benjamin wrote it in 1936 the First World War was recent enough for death to be firmly located in the conceptual world of his contemporaries. Nonetheless the point stands that in this period death had become an event that for most people occurred offset; cadavers were a far less frequent sight than they had been in previous centuries. The Blitz changed this by bringing the dead closer to home than they had been in earlier wars. Most Londoners – and certainly those involved in the Civil Defence services – were now confronted by corpses on a relatively frequent basis.

Perhaps one of the few positive effects of this harrowing destruction was to rejuvenate the short story as a form and to enable ghosts to take their place within otherwise realistic, even documentary narratives.[34] Bowen's suggestion that her ghost stories formed the diary not only of her own but of the collective unconscious is supported by the large number of ghosts in the short fiction of this period. Indeed these wartime ghosts seem to be apotheosis of what I am terming 'unrealistic realism' or could with Bowen term 'lucid abnormality'. The ghosts were an unrealistic detail used realistically to evoke a wartime state of mind.

The majority of wartime ghosts were psychologically explicable either as hallucinations or as ghost-like figures. In a world in which there is very little distinction between yesterday's living and today's dead, it is easy to incorporate ghosts without troubling the reader. Perhaps the saddest of the ghostly figures in wartime stories is Miss Anstruther, the heroine of Rose Macaulay's account of a woman whose life is 'cut in two' when her flat is bombed on the night of 10 May 1941, leaving her 'a ghost, without attachments or habitation'.

Like so many short stories from this time, 'Miss Anstruther's Letters' is autobiographical. On the night of 10 May 1941 Rose Macaulay's own flat had been completely destroyed by a bomb though Macaulay, unlike Miss Anstruther, was not around to witness it. Miss Anstruther, like her creator, is a successful novelist who is working as an ambulance driver during the war and crucially Miss Anstruther like Macaulay herself has been engaged in a long and passionate affair with a man whose letters are destroyed in her flat. When Macaulay wrote the story in the spring of 1942 her own lover, Gerald O'Donovan, was dying; in the story Miss Anstruther's lover is already dead. Publicly, Macaulay was unable to grieve for O'Donovan's impending death and so seems to have taken refuge at this time in grieving vehemently for the books that she had lost in the bombing. Some of her acquaintances found her grief for her books excessive, given that all around her there were people dying each day in the war. In this story, written for publication in America but not in Britain, it becomes clear that in fact she was grieving for O'Donovan's letters, rather than her books, and that she was devastated by the prospect of secretly mourning the man she loved without having recourse to his letters to restore his voice and reassure her of his feelings.

For our purposes here, the story is especially interesting in its combination of realist detail and ghostliness. The style is casually loquacious and hypotactical, as though to emphasise that this is a report of ordinary life rather than a gothic tale. This makes the description of Miss Anstruther as a ghost in the first sentence seem oddly literal, as though it is quite normal for people to experience themselves as ghosts:

> Miss Anstruther, whose life had been cut in two on the night of May 10th, 1941, so that she now felt herself a ghost, without attachments or habitation, neither of which she any longer desired, sat alone in the bed-sitting room she had taken, a small room, littered with grimy, broken and useless objects which she had salvaged from the burnt-out ruin round the corner.[35]

And the story continues in this vein, mingling practically detailed explanation with mysterious horror. We learn that on this wild night of bombing both high explosives and incendiaries rained on London and the water ran short in the same paragraph that Miss Anstruther's former flat is described in gothic terms as 'a gaunt and roofless tomb, a pile of ashes and rubble and burnt, smashed beams' (p. 161). Later she recalls waiting desperately for a fire engine on that night when prosaically there were 'a hundred fires, the water given out in some places, engines helpless' and more apocalyptically Miss Anstruther sits on the wreckage of the road 'with hell blazing and crashing round her', 'sick and shaking, wholly bereft' (p. 167).

Macaulay wrote no fiction or diary after 1941 and, apart from a small amount of journalism and a handful of letters, this is her only attempt to witness the war that she was participating in night after night as an ambulance driver. It is revealing that it is both a relatively accurate account of the bombing of her flat on 10 May 1941 and an accurate depiction of her state of mind in the spring of 1942, mirroring letters from this time where she wishes repeatedly that she could have been bombed too, but that in order to do this she writes a form of short story in which, at the same time as the realist details proliferate, a visionary register is used, allowing hell to blaze around her and the bombed flat to become a gaunt tomb.[36] By the end of the story Miss Anstruther has gone from 'feeling herself' to be a ghost to being a ghost. As she blames herself for a moment when, twenty years ago, she disappointed her lover, she finds that 'the twenty years between were a drift of grey ashes that once were fire, and she a drifting ghost too' (p. 170).

Macaulay seems to have been thrown by the war into a version of the state described by Henry Green in 'Mr Jonas' as 'betwixt coma and the giving up of living'. This is a deathly form of the suspended present that also characterises the atmosphere of William Sansom's story 'Fireman Flower' (the title story in his 1944 collection of stories), an account of a fireman's experiences in a burning building. If for Sansom the challenge for the writer was to overcome the dulling of the senses that seemed to make recording the war impossible, then he responded to this here by describing just that state in which the nerves are 'stretched and battered, torn and bruised beyond sensibility' as accurately as possible. Once again, this accuracy entailed a visionary mode of writing akin to the 'lucid abnormality' described by Bowen and, as in 'Miss Anstruther's Letters', it involved turning the protagonist into a figure so ghostly that he might as well be a ghost.

'Fireman Flower' documents a fireman's attempt to locate the kernel of a fire that is ravaging 'a black-bricked warehouse of hideous design'.[37] As he wanders through the smoke he finds himself encased in a 'dull luminosity', blinded like the fireman in 'Mr Jonas' by the 'white veil' of smoke. Feeling 'fogged and lost' (p. 132) he is surprised to find that occasionally the smoke clears to reveal 'some object of the surrounding chaos' that appears to be 'a half-remembered episode from the dreamed past' (p. 133). In this odd, timeless world, he starts to feel helpless, as though he has no volition; as he wades through a strangely luxurious flood of warm water and then encounters the smell of perfume where hundreds of bottles have been burst by the flames, he becomes drunk on the fumes and collapses elated onto the warm foam behind him.

This is an appropriate state in which to encounter ghosts. First, stopping 'dead', a few feet away from a mirror, Fireman Flower sees 'the ghost of himself' in the bare corridor, 'the reflection of his past masqueraded as the darkling ghost of the future' (p. 146). Then, entering a moonlit deserted room, he plunges through a wardrobe into a room filled with objects from his own past where he finds an old friend sitting waiting for him in a chair, wanting to reminisce about their childhood. Jolted back into the present when his helmet falls over his face, Flower then rejoins his crew in fighting the fire, only to find that his friend is now among them. Now at last, he and his companions locate the kernel of the fire and he feels infused by love, loving 'a single rusted nail as he loved the Giaconda smile', transformed by the strange timeless world of the smoke (p. 163).

'Fireman Flower' fulfils Bowen's criteria for the mysterious short story, conjuring amazement and refusing analysis: this is 'an affair of reflexes, of immediate susceptibility, of associations not examined by reason'. It also fulfils Lehmann's demand that in order to be truly realistic, wartime writing should allow for the unseen or ghostly. At the same time, though, it remains psychologically explicable in that this can all be read as a hallucination, brought on by the fire's assault on the senses. If this is unrealistic realism then it is unrealistic in the service of documenting the peculiar mental state that can be occasioned by firefighting, serving as a strange form of diary. The bombing war occasioned experiences extreme enough to turn the visionary short story and even the ghost story into a form of life-writing, better suited than ordinary reportage to documenting these heightened mental states.

As Bowen suggested in her 1945 postscript, the same possibility for documentary authenticity can be seen in some of her own wartime ghost stories. Here she described the ghosts in 'Pink May', 'The Cheery Soul' and 'The Demon Lover' as 'questionable' ('for are they subjective purely?') (p. 98). But if the ghosts in these stories are hallucinations, then the reader is not encouraged to think of them in this way. Like Benjamin's storyteller, by refusing analysis, both Sansom and Bowen give a physical actuality to their ghosts. Fireman Flower's old friend is too chatty and familiar to seem like a mere smoky vision. Similarly, the ghost in 'Pink May' swishes around bossily disapproving of the way the protagonist does her makeup and the ghost in 'The Demon Lover' whisks Mrs Drover off in his taxi, 'accelerating without mercy' as they speed off into the deserted streets.[38] Both writers conjure a world in which the dead have a physical presence no less corporeal than the living; in which the living cannot trust themselves to be any more real than the ghosts who haunt them.

This is made more explicit in 'Green Holly', published in *The Listener* in 1944, which Bowen described in her postscript as the only story in her wartime collection where the ghosts are 'definite' (p. 98). I will end with a discussion of this story, although its action takes place outside London, in a dilapidated country house called 'Mopsam Grange' where a group of decidedly ghost-like civil servants are engaged in top secret war work, having 'dropped out of human memory' in London.[39] The moment of the story occurs on Christmas Eve some years into the war and it is a moment when three ghosts fall in love. Two of these are ghostly living figures, civil servants called Mr Winterslow and Miss Bates. The third is an unusually vibrant ghost, who sports a feather boa and quivers with excited sexual energy. Unusually, this ghost is given a large section of the narrative from her point of view. We see her hesitating in the familiar corridor, summoning herself into visibleness in a mood of 'flamboyance and agitation'. Discarding her feather boa, she exposes shoulders around whose bareness 'shimmered a thousand evenings'. She is haunted (for 'it is the haunted', Bowen tells us, 'who haunt') by her own embodied past: the scent of her corsage fills her nostrils, remembered bracelets slip on her forearm, warmed by remembered blood (p. 723).

The ghost has just fallen in love with Mr Winterslow, balding, tired, with stain-reddened eyelids but worthy nonetheless of '*the* illusion' of love, and as the story begins he is falling in love with her in turn, his eyes 'bright and vacant' as he describes her to his colleagues (pp. 724, 722). But Mr Winterslow does not prove equal to the moment of excited crisis with his bare-shouldered spectre on the stairs. He rushes off to get his spectacles and, haughtily perturbed, the ghost stills him by putting out the electric lights. They are left in a 'fog-dark but glass-clear veil of hallucination' not unlike Fireman Flower's state in Sansom's story (p. 725). In this moment Miss Bates appears and falls in love with the ghost's dead husband, who is lying in the hallway where he killed himself on an earlier Christmas Eve after discovering his wife's infidelity. Previously, Miss Bates has engaged in desultory love affairs with Mr Winterslow and other members of their cohort. Now she, like Mr Winterslow, finds that in these strange, enervated times love can be more fulfilling and vivifying when the loved one is dead. 'Here I am, left, left, left, to watch dust gather on Mr Ranstock and you', she complains to Mr Winterslow, bemoaning the ghostliness of the living. She can sense on her dead lover's lips the trace of kisses lately bestowed on the white rose he clutches in his hand and finds that 'the ideality of those kisses, for the last of which I arrived too late . . . will haunt, and by haunting satisfy me' (p. 726).

As the only story with indisputable ghosts, 'Green Holly' is the most unrealistic example of the unrealistic realism discussed here. Circumstantially, it bears almost no resemblance to Bowen's war. The atmosphere of her nights on duty in London as an ARP warden is much more obviously present in 'In the Square', with its bombed out houses, or 'Mysterious Kôr', where London becomes 'the moon's capital'.[40] But nonetheless the story engages in an act of war witnessing, observing what Bowen described in her postscript as the need 'to survive, not only physically, but spiritually', and to retrieve the 'I' 'at the cost of no little pain'. What is being witnessed is a suspended moment in which the wall between the living and the dead has crumbled, like the wall that falls so heavily and viscerally in Sansom's first war story. The perspective of the dead is now no less insistent than the perspective of the ghostly living who dwell in their house. And with the psychic walls removed, the living and the dead are left an atmosphere of yearning. This is a moment of vulnerability in which hearts can be broken but in which the lucid abnormality enabled by the 'glass-clear veil of hallucination' is unusually lucid.[41]

In her postscript Bowen states that during the war she lived 'both as a civilian and as a writer, with every pore open'. Ultimately it is this that is being documented in these short stories that she described as 'the only diary I have ever kept'. And it is this peculiar open-pored receptivity to the environment that is being witnessed in all these short stories by writers whose nerves and senses were brutally exposed and who in strange, visionary, hallucinatory writing were fulfilling Sansom's injunction to 'write down exactly what all this feels like'.

King's College London

Disclosure statement

No potential conflict of interest was reported by the author.

Notes

1 Willliam Sansom, *The Birth of a Story* (London: Chatto & Windus, 1972), pp. 9–10.
2 Richard J. Aldrich (ed.), *Witness to War: Diaries of the Second World War in Europe and the Middle East* (London: Doubleday, 2004), pp. 1, 3.
3 Henry Yorke, letter to Rosamond Lehmann, quoted Rosamond Lehmann, 'An Absolute Gift', *Times Literary Supplement*, 6 August 1954, p. 41.
4 Henry Yorke, letter to Rosamond Lehmann, 9 January 1941 (Rosamond Lehmann archive, King's College Cambridge).
5 In his essay 'Broken Glass' Rod Mengham does describe the 'new enthusiasm for short stories' in this period, suggesting that the kind of short story most popular was 'the kind that did not present an understanding of what was happening *now*, but which merely provided a record of events to be used as material *later on*'. For Mengham the short story's popularity is due partly to its fragmented nature, which reflected the fragmentation engendered by the Blitz (in Rod Mengham and N.H. Reeve (eds.), *The Fiction of the 1940s: Stories of Survival* (Basingstoke: Palgrave, 2001), p. 126). In *Under Siege: Literary Life in London 1939–45* Robert Hewison explains the popularity of the short story more in terms of paper shortages (London: Weidenfeld and Nicolson, 1977, p. 80).

6 Cyril Connolly's editorial in the June 1940 *Horizon* professed hope that the paper shortage would usher in the era of the short story (*Horizaon* 1.6, p. 392). That March he had announced that 'the three most neglected forms to-day are the long poem, the critical essay and the long short story' and expressed his commitment to publishing stories (*Horizon* 1.3, p. 149). The success of magazines like *Horizon* and *New Writing* at this time no doubt played its part in making short stories a more prestigious genre.
7 Elizabeth Bowen, postscript to the US edition of *The Demon Lover and Other Stories, The Mulberry Tree*, ed. Hermione Lee (London: Virago, 1986), p. 99. All subsequent page numbers refer to this edition.
8 Kate McLoughlin, *Authoring War: The Literary Representation of War from the* Iliad *to Iraq* (Cambridge: Cambridge University Press, 2011), p. 137.
9 Sansom, *Birth of a Story*, p. 10; John Lehmann (ed.), *English Stories from New Writing* (London: AB Ljus Publishers, 1946), p. 8.
10 William Sansom, *Westminster in War* (London: Faber and Faber, 1947), p. 49.
11 Elizabeth Bowen, *The Heat of the Day* (London: Jonathan Cape, 1949), p. 95. All subsequent page numbers refer to this edition.
12 Harold Nicolson, *Diaries and Letters 1939–45*, ed. Nigel Nicolson, 3 vols (London: Collins, 1967), Vol. 2, p. 96.
13 Graham Greene, *The Ministry of Fear* (London: Vintage, 2001) p. 28.
14 Graham Greene, Blitz notebook, 16 April 1941, reprinted in *Ways of Escape* (London: Vintage, 1999), p. 110.
15 Mary Rohrberger, 'Origins, Development, Substance, and Design of the Short Story', in Per Winther, Jakob Lothe and Hans H. Skei (eds), *The Art of Brevity: Excursions in Short Fiction Theory and Analysis* (Columbia: University of South Carolina Press, 2004), p. 8.
16 Sansom, *Birth of a Story*, p. 4.
17 William Sansom, 'From a Fireman's Journal', *Pleasures Strange and Simple* (London: The Hogarth Press, 1953), p. 193.
18 Greene, *Ways of Escape*, pp. 109, 110, 113.
19 Greene, *Ways of Escape*, p. 107.
20 Henry Green, 'Mr Jonas', in Matthew Yorke (ed.), *Surviving: The Uncollected Writings of Henry Green* (London: Harvill, 1993), p. 83. For this and all subsequent stories, all page numbers refer to the edition given in the initial reference.
21 William Sansom, 'The Wall', *Fireman Flower and Other Stories* (London: The Hogarth Press, 1944), p. 109.
22 See Mengham, for whom both this story and 'The Witnesses' 'examine the limits of conventional perception', imagine specifically 'a vision that is incommensurate with a camera' ('Broken Glass', p. 126).
23 For the Second World War gothic see Sara Wasson, *Urban Gothic of the Second World War: Dark London* (London: Palgrave Macmillan, 2010) and for surrealism see Leo Mellor, *Reading the Ruins: Modernism, Bombsites and British Culture* (Cambridge: Cambridge University Press, 2011) and Adam Piette, *Imagination at War: British Fiction and Poetry, 1939–1945* (London: Papermac, 1995).

24 In a 1943 memoir Inez Holden described a surrealist painter surveying a bombsite and saying to her 'of course we were painting this sort of thing years ago, but it has taken some time to get here' (*It was Different at the Time* (London: John Lane The Bodley Head, 1943), p. 69).
25 William Sansom, 'In the Morning', in *Something Terrible, Something Lovely* (London: The Hogarth Press, 1948), p. 101.
26 Sansom, 'From a Fireman's Journal', pp. 199–200.
27 William Sansom, 'The Witnesses', *Fireman Flower*, p. 86. For Sansom's stories as an attempt to overcome 'the unrepresentableness of the violent sublime' see Mark Rawlinson, *British Writing of the Second World War* (Oxford: Oxford University Press, 2000), p. 97.
28 John Lehmann, 'The Armoured Writer IV', *New Writing*, winter 1943–spring 1944, pp. 164–5.
29 Terry Eagleton, *Heathcliff and the Great Hunger: Studies in Irish Culture* (London: Verso, 1995), p. 150.
30 Walter Benjamin, 'The Storyteller: Reflections on the Works of Nikolai Leskov', in *Illuminations*, ed. Hannah Arendt, trans. Harry Zohn (London: Jonathan Cape, 1970), p. 89. All subsequent page numbers refer to this edition.
31 Charles E. May, 'Why Short Stories are Essential and Why They are Read', in Winther, Lothe and Skei, *The Art of Brevity*, p. 17.
32 Elizabeth Bowen, introduction to *The Faber Book of Modern Short Stories* in Charles E. May (ed.), *Short Story Theories* (Athens: Ohio University Press, 1976), pp. 153, 155.
33 Elizabeth Bowen, introduction to *The Stories of William Sansom* (London: The Hogarth Press, 1963), p. 9. For a discussion of Bowen's theories of the short story see Allan Hepburn, introduction to Elizabeth Bowen, *The Bazaar and Other Stories* (Edinburgh: Edinburgh University Press, 2008), pp. 1–26. Hepburn includes a particularly helpful discussion of Bowen's thinking about the ghost story and of the role of the irrational in short story (pp. 15–7).
34 See Bowen's introduction to Cynthia Asquith (ed.), *The Second Ghost Book* (London: James Barrie, 1952) for a discussion of the realism of the modern ghost story.
35 Rose Macaulay, 'Miss Anstruther's Letters', reprinted in Constance Babington Smith, *Rose Macaulay* (London: Collins, 1972), p. 161.
36 For Macaulay's letters and for a general biographical sketch of Macaulay at this time see Lara Feigel, *The Love-charm of Bombs: Restless Lives in the Second World War* (London: Bloomsbury, 2013), pp. 149–57.
37 William Sansom, 'Fireman Flower*Fireman Flower*, p. 129.
38 Elizabeth Bowen, 'The Demon Lover', in *The Collected Stories of Elizabeth Bowen* (London: Jonathan Cape, 1980), p. 666.
39 Elizabeth Bowen, 'Green Holly', *Collected Stories*, p. 719.
40 Elizabeth Bowen, 'Mysterious Kôr', *Collected Stories*, p. 728.
41 For a discussion of Bowen's ghosts see Mellor, *Reading the Ruins*, pp. 157–61 and Stefania Porcelli, 'City of Ghosts: Elizabeth Bowen's Wartime Stories', in

Lisa B. Kröger and Melanie Anderson (eds), *The Ghostly and the Ghosted in Literature and Film: Spectral Identities* (Plymouth: The University of Delaware Press, 2013), pp. 15–27. Porcelli sees Bowen's ghosts chiefly as representing the uncertainty of the Blitz through lingering in a 'liminal space' where 'the categories of "certainty", "finality" and "reality" are repeatedly put into question' (p. 24). Her brief discussion of 'Green Holly' reads this somewhat oddly as a story about women (the ghost) learning to turn from being 'objects of others' gaze' into 'subjects of their own actions' (p. 23).

Victoria Stewart

Representing Nazi crimes in post-Second World War life writing

As the concept of the 'Home Front' reflected, the war against Nazism was conceived in Britain as a collective endeavour, and in biographical accounts of wartime experience, this collective aspect is held in tension with the individuating details of the protagonist's own war. When the story told involves extreme danger, hardship, or even torture, questions of authenticity become increasingly pressing. This article captures a particular moment in the ongoing construction of the British narrative of the Second World War, addressing how authors of biographies of female Special Operations Executive agents attempted to encompass Nazi atrocities within narratives that are principally intended to laud the heroism of individuals who had direct and in some cases prolonged contact with the Nazis during the conflict. I will consider the strategies employed by authors to give credibility to what might seem to be unbelievable events, a process complicated by the fact that these authors are in most cases writing after the death of their subject, and I will ask how such atypical stories might fit into existing narratives, however fragmented these might be, of the war.

As the concept of the 'Home Front' indicates, the war against Nazi Germany was conceived in Britain as a collective endeavour, but this did not mean that the heroism of particular individuals was ignored in popular discourse. Biographical and autobiographical accounts of war experience aimed at a general readership preceded official histories which demanded more thoroughgoing research and planning. This is perhaps not surprising given the war's scope and scale, but it means that, when biographers and autobiographers desired to present the war as a group endeavour, this had to be held in tension with the individuating details of the subject's own war. The singling out of individual stories can become problematic from an historiographic perspective when it serves to overshadow or diminish the scope of the events that are being represented. Mark Rawlinson has suggested that narratives of 'heroic individualism', drawing as they do on existing tropes, are prone to leech away the political realities of the war and exert too strong an influence on 'the postwar conception of the ethical universe in which the war took place'.[1] To an extent, biographies of female Special Operations Executive agents that appeared in the postwar period might be seen as perpetuating this rhetoric of 'heroic individualism' while at the same time, perhaps paradoxically given the nature of the activities they describe, reinforcing the 'back to home and duty' ideology that prevailed during these years. Women such as Odette Sansom and Violette Szabo undertook highly dangerous work, performing a traditionally masculine martial role to an extent not required of women on active service in other forces; but in many postwar representations, they are nevertheless shown to retain their femininity and continue, even in extremis, to embody hegemonic ideals of the feminine.[2] Thus narratives with an ostensible focus on an individual both engage with and, in some cases, help to perpetuate, these sorts of wider cultural beliefs and expectations.

Texts such as Jerrard Tickell's *Odette: The Story of a British Agent* (1949) and R. J. Minney's *Carve her Name with Pride: The Story of Violette Szabo G.C.* (1956) have been criticised by M. R. D. Foot, author of the official history of SOE, published in 1968, as 'good thrillers, but bad history',[3] and historian Mark Seaman concurs, commenting of *Odette* that 'at times the book reads like a novel'.[4] In these comparisons, the fictive realm is constructed as unreliable and inauthentic: it has no place in an account of historical events. Tickell's and Minney's biographies, though sometimes bracketed together by Foot and others, differ greatly in tone and approach, these differences arising at least in part from the fact that Minney's subject, Violette Szabo, did not survive the war. Foot's and Seaman's dismissal of the fictional downplays the extent to which the techniques associated with fiction, such as figurative language, may enrich historical or biographical writing, but, whether or not these texts may be judged 'good', that is, reliable, history, they can nevertheless be highly revealing of the temper of the period when they were produced. Focusing on the sections of these and other texts that describe the time the agents spent in Nazi captivity, I will argue that their supposedly fictive aspects are symptomatic of attempts to describe historical events that are only partially understood and indeed, at the times these texts were published, only partially accessible via official sources. Attributing thoughts, feelings, even dialogue to their subjects may not strike historians as good practice, but for these biographers, this is a legitimate means of creating a coherent account of their subject's behaviour, and of bridging the gaps in the historical record. Narrative coherence, centred on character, substitutes for historical accuracy.

Odette and *Carve her Name* were both filmed (in 1950 and 1958 respectively) and received paperback reissues by the publisher Pan, which, during the late 1940s and into the 1950s, developed a popular list of reprints of war-related texts with striking illustrated covers. Jean Overton Fuller's *Madeleine* (1952), the biography of Noor Inayat Khan, another agent who died in Nazi captivity, also appeared as a Pan volume, revised and renamed *Born for Sacrifice* (1957), but along with Elizabeth Nicholas's exploration of the fate the agent Diana Rowden, *Death be Not Proud* (1958), Fuller's text takes a radically different approach to the problem of representing events that are either undocumented or have no surviving witnesses. Broadly speaking, where Tickell and Minney take a 'fictionalising' route, smoothing over narrative gaps in such a way as to render them almost invisible to the reader, Fuller and Nicholas insert themselves as researchers into their narratives, describing the problems they encounter in the course of their investigations. These choices have an impact on both content and form. Tickell and Minney are less inclined to critique systems, focusing as they do on individuals' motives and actions. Their wartime activities are the reason for these individuals becoming the subjects of biographies, but Minney's *Carve her Name* and Tickell's *Odette* de-emphasise the collective aspects of the war and therefore depoliticise their narratives. Although both Fuller, in *Madeleine*, and Nicholas, in *Death be not Proud*, set out to trace the story of an individual, in each case the research leads to the exposure of the complexities and indeed deficiencies of SOE as an organisation. In their vacillations between consideration of these agents as individuals and their contextualisation within groups of different kinds, these texts engage variously with wider debates of the period about agency, responsibility and the relationship between the individual and the collective in wartime and after.

For Fuller and Nicholas in particular, an important part of the quest to uncover the wartime activities of their subjects is a desire to find out how they died. Considered by their captors to have committed espionage, some agents, including all those discussed here, were sent, following capture, to concentration camps. This means that each author must, in his or her narrative, pass into the concentrationary realm, itself only partially understood at the time when they were writing. British attempts at discovering the fate of agents who had fallen into German hands during the war intersected with investigations into what were broadly termed 'Nazi crimes', and as the complex process of prosecuting individuals for war crimes got underway, the torture and murder of British agents were among the charges laid. As Donald Bloxham has shown, however, the desire to undertake prosecutions was tempered by a wish to get them over and done with as swiftly as possible and to begin the process of establishing good postwar relations with Germany. Tribunals were organised within each of the Allied zones of occupation and, with some exceptions, related to events that had taken place on that particular territory: the women's concentration camp, Ravensbrück, was in the Soviet zone, but some of its personnel were prosecuted by the British, because British prisoners, including Odette Sansom, had been held there.[5] Bloxham notes that the desire to prosecute those responsible for the executions of the Stalag Luft III escapers (who were recaptured after the so-called 'Great Escape') was one factor in the prolongation of the British tribunal process and sees this as representative of the extent to which '[m]ost of the little interest [. . .] regarding the trials shown by the British public was on matters relating directly to Britain'.[6] Despite the shocking images of death camps and concentration camps that were shown in cinemas and widely circulated in the press in Britain, it was the prisoner of war camp, as exemplified by Stalag Luft III, that held a more prominent place in the British cultural imagination.[7] All four authors, then, have to address the issue of how the fate of an individual in the grip of a barely comprehensible system can be represented within the narrative frameworks available to them. Furthermore, and more problematically, Minney, Fuller and Nicholas face the challenge of incorporating into their narratives their subjects' deaths.

Bearing witness?

Foot's and Seaman's concerns about crossing the boundary between the construction of an engaging historical narrative and 'fictionalisation' are acknowledged in the Foreword provided by former SOE F-section recruiting officer Selwyn Jepson to Fuller's *Madeleine*, where he notes the author's 'painstaking and successful efforts to avoid the taint of fiction'.[8] Fuller describes her researches as having been hampered by a lack of assistance from the War Office, leading her to resort to 'methods which would grace a detective story',[9] a reference to her interviewing of witnesses and footslogging around England and France. (Jepson had first-hand knowledge of the 'taint of fiction', having established himself as a successful writer of detective novels in the interwar years; detective fiction was another genre in which Pan Books had a successful list.) There may appear to be a contradiction between Jepson's and Fuller's characterisations of her work, but there is evidently a distinction being made between content, which Jepson refers to, and form, or indeed research method – the latter in fact dictates the former – as described by Fuller. Foregrounding the silences, evasions, unanswered letters and dead ends that she encounters during her search for what happened to her friend Noor Inayat Khan serves not to diminish the credibility of Fuller's account, I would argue, but rather to increase it; her reliability is reinforced even as the gaps in her knowledge are exposed.

However, Foot takes issue with 'passages in quotation marks' which he feels 'render' the 'authenticity' of certain scenes 'doubtful'.[10] For instance, Fuller reports what she was told by another agent who noticed that Khan carried around an exercise book containing messages she had sent to London:

> 'That is a very dangerous document,' he said. 'Anybody into whose hands it should fall would be able to work out your code from it.'
>
> 'I know,' she said. 'That is why I carry it about with me everywhere.'
>
> 'But this means that if the Germans capture you, they capture this on you!'
>
> 'Yes, but there is nothing I can do about that.'[11]

This is Fuller's rendering of a conversation that has been reported to her by a third party, perhaps in 'I said, she said' form. While quotation marks are usually a sign guaranteeing that the material within is a direct record of speech, Foot's argument is that, within the context of what purports to be a truthful account, they are in fact a sign of falsity: who can remember the detail of a conversation years after the event? Of course what matters is not the exact wording but the substance; according to this account, Khan was carrying round with her a highly compromising document, a mistake Rita Kramer attributes to her misunderstanding of the term 'file'. Kramer suspects that Khan might have been told in training to:

> '[B]e extremely careful in the filing of your messages.' Evidently she was unfamiliar with the use of 'filing' in the sense in which a journalist 'files' – that is 'sends' – a story, and thought she was meant to keep them in some sort of filing system.[12]

Fuller has already acknowledged that some of those in training with Khan did not believe she was a suitable person to be sent undercover, and raised their concerns with Vera Atkins,[13] the F-section intelligence officer who 'coordinated the preparation of more than four hundred secret agents who were to be dropped into France' over the course of the war.[14] Fuller's investigation was itself prompted, in part, by her disbelief that her gentle, spiritual friend could have been chosen to undertake such work. Such concerns are largely overshadowed by Khan's refusal to give anything away to her captors, a staunchness which seems to guarantee the rightness of the decision to send her, albeit that this can only be demonstrated when she has in fact, to some extent, failed by being captured. The conversation Fuller 'records' about the messages may or may not be an exact transcript, but in any case exposes not certainty but uncertainty because Fuller can offer no convincing explanation for Khan's apparently dangerous behaviour.

Fuller's introduction of herself into this narrative as both an acquaintance of Khan and an investigating author, a double role that is also foregrounded, through similar means, by Elizabeth Nicholas when she decides to find out what happened to her old school friend Diana Rowden, can be characterised as an attempt to answer a question that has long concerned those engaged in work on the representation of the Holocaust: who has the right to speak, and on behalf of whom? If, as Primo Levi maintains, the 'survivors [. . .] are not the true witnesses',[15] then how can the fate of those who did not return be articulated? Fuller seems to cast herself as, in Dominick LaCapra's term, a 'secondary witness',[16] one who undertakes 'critical work' to transform the 'primary memory' of those who 'initially had the relevant experiences' into 'secondary memory', to be imparted 'to others who have not themselves lived through the experience or events in question'.[17] Fuller charges herself with constructing a narrative of Khan's life through interviews with those who knew her, even those involved in her interrogation, but she is not a neutral vessel through which this information passes, and she foregrounds the practical and emotional difficulties of her 'critical work'. There is a danger here of the focus of the narrative being shifted from its ostensible subject – Khan – to its narrator, but through this technique Fuller can acknowledge the distance between Khan's experience and her own, and by extension the readers', rather than this distance being foreclosed. In this way she avoids appropriating Khan's experience, achieving instead an effect approaching what LaCapra calls 'empathic unsettlement',[18] refusing to smooth over difficulties or dissonances in the account and avoiding the imposition of a false sense of completion on the narrative.

Such foreclosure of the distance between narrator and subject is in fact more of a danger in third-person accounts, as focalisation can create a misleading sense of proximity to the events narrated. When R. J. Minney describes the capture of Violette Szabo by an officer from an SS Panzer Division following an armed stand-off, events initially appear to be described from the perspective of another agent, Anastasie (René Dufour), who managed to escape and hid under a woodpile in a farmyard, with the help of the farm's inhabitants:

> They brought her, hot and dishevelled, to the heap of logs under which Anastasie was hidden and stood within a pace of him. [. . .] A young officer, eyeing Violette with admiration, said: 'I like your spirit. You put up a wonderful fight – right up to the end.' Then, motioning to his men to let go her arms, he took out his cigarette-case, selected one for her and stuck it between her lips. [. . .] Her eyes blazing with fury, she said: 'You dirty cowards. You filthy German swine. I don't want your cigarettes –' and with that, leaning forward, she spat full in the young officer's face. [19]

While the challenge to Khan about the notebook is material in that it seems to expose a mistake on her part, the purpose of this focalisation is to reinforce Szabo's status as defiant to the extent of recklessness; the German officer also acts true to stereotype. Having had his 'gentlemanly' offer so rudely rejected, '[h]is eyes narrowed [. . .] Then suddenly he threw back his head and laughed. "All right," he said. "Take her away"'.[20] There is, as Foot might argue, 'novelisation' here, inasmuch as a third-person and apparently omniscient narrator attributes thoughts, feelings and actions to protagonists, basing these descriptions principally on imagination rather than observation. Notably, Minney evokes the sentiments not just of Szabo but of the 'German' (throughout the narrative he more often refers to Germans than to Nazis, itself a weighted choice). On the one hand, the implication is that even after being insulted by her, the German admires her spirit; on the other, he is offered, if only momentarily, as an object of identification for the reader, as his actions are more precisely described than hers in this incident. The focalising presence of Anastasie under the woodpile is soon abandoned; in fact Dufour, who joined the French army at the end of the war, was killed in Indo-China in 1946, and, although he produced a written account of Szabo's capture for the head of his resistance group, postwar recollections of the inhabitants of the farm are likely to be Minney's main source for this incident. Nevertheless, this moment echoes the perpetrator-victim-bystander triangulation that, in the wake of Raul Hilberg's work, is often seen to structure Holocaust narratives: the bystander position may, on the surface, seem to be the least ethically problematic for the reader to adopt, but can instead 'reinforce the tendency to see [the Holocaust] in Manichean terms', offering support for 'the rather complacent assumption that few of us will become perpetrators' and reinforcing our 'optimism that we will not become victims' either.[21] Like Minney himself, the reader vacillates between two seemingly impossible points of identification: the peerless Szabo and the cruel German, retreating finally to the only apparent neutrality of the bystander.

Minney is also explicitly assisting in the transformation of Szabo into a mythic figure: as his Introduction notes, Szabo was a 'humble' individual with 'no discernible talents', with a 'haunting beauty' which she 'did not exploit', who nevertheless had 'qualities, noticeable only to a few, which, in a moment of crisis and peril, made her resolute, fearless, unresponsive under agonising torture, so that in Britain's proud story she has her place as a heroine'.[22] There is no question of his being an account which contests this perception of Szabo; nor, indeed, does Fuller downplay the beauty or bravery of her own subject, Noor Inayat Khan. The key difference is that Fuller's chosen narrative technique does provide her with space to question the organisational methods of SOE and indeed postwar information management: the reason she embarks on her 'detective'-like quest for individual testimony about Khan is the paucity of the official record. Her book about Khan in fact raised more questions than it answered for Fuller and led to her writing a series of books, each based on the loose ends of the previous one, uncovering possible double agents and questioning official intransigence. Minney and, to an extent, Tickell focus on individual testimony because their interest lies precisely and squarely on the individual. The agents' involvement in SOE necessitates their actions and creates the circumstances of their dire predicaments, but it is the depoliticised, even to an extent decontextualised 'human story' that is the focus of their biographies. By contrast, Fuller, and indeed Nicholas, use their self-referential accounts to interrogate this style of life writing.

Prolepsis and the anticipation of horror

In another respect, the lives of these women are very precisely contextualised by Minney and Tickell. Both textual and paratextual material indicates to the reader how the narrative will end; that is, whether the subject will survive. Public knowledge of the fates of these women was first awakened by newspaper reports of the trials of those believed responsible, or of the award of honours: Odette Sansom in particular became well-enough known to be referred to by only her first name in newspaper headlines. (There was also an element of convenience in this as she was born Odette Brailly, married Roy Sansom in 1931, divorced him after the war to marry Peter Churchill in 1947, eventually separated from Churchill, remarried, and ended her life as Odette Hallowes.) Even for those who did not approach these texts with existing knowledge of their subjects' fates, jacket copy would often reveal what to expect:

> Violette Szabo. London shop assistant who became a secret agent, was captured and shot by the Gestapo, and was the only British-born girl to be awarded the George Cross. "She was the bravest of us all" said Odette Churchill, G.C."[23]

But the narratives themselves make no virtue of suspense where the fate of the subject is concerned; not only in prefaces and opening chapters but in some cases throughout, prolepsis is used to ensure that the reader understands what the eventual consequences of particular decisions, on the part of the agents or of others, will be. In *Carve her Name*, following her capture, Szabo is taken from Fresnes prison by van: 'She knew where she was being taken, for they had talked of it in England. It was to the Avenue Foch where the Gestapo did their harsher questioning, aided by the persuasive refinements of torture.'[24] The purpose of the (unprovable) attribution of this knowledge to Szabo is both to reinforce that she embarked on her mission fully understanding what the consequences might be, but also to indicate her preparedness, and by extension, to prepare the reader, for what is to come. In the event, Minney gives only hints, introducing a gap in his narrative, presumably to protect the reader, but actually licensing horrible imaginings:

> As the questioning proceeded and she still proved recalcitrant, implements of torture were produced and each was hold up before her. The inquisitor said: 'Will you answer now?' and, just as defiantly as when she was a child, she replied: 'I won't. I *won't*.' The young German then gave the sign. There followed the most atrocious torture.
>
> She winced and bit her lips. Her face was contorted in horrible agony. But still [. . .] she repeated, almost inaudibly: 'I won't. I won't.'[25]

The paragraph break is important here: it is in the gap between the paragraphs that the torture occurs, but the reader sees only its consequences, or at least, its consequences are legible in Szabo's face. Notably, Minney does not attempt to describe, from Szabo's perspective how it *felt* to be tortured: both the narrator and therefore the reader are observing, spectating, and an attempt is made to foreclose the possibility of a dangerous identification with the perpetrator by the agentless nature of the statement: 'There followed the most atrocious torture.' The bystander position is again adopted as apparently less problematic than the position of either perpetrator or victim.[26]

Minney ends his account with Szabo's George Cross citation, a document described by Elizabeth Nicholas as 'giving in detail a description of events that never in fact took place',[27] but which in *Carve her Name* stands as an official guarantee of the trustworthiness of the text itself. Tickell opens *Odette* with a description of the Ravensbrück trial, his chapter culminating in Odette's confirmation of her identity when she takes to the stand. Thus the narrative which follows, beginning with Sansom's family background, is framed by the validatory force of courtroom witness testimony. Of course, her evidence did not consist of her recounting her whole history in the detail which Tickell does, but in using the courtroom as a frame, Tickell authenticates his account. Testimony is here shorn of its subjectivity, or, more precisely, its potential unreliability. Sansom's physical presence in the courtroom is important because her body itself testifies to her resilience under torture. (The back cover of the Pan paperback does not pull its punches in describing what, infamously, happened to her in captivity: 'The Gestapo put certain questions to her; she had nothing to say, even after they had pulled out all her toenails.'[28]) She embodies survival: 'Her face, pale in the strong light, was small-featured, delicate and oddly child-like. Her eyes were bright. A mass of dark hair swept upwards from her forehead, almost concealing the slanting beret, and fell thick upon her shoulders.'[29] Despite what she has endured, her essential femininity, signified by her 'child-like' face and luxuriant hair, is essentially undamaged. Positioned at this early point in the narrative, this is a guarantee for the reader that Sansom will emerge from her ordeal, and, having kept silent under torture, will eventually, in the safe confines of the courtroom, be able to speak about what she has endured.

Tickell's penchant for what now seem like horribly inappropriate images in his descriptions of, in particular, events that take place while Odette Sansom is in Nazi captivity, emerges early on in *Odette*. During the account of the trial, the organisation and running of Ravensbrück is explained, including the process of *Selektion*, the identification of those who would be gassed, which is described by Tickell as a 'fiendish Folies Bergères'.[30] This is an allusion apparently justified by his description of the women's attempts to make themselves appear younger and healthier prior to the *Selektion* itself; this tactic is depicted in the film *Schindler's List* (1993), where women pinch or rub blood onto their cheeks to mimic a 'healthy glow'. Tickell's analogy points to the fact that in each case, men are looking and women being looked at, but the comparison is nevertheless shocking because it brings into conjunction two things – a Parisian nightclub that has become a metonym for a particular kind of illicit entertainment and the choosing of individuals to undergo death by gassing – that seem utterly incomparable. The ethical problems of comparing the concentration camps with anything and indeed of using figurative language to describe them at all are now familiar, and even in early representations, an emphasis on indescribability and the paucity of existing comparators were characteristic. Barbie Zelizer quotes a news editor's comment on task facing the media as information about the camps emerged: 'In the presence of these German horror camps, language breaks down.'[31] Tickell, writing at a distance from the events he is describing, seems determined to resist such a breaking down of language, albeit that the results now seem distasteful. His choice of the image of the Folies Bergères sexualises the process he describes, but it is not impossible that this is precisely the point. Tickell (perhaps) attempts to indicate that, for the Nazis, this process was akin to looking at women in a nightclub; looked at this way, the choice of analogy seems (marginally) more explicable, but it underlines the difficulty that Tickell, like Minney, has in establishing a consistent narrative voice and perspective, a difficulty that refracts the nature of the events described. His use of the phrase 'fiendish Folies Bergères' is in fact embedded in a sentence that attempts to evoke the women prisoners' emotions: 'those who were forced to take part in this fiendish Folies Bergères were fully conscious of its dread purpose'.[32] In this context, the implication is that the women might have conceived the selection in this light, itself both improbable and unprovable. This image, then, disjunctive as it is, stands as a sign of the difficulties of representation that it precisely attempts to solve.

Odette Sansom herself was not subject to the *Selektion* process, as although she was kept prisoner at Ravensbrück, she was in solitary confinement for most of her captivity. Tickell does not elaborate on the fact that Odette Sansom, contrary to SOE regulations, was having an affair with Peter Churchill, the organiser of her circuit, prior to her capture; she married him after the war, once she had divorced her first husband, who disappears early on and without explanation from the narrative of *Odette*. After being captured, she decided to pretend that she was married to Churchill and that he was related to Winston Churchill, a tactic which meant she was considered to have some exchange value. This pretence, which involved Odette foreshadowing her actual postwar marriage to Peter Churchill as well as adopting a further false identity on top of the one that had been constructed for her by F-section, did not however save her from torture prior to her incarceration at Ravensbrück.

Whereas Minney is reticent in his account of Szabo's treatment, Tickell does not draw a veil over what happened to Odette. He is also describing events that have been recounted to him by a living witness, indeed, a survivor:

> A man knelt at her feet. He was a young man, under thirty, very good-looking in a dark Mediterranean handsomeness, and he glanced up at her with blind, brown eyes. He did not see her as a woman but only as a living, sensitive adjunct to her naked foot. His impersonality was terrifying. [. . .] Then, with a slow, muscular drag, he began to pull. A semi-circle of blood started to the quick, oozed over the skin, flooded after the retreating nail.[33]

When all her toe-nails have been removed, we are told: 'Odette gazed incredulously at the bloody furnace of her feet and at the red litter on the floor, litter of a diabolical chiropody.'[34] This latter phrase stands out, like 'fiendish Folies Bergères', on account of its inaptness: chiropody has mundane, even suburban connotations that are hard to dispel, even by the word 'diabolical'; the phrase has the ring of bathos. And yet what is described here is abject and horrific, albeit that, like the description of Szabo's torture, it conceals more than it reveals, and its point of view wavers. The handsomeness of the torturer is framed as being observed from the victim's point of view: how incongruous that a handsome man should be a torturer, and that he should be oblivious to his victim as a sexual being. Yet his 'impersonality', his detachment from his task, seems echoed in the description of the removal of the first nail, which is described as though being coolly observed rather than felt. The purpose here could be to emphasise the victim's shocked detachment from the reality of what is happening; when, after she still refuses to answer questions, the procedure is repeated, more emotive language is used: 'The enclosing flesh ripped and yielded in agonizing pain as the nail was dragged out.'[35] Even here, though, the 'agonizing pain' is not attributed directly to Odette, a tactic which echoes Minney's impersonal statement: 'There followed the most atrocious torture.' In both instances, torture seems to float free of both perpetrator and victim: the problem of where the narrator can or should be positioned, a problem that is fundamentally linked to notions of trustworthiness and reliability, seems insoluble.[36]

'Quest' narratives and the search for evidence

In Minney's and Tickell's accounts of Szabo's and Sansom's experiences, prolepsis is used to situate the narrator as a figure of authority. Fuller's use of foreshadowing in her Preface to *Madeleine*, which largely serves to describe her own investigative technique, is less explicit, although her subject is referred to in the past tense, and the description of the summer of 1943, leading up to Khan's capture, as 'fateful' provides the reader with clues.[37] Later, Yvonne Beekman and Cecily Lefort, other agents who train with Khan, are described as 'doomed to die'.[38] Elizabeth Nicholas, the most polemical of the authors under consideration here, chooses for the title of her book about Diana Rowden and her associates a quotation from John Donne which itself foregrounds mortality, but also bluntly explains, at the start of her prologue, the purpose of her narrative:

> This is a book about seven women who served with the French Section of the Special Operations Executive, were captured by the Germans, and put to death in a manner shameful to their captors, yet ennobled by the courage with which it was endured.[39]

This final clause, and Nicholas's title, might seem to make her liable to be bracketed alongside Minney and Tickell as dealing in novelisation or fictionalisation, although Nicholas's relative bluntness here in fact indicates a desire to distance herself from those earlier examples, a desire that is made explicit early on in *Death be not Proud*:

> reading some books about, or by those who survived, I have been astonished by the facility they reveal for retaining in the memory, over long periods of years, great slabs of detailed dialogue [. . .] I have felt it best not to be lured into the entrancing glades of semi-fiction; I have recorded nothing in this book as having happened unless it were repeated to me as first-hand-evidence.[40]

It would be easy enough to be cynical about Nicholas's faith in 'first-hand-evidence', but her comments indicate not only a contemporary awareness of the deficiencies of accounts such as Tickell's but also their incredible resilience. (Her book did not get a paperback run.) Nicholas accuses Tickell of 'facetiousness', and observes that *Odette* 'was written in a style that suggested it was fiction; it simply reeked of the cops and robbers approach to subversive activity'.[41] With regard to this latter accusation, it is notable that Nicholas, like Fuller, is aware of the danger of such a binary approach and points, albeit implicitly, towards both the problems and the responsibilities for writers who engage with these events.

Some of Nicholas's comments about *Odette* echo the kind of criticism levelled at Anne Frank's *The Diary of a Young Girl*, first published in Britain in 1954 by Vallentine Mitchell and also issued as a Pan paperback, in 1958. In their focus on the experience of sequestration, both texts present the war and the Holocaust aslant, rather than face-on. Just as the diary has become an iconic text of the Holocaust despite being an account of an atypical experience, so *Odette*, in Nicholas's view, is taken to be the representative text of SOE's F-section despite its lack of attention to the

> subterfuge and deception [. . .] the errors, the confusions and the betrayals [. . .] The story revealed was uncomplicated; it was [. . .] the story of one women, and no attempt was made to disentangle the strings that had manipulated her life and led her, ultimately, to the grotesque and mediaeval horrors of Ravensbrück.[42]

As Nicholas makes clear from the outset, her initial investigation into the life of her former schoolfriend Diana Rowden leads to what is essentially a group biography; she cannot write about Rowden without exploring the fates of those who went to France, worked with and died alongside her; indeed, Nicholas was the first to identify the Frenchwoman Sonia Olschanezky as one of those who was executed with Rowden at Natzweiler.[43]

Nicholas aimed to offer not just a corrective to *Odette*, but also a contexualisation of information about Rowden and her fellow agents that was already in the public domain. In the first chapter of her *Death be not Proud*, she quotes newspaper articles, published trial reports and even the inscription on the FANY memorial, unveiled in May 1948 in Knightsbridge. Each of these texts is found by Nicholas to be deficient or problematic: one newspaper report cited indicates that Rowden was 'burned alive in [the] crematorium at Natzweiler', and these words 'still had the power to shock almost beyond endurance'.[44] As Nicholas soon established, the women were given lethal injections and were unlikely to have been conscious when they were taken to the crematorium.[45] For various reasons, despite her desire to know more being piqued, Nicholas does not begin a concerted investigation into the fate of Rowden and the other women until 1955. She recalls reading an article, at this time, about the release of the film *The Dam Busters*, in which the author suggested 'that it was, perhaps, inopportune to remind the Germans of disaster [. . .] Too much, I thought, was being forgotten too quickly; to forgive was one thing, to forget another'.[46] Nicholas is not setting the war as represented by the 'dam busters' raids, a technologised, masculine enterprise, as a counter to the war of women on active service: however compromised their memorialisations might be, the women have been remembered. Rather, she brackets both these aspects of the conduct of the war together; both are still worthy of attention and remembrance, and she is critical of those who would kick over the traces. She could not have known, at this point in her researches, that the full-scale biographical and filmic commemoration of Szabo was yet to come.

The transcripts of the Natzweiler Trial provide Nicholas with a full account of the circumstances of Rowden's last days and her narrative therefore focuses on attempting to retrace her friend's steps in France, interviewing those who had contact with her during this period. Jean Fuller's biography of Khan proceeds in a similar fashion; the same trial transcript in which Rowden's death is described also mentions 'Nora Baker', a name by which Khan was known, as having been taken from a civilian prison at Karlsruhe to Dachau for execution in July 1944.[47] While at Karlsruhe, Khan was kept 'in chains by day and by night, in solitary confinement',[48] or so Fuller learns from an interview with the former prison governor, Wilhelm Krauss. Fearful of defying the Gestapo, Krauss claims that he nevertheless eventually decided to ease the conditions of Khan's captivity: 'It is impossible to tell how long she was kept completely chained [. . .] That the conditions of her detention were gradually eased emerged from the statements of all my informants, though they naturally do not tally in every detail.'[49] This brisk, almost business-like tone is typical of Fuller, who never resorts to the shock tactics of Tickell.

Although Fuller does indicate to the reader when she feels her 'informants' are prevaricating, she adopts a deliberately objective-seeming stance. Shortly after recounting the nature of Khan's imprisonment at Karlsruhe, and in search of more information about Khan's final hours, she decides to contact 'a certain Wassmer', a Gestapo clerk, who transported both Rowden and Khan from prison to Natzweiler and Dachau respectively. The account she receives from Wassmer forms the short final chapter of the biography. Fuller hesitates to contact Wassmer, who, she reflects, with little discernible irony, 'must be weary of interrogations', and, when she finally writes to him, her 'hope of receiving a reply was not very great'.[50] However, she soon receives a reply, the 'obvious sincerity' of which she 'finds touching: it was clear that he was anxious to help me as best he could to complete my picture of Noor, and to show that her wonderful bravery had not failed her at this time'.[51] Fuller's kid-gloves attitude towards a former Gestapo official might seem peculiar, but throughout the text, Fuller reserves judgement on individuals who she believes can help her with her quest. Her place, it seems, is not to pass judgements on what was done or not done. Rather, her focus is on gleaning as much information as she can from whatever source, to write 'impartially' and not 'against the Germans – or for them'.[52] Wassmer can describe the final journey taken by Khan and her fellow prisoners, and tells Fuller that they 'talked together in a very lively and spirited fashion' but his narrative ends once he has delivered the women to Dachau: 'Later, official information was received in Karlsruhe that the women had been shot.'[53] This is the final sentence of the body of the text; it is followed by two appendices which transcribe Khan's posthumous citations for the George Cross and the Croix de Guerre. The impersonal framing of the statement: 'information was received' is an indication that Fuller can go no further. Fuller is not willing to project emotions onto Khan, to imagine how she might have felt, or, to put it another way, to fictionalise her.

The starkness of Nicholas's and Fuller's accounts stand in contrast to Minney's description of the final moments of Szabo's life. Minney weaves together the testimony of a fellow prisoner of Szabo's at Ravensbrück and the account gleaned from the camp's second-in-command, Johann Schwarzhuber, by Vera Atkins. The commandant, Fritz Suhren, fled the camp by car taking Odette Sansom with him and attempted, unsuccessfully, to use her to bargain his way to freedom. Schwarzhuber's account states:

> The shooting was done [. . .] with a small-calibre gun through the back of the neck. [. . .] All three were brave and I was deeply moved. Suhren was also impressed by the bearing of these women. He was annoyed that the Gestapo did not themselves carry out these shootings.[54]

This final buck-passing remark could be intended to exculpate Suhren, but of course his annoyance does not go so far as condemning the fact that the executions are carried out at all, only that he has to take responsibility for them. Minney supplements this account with his own imaginative reconstruction of the execution, from the perspective of other prisoner-witnesses, but also of Szabo herself:

> Violette, they say, was the last to be executed and had to suffer the agony of seeing her friends put to death, aware all the time that the same fate awaited her. She did not flinch. Her spirit was indomitable. Again and again in the past, when all seemed lost, she had fought her way out [. . .] Even in captivity she tried repeatedly to break away so that, returning she could fight on. But now there seemed to be no way out at all. [. . .] Lifting her head with haughty scorn, she walked the last few paces to her death.[55]

Given how Minney has characterised Szabo throughout the narrative ('again and again [. . .] she had fought her way out') her 'haughty' raising of her head is a necessary culmination. The whole framing of Szabo's life has been gravitating towards this end. Her death is not the result of particular historical circumstance, but something less contingent: it is her fate. (In this regard, it seems ironic that the paperback reissue of *Madeleine* was retitled *Born for Sacrifice*; Fuller, while considering the events in Khan's early life that might have led her to enrol in SOE, sees her 'doom' as historically contingent.) The various documentary, eyewitness and other accounts that underpin *Carve her Name* are subsumed to a character study, as is made plain by the juxtaposition of these two descriptions of Szabo's death. Schwarzhuber describes the women as 'brave', but could himself be telling Atkins what he believes she wishes to hear.

Conclusion

Speaking in the 1970s, C. B. Townshend, who was then overseeing the SOE archives, commented that the material under his aegis consisted of 'the surviving files of a collection of files of which we have documentary evidence that at least 87 per cent were destroyed in London between 1945 and 1950'.[56] The authors I have discussed here had varied experiences of working with official sources; Tickell was given assistance that Fuller, just a few years later, could only envy. It would be misleading to describe Fuller's and Nicholas's accounts as counter-narratives, as they were writing a number of years before the 'official' narrative of SOE's activities in France was produced, but both were evidently motivated not by a desire to produce hagiographies of women who were known personally to them, but to acknowledge the bravery of their actions and the horror of their deaths without resorting to the hyperbole or shock tactics that characterise Tickell's work in particular. Nicholas's and Fuller's refusal to attribute feelings or emotions to their subjects means that their narratives have gaps, but it also means that the particularity of what Khan, Rowden and others experienced is respected. These differing approaches prompt us to consider where the boundaries of biography as a genre lie, shading off as these texts do into fictionalising on the one hand and confronting the reader with gaps in the historical record on the other. Any biography might provoke questions about genre, but these questions become far more pressing in the context of war, when the personal and ideological importance placed on truth and authenticity are so much greater than in peacetime. In Nicholas's and Fuller's cases, not representing an event, or representing it as an absence, is chosen as more honest than either speculation or the elaboration of the testimony of often self-serving eyewitnesses. This is not so much a case of refusing to try to 'represent the unrepresentable' as an acknowledgement that even when it comes in the line of duty, one's death should remain one's own.

University of Leicester

Disclosure statement

No potential conflict of interest was reported by the author.

Notes

1 Mark Rawlinson, 'This Other War: British Culture and the Holocaust', *Cambridge Quarterly*, 25.2 (1996), pp. 1–25, p. 11.
2 Deirdre Osborne, '"I do not know about politics or governments . . . I am a housewife.": The Female Secret Agent and the Male War Machine in Occupied France (1942–5)', *Women: A Cultural Review*, 17.1 (2006), pp. 42–64, p. 51.
3 M. R. D. Foot, *SOE in France: An Account of the Work of the British Special Operations Executive in France 1940–1944* (London: Her Majesty's Stationery Office, 1968), p. 453.
4 Mark Seaman, 'Good Thrillers, But Bad History: A review of Published works on the Special Operations Executive's work in France during the Second World War', in K. G. Robertson, (ed.), *War, Resistance and Intelligence: Essays in Honour of M. R. D. Foot* (London: Leo Cooper, 1999), pp. 119–33, p. 121.
5 Donald Bloxham, 'British War Crimes Trial Policy in Germany, 1945–1957: Implementation and Collapse', *Journal of British Studies*, 42.1 (2003), pp. 91–118, p. 105.
6 Ibid., p. 106.
7 Rawlinson, pp. 16–17.
8 Selwyn Jepson, 'Foreword', in Jean Overton Fuller (ed.), *Madeleine: The Story of Noor Inayat Khan George Cross, M. B. E., Croix de Guerre with Gold Star* (London: Victor Gollancz, 1952), pp. 7–8, p. 7.
9 Fuller, p. 9.
10 Foot, p. 339 n. 3.
11 Fuller, p. 127.
12 Rita Kramer, *Flames in the Field: The Story of Four SOE Agents in Occupied France* (Harmondsworth: Penguin, 1996), pp. 141–2.
13 Fuller, pp. 77–8.
14 Sarah Helm, *A Life in Secrets: The Story of Vera Atkins and the Lost Agents of SOE* (London: Abacus, 2006), p. xx.
15 Primo Levi, *The Drowned and the Saved.*, trans by Raymond Rosenthal (London: Abacus, 1989), p. 63.
16 Dominick LaCapra, *History and Memory After Auschwitz* (Ithaca and London: Cornell University Press, 1998), p. 21.
17 Ibid., pp. 20–21.
18 Dominick LaCapra, *Writing History, Writing Trauma* (Baltimore, MD: Johns Hopkins University Press, 2001), p. 41.
19 R. J. Minney, *Carve her Name with Pride: The Story of Violette Szabo G. C* (1956; London: Pan, 1958), pp. 147–8.

20 Ibid., p. 148.
21 Tony Kushner, '"Pissing in the Wind?": The Search for Nuance in the Study of Holocaust "Bystanders"', in David Cesarani and Paul S. Levine (eds.), '*Bystanders' to the Holocaust: A Re-evaluation* (London: Frank Cass, 2002), pp. 57–76, p. 61, p. 60.
22 Minney, p. 9.
23 Ibid., jacket blurb.
24 Ibid., p. 159.
25 Ibid., p. 160.
26 This description is further complicated by the fact that post-Minney accounts of Szabo's experience maintain that, unlike Odette or Eileen Nearne, another F-section agent who survived Ravensbrück, Szabo was not in fact subject to torture. See Juliette Pattinson, *Behind Enemy Lines: Gender, Passing and the Special Operations Executive in the Second World War* (Manchester: Manchester University Press, 2007), p. 163. Osborne cites a claim, first made many years later by a former cellmate of Szabo's, that Szabo was raped during her time in Ravensbrück. See Osborne, p. 52. Minney is referring to an earlier point in Szabo's captivity.
27 Elizabeth Nicholas, *Death be not Proud* (London: Cresset Press, 1958), p. 271.
28 Jerrard Tickell, *Odette: The Story of a British Agent (Odette Churchill G. C. M. B. E.)* (1949; London: Pan, 1955), jacket blurb.
29 Tickell, p. 16.
30 Ibid., p. 15.
31 Barbie Zelizer, *Remembering to Forget: Holocaust Memory Through the Camera's Eye* (Chicago, IL: University of Chicago Press, 1998), p. 85.
32 Tickell, p. 15.
33 Ibid., p. 223.
34 Ibid.
35 Ibid., p. 223.
36 In the first edition of *SOE in France*, Foot cast doubt on Odette Churchill's description of her torture, an accusation that culminated in damages being paid both to Churchill and to R. J. Minney, who Foot suggested was guilty of sensationalism in his description of Szabo's treatment by the Gestapo, and in the removal of the offending remarks from subsequent editions. See Christopher Moran, *Classified: Secrecy and the Secret State in Modern Britain* (Cambridge: Cambridge University Press, 2013), p. 307.
37 Fuller, p. 10.
38 Ibid., p. 70.
39 Nicholas, p. 13.
40 Ibid., pp. 20–21.
41 Ibid., p. 30.
42 Ibid., p. 31.
43 Kramer, p. 183.
44 Nicholas, p. 29.
45 Ibid., p. 71.
46 Ibid., pp. 32–3.

47 Fuller, p. 186.
48 Ibid., p. 180.
49 Ibid., p. 181.
50 Ibid., p. 187.
51 Ibid.
52 Ibid., p. 9.
53 Ibid., p. 187.
54 Minney, p. 185.
55 Ibid., p. 186.
56 Qtd in Duncan Stuart, '"Of Historical Interest Only": The Origins and Vicissitudes of the SOE archive', in Mark Seaman, (ed.), *Special Operations Executive: A New Instrument of War* (London: Routledge, 2008), pp. 217–29, p. 228.

Lyndsey Stonebridge

Statelessness and the poetry of the borderline: André Green, W.H. Auden and Yousif M. Qasmiyeh[†]

Every conflict brings its refugees, but the wars of the twentieth century produced population movements on a new scale. The peace of these wars was almost as bad as the fighting: for every border re-drawn, every treaty signed, millions shifted. They shift still. Traumatic testimony has long been the life-writing genre of choice for those wanting to give voice to the dispossessed. But can trauma really capture the complexity of this territorial violence? There are many ways of moving across a border, or, as is the case for millions today, living on a border. In his 1976 essay, 'The Borderline Concept', the psychoanalyst, André Green wrote: 'I can *be* a citizen or *heimatlos* (homeless), but to "be" borderline – that is difficult for me to imagine'. This article takes Green's writing on the borderline as a starting point for reflecting on the condition of statelessness. For Green, to think seriously about the borderline is to risk an imagination adequate to its shifting geographies – frequently, he compares the task of imagining borderline states to the writing and reading of poetry. How might we describe a poetry of the borderline? And how might such descriptions help us think again about the geographies of modern writing? The second part of this article turns to two poets from different ends of the same history of exile and displacement: Auden, whose voluntary 1939 departure from England coincided with the first convulsions of national frontiers in Europe, its colonies, protectorates and mandates, and the Oxford-based Palestinian, Yousif M. Qasmiyeh, whose writing captures the reality of borderline existence with a particular clarity.

[†]My thanks to Yousif M. Qasmiyeh for permission to quote from his poem here, and for generously discussing his writing with me.

Proving statelessness is like establishing a negative. The individual must demonstrate something that is *not* there.

Carol Batchelor, UNHCR,
'The 1954 Convention relating to the Status of Stateless Persons'

How will I die
While all
Can see me?

Yousif M. Qasmiyeh
'Holes'

More than any other field, psychoanalysis has the particularity of being the kind of work which makes the negative visible.

André Green
The Work of the Negative

Every conflict brings its refugees, but the wars of the twentieth century produced population movements on a new scale. The peace of these wars was almost as bad as the fighting: for every border re-drawn, every treaty signed, millions shifted. They are shifting still. Yet even though displacement is one of the most common experiences of war, it often remains an invisible condition. This is a particularly charged kind of invisibility. *The Scum of the Earth* (1941) was the title Arthur Koestler gave to his autobiographical account of life in the internment camps and on the refugee rat runs of wartime Europe.[1] It is not only their own misfortunes they bring with them, Hannah Arendt remarked of refugees in the same period, but the misfortunes of the whole world.[2] Mass displacement unnerves.

What is it, then, that rises to the surface when large populations of people are pushed outside nation states? One answer is the frailty of the category of the nation state itself, its sovereignty and its borders. The most potent threat the refugee carries with her is that of her own statelessness – the negative image of citizenship. Most refugees are de facto stateless in that by fleeing they have also relinquished the legal protection of their home nation. International legislation strives to ensure that statelessness is only ever temporary: far better to view the refugee as a citizen in transition, either on her way to a new country or back home, than admit a condition of permanent non-citizenship. But the negative condition of statelessness exists nonetheless, as today's rapidly proliferating refugee camps, UN protectorates, immigration removal centres and migrant borderlands all attest. Were statelessness not a condition to be feared, there would be little point in governments threatening to withdraw citizenship from those it finds troublesome (Kuwait, Bahrain, Saudi Arabia, Norway and the UK have all recently re-discovered a taste for punitive de-citizenship).[3]

The dominance of traumatic testimony as the genre of choice in much recent wartime life writing and scholarship, to my mind at least, has not done justice to the complexity of statelessness, either as it is experienced as a brutal reality or as it appears as an existential and political threat. While the rise of testimony has given the asylum claims of refugees a powerful form of advocacy, the emphasis on individual suffering required not only by the genre but also, implicitly at least, often by the law too, tends to push the global politics of mass displacement back into the dark. The United Nations' 1951 Convention Relating to the Status of Refugees defines a refugee as someone who flees in fear of persecution. Today in France asylum seekers are asked to produce 'certificates of trauma' to authenticate that fear.[4] France is not unique: many nations will only grant legal recognition on receipt of a convincing enough victim testimony.

In what follows I propose a shift of emphasis away from testimonies of individual fear and suffering and back to the borderline territories, to the stateless, and to the threat they pose to fantasies of sovereignty. What does it mean to have statelessness in mind?[5] This is my first question. It is a question that cuts in two directions at once. On the one hand, statelessness was (and is) a condition lived by millions: it is therefore a condition that lived in the minds of the homeless, a borderline condition. On the other hand, statelessness disturbs those within states: it is borderline condition that in turn disrupts national, cultural and psychic borders. 'Whoever is uprooted, uproots others', Simone Weil warned Charles de Gaulle in 1943.[6] What kind of writing is capable of capturing this kind of political and psychic complexity? That is my second question.

As devastating as they are, the testimonial life stories required of refugees (although less often actual lives) at the very least offer a story of beginnings, and endings, of persecution and asylum, of trauma and, perhaps even, recovery.[7] These stories are plausible even as they are disturbing; often they disturb precisely because they are plausible. As we will see, the borderline condition offers no such narrative comfort, but challenges us instead to imagine what United Nations High Commission for Refugees representative, Carol Batchelor, has eloquently described as 'a negative': 'Proving statelessness is like establishing a negative. The individual must demonstrate something that is "not" there'.[8] Statelessness is a condition, at once legal, geopolitical and psychical, that requires a particular stretch of the mind.

In his 1976 essay, 'The Borderline Concept', the psychoanalyst best known for his work on the negative, the late André Green described just how difficult this stretch can be: 'I can "be" a citizen or *heimatlos* (homeless), but to "be" borderline – that is difficult for me to imagine' (*On peut être citoyen ou apatride mais il est difficile d'imaginer qu'on est un frontière*).[9] Crossing borders or even living on them can at least be pictured in a story, or on a map; 'being a border', by contrast, is an odd and, indeed, a hard thing to think. Yet as the political philosopher, Étienne Balibar, notes of this passage, being a border is exactly what many people today are struggling with, day in day out, often without end in sight: 'It is precisely what they are living, what most intimately affects their "being" insofar as it is neither this nor that'.[10] Neither this nor that, existing neither here nor there; the borderline condition is not only a lived reality for millions, it haunts contemporary fantasies of sovereignty, both in geopolitical terms and in the most intimate places of being – in our minds.

It is perhaps no coincidence that the first published discussion of the borderline patient in psychoanalysis appeared in 1938, the same year as the major powers met in Evian, France, to discuss the urgent problem of Europe's new refugees, the minorities created by the Peace Treaties of 1919 and the rise of National Socialism.[11] Neither citizens nor refugees with rights to asylum, this generation of the stateless were the first occupants of the borderline territories of the camp and detention centre, and the first to understand how living in a borderline place can turn one into a borderline case. It is Hamlet, not Oedipus, who is the true psychoanalytic prototype of our age, Green remarked ('BC' 60). Hamlet was driven mad by (among other things) a tormenting uncertainty about legal and political sovereignty. André Green was better placed than many to comprehend that uncertainty: born to a non-practising Sephardic family in Cairo, Egypt, in 1927, he moved to Paris in 1946 to study psychiatry, and spent a lifetime occupying the frontiers between competing psychoanalytic institutions and languages, pushing the work of Jacques Lacan into dialogue with that of Donald Winnicott and Wilfred Bion. In a later interview with Gregorio Kohon, Green explained that he had wanted to study philosophy in Paris, but was barred from teaching in France as he had no nationality. 'No nationality? . . . How did you travel?' '*Apatride*! I was a stateless person'.[12]

In this first part of this article, I take Green's writing on the borderline as a starting point for reflecting on what it might mean to write about statelessness today. The borderline condition itself is a category that notoriously causes trouble for theoretical boundaries and distinctions. The borderline case presents symptoms that exist on the border between neurosis and psychosis: often the patient will disguise her psychotic detachment from reality with a set of neurotic symptoms, inhibitions, phobias and actings out. The borderline struggles to look like a plausible person when the ground for appearing plausible has shifted beneath her feet.

This psychic and theoretical complexity is what fascinates Green. One reason for turning to his writing today rests with his refusal to sacrifice what he describes as 'the complexity of the concept of the borderline' ('BC' 61). For Green, to think seriously about the borderline is not so much to establish it as a category as to risk an imagination – a kind of writing and thinking – adequate to its shifting geographies. Like a person attempting to demonstrate the condition of statelessness to immigration control, Green insists that what does not appear visible matters, is significant, conditional even, for a certain way of existing.[13]

Border control is all about establishing sovereignty for both the mind and for nation states. Green begins not by assuming what a border is, or even where a border should be, but by asking what kind of mental work is involved in representing borders in the first place, for both the patient, the analyst and the theorist-as-writer. This also requires suspending the idea of what sovereignty is or should be (earned in exchange for a convincing refugee victim testimony, for example), and focusing instead on the gaps in experience, time and speech. In a typically arresting image he compares the language of the borderline patient to a 'pearl necklace without a string' ('BC' 79). The defining quality in this image is the state of being 'without': the necklace once had or may in the future have a string; it is the absence Green wants us to notice (this is not the same as finding a set of pearls scattered randomly across the seabed). There is meaning to be had, but only in the missing links of thought, action, speech and dream. Frequently, Green compares this work of attending to the negative, of seeing what is both there and not there, to listening and writing poetry. In the context of the theme of this special issue, were Green asked what kind of life writing best captures the experience of 'being a border', poetry, no doubt, would be his answer.

Like the experience of statelessness itself, the exilic conditions of poetry are so obvious that often they barely seem worth noting. From epic to elegy, poetry has always been about departures and loss. But the poetry of exile is a wide field. And, as Edward Said argued in his famous 1984 essay, 'Reflections on Exile' (writing in the one of the bleakest periods of the Palestinian struggle) to subsume the experience of statelessness under the humanising aesthetics of the literature of exile, is to risk rendering 'its mutilations' banal.[14] In the second part of this article, I turn to two poems written by late modernist poets writing from different ends of the same history of exile and displacement: Auden, whose infamous voluntary 1939 departure from England coincided with the first convulsions of national frontiers in Europe, its colonies, protectorates and mandates, and the Oxford-based Palestinian Yousif M. Qasmiyeh, whose writing captures the reality of statelessness, and its ever expanding history, with a particular clarity. Both poets can be described as attending to the negative in a sense that Green might have recognised. I contrast them here to respond to the challenge I read in his writing of discovering a mode of psychic – and possibly political – being in which the borderline cannot only be understood, but thought as the basis for imagining new kinds of geographical and historical belonging.

A late twentieth-century psychoanalyst from Cairo and Paris, a mid-century Oxford poet in voluntary exile, a contemporary Palestinian poet in Oxford: to bring these three disparate writers together is to begin to track the emergence of a new condition, the borderline condition, from the last century to our own time. As Qasmiyeh's poetry demonstrates, in an anxiously border phobic world finding a language for the condition of statelessness is a creative, as well as a legal and political imperative.

The borderline concept

As Jacqueline Rose was the first to argue, sometimes it seems as if psychoanalysis has been writing a clandestine history of the shifting frontiers of the nation state all along.[15] In Freud's writing, egos, like states, require defence mechanisms to ward off intruders that more often than not come from within their own walls; those unwanted guests, the drives, are 'frontier creatures' (Freud's image) scuttling across the railway station concourses of the psyche with their conspicuous libidinal luggage; our minds are quite literally 'occupied' by 'foreign bodies', annexed to an absolutist power that brooks no resistance. At the heart of Green's 1976 essay, 'The Borderline Concept' is a passage typical in this respect from Freud's *New Introductory Lecture* on 'The Psychical Dissection of the Personality', first published in that most conspicuous of years in the history of the borderline, 1933:

> In thinking of this division of the personality into an ego, a super-ego and an id, you will not, of course, have pictured sharp frontiers like the artificial ones drawn in political geography. We cannot do justice to the characteristics of the mind by linear outlines like those in a drawing or in a primitive painting, but rather by areas of colour melting into one another as they are presented by modern artists. After making the separation we must allow what we have separated to merge once more. ('BC' 71)[16]

As Freud well knew, in fact his interwar audience was far more likely to have pictured the second topography as comprising different territorial states distinguished by 'sharp frontiers' than as the deliquescent colour fields of a modernist painting. As with the politics of national sovereignty, theories of the mind prefer maps to melting pots. In this context, and with historical hindsight, Freud's stern injunction ('you will not, of course') carries a very clear political resonance. At the very moment the borders of Westphalian Europe began to tremor, Freud was insisting that the psychoanalytic imagination is capable of a different kind of 'justice' to that of crude nation division. In place of the absolutes of the politics of national sovereignty, he was calling for a thinking that would allow 'what we have separated to merge once more'.

Forty years later, after Europe's tremors had erupted to produce what Arendt described as the 'calamity' of the stateless,[17] Green makes the problem of 'merging' the focus of his 1976 essay, and develops Freud's analogy for an age of mass displacement through a series of arresting geopolitical metaphors: '[t]he borderline case is less of a frontier than a no-man's land, an entire field whose borders are vague. Its population needs to be sorted out', he begins ('BC' 74). The merging between the language of geopolitics and states of mind is deliberate in this essay: no mere analogising, Green means for us to understand how the language of global politics quite literally gets inside our heads. But while implementing rigid border control is one way of sorting populations for the nation state, in the psyche nothing ever stays sorted. Try as it might, the mind can never entirely get rid of its previous inhabitants: what we expel always remains as a trace in the homeland. For psychoanalysis, negation is a primary form of border control. The first 'no', Freud argued in 'On Negation' (1925), coincides with the first border – 'no, not me', and the first expulsion with the first demarcation between inside and outside – 'no, not inside me'. But, as Green insists, this is not a once and for all narrative moment in the development of the ego; that original scene of judgement and separation can only be grasped retrospectively by an act of thought that has to acknowledge not just the 'no', but the state of merging that preceded it. Capturing the complexity of that act of thought – of merging – is the wager of Green's writing on the borderline after Freud: 'The major difficulty lies in the co-existence of different ego-states: tolerance of "shadows, doubts and mysteries" and/or capacity to decide between the Yes and the No, the existent and the non-existent' ('BC' 71). This is a major difficulty not only for the borderline case, but also for 'normality'. For Green, the borderline is nothing less than 'the basic concept in psychoanalysis' ('BC' 73). We are all constantly on the border, struggling to inhabit a state that cannot be imagined completely, one that haunts us from within even as we experience it as menacing us from without.

As Rose argued, such states of mind also underpin the fantasies of nation states. Establishing borders, building walls and security fences, is one way of banishing the shadows, doubts and mysteries, of terminating the pressures on the mind with the erection of a giant symbol or picture; re-establishing a primitive political geography of the mind (in Freud's terms) which also happens to be a lived political geography for millions. In *Walled States, Waning Sovereignty* (2010), Wendy Brown suggests that our contemporary obsession with wall and frontier building directly corresponds to a waning sense of national sovereignty.[18] The nation state no longer binds us, hence our panicked devotion to fences and ditches, barbed wire and concrete. Brown's psychoanalytic reference points are the Freud of 'The Psycho-Neuroses of Defence' and Anna Freud's classic 1936 text on defensive ego manoeuvring, *The Ego and the Mechanisms of Defence*. Coming from a different tradition in psychoanalytic theory – from between object relations rather than from behind ego defences – Green's focus on the border prompts a related but different question: if one part of the world is engaged with the desperate building of defensive borders, what does it mean for others to 'be' this border? How is it possible to inhabit a place that is at once a crudely drawn geopolitical line in the eyes of some, but experienced as a no-man's land by those who live there? 'One might think of isolated pieces of land delineated by void space', Green writes of the borderline at one point, evoking not only a mental border, but the contested territories of today's political maps; shifting 'archipelagos' (the image is Green's again), makeshift homes for many that can only be imagined as an impenetrable barrier by others ('BC' 79).[19]

Being a border, in this respect, is also a method of defence. Indeed, it is, perhaps, one of the few defences left to the totally defenceless. If one cannot have one's own borders, Green writes, one becomes instead 'a moving border' and hence inviolable: nobody can cross *into* a border. But this defence comes with a heavy price. To be a border is also to perform a vanishing act, to disappear into what elsewhere Green calls a 'psychic hole'. Pushing the psychic and political analogies a little further, we might claim that something similar happens to those who slip into what Carol Batchelor describes as a political and legal hole: statelessness or 'something that is "not" there'. While the tremulous sovereign subjects of the waning nation state anxiously shore up its ruins by erecting concrete slabs, those they intend to keep out do not so much scratch at the walls demanding entrance (as the wall fantasy fears), as disappear into them.

But Green refuses to let the complexity of the borderline disappear into the border – which is why his writing deserves a place in contemporary discussions about the psychopathology of national sovereignty and statelessness. That complexity demands an act of analytic and, one might also say, moral imagination. One would have to be a poet, he notes at one point, to capture what is experienced in the analysis of a borderline patient. Green is not a poet, but making the work of the negative visible in his writing involves a particular attentiveness to the ways in which analogies push one another around. If psychoanalysis has indeed been writing a clandestine history of the nation state in its geopolitical metaphors all along, with Green the historical stakes of that traffic in language become very clear. There are of course other languages that psychoanalysis can and does use to describe borders: Green, for example, also writes of the way an 'osmotic border can open up to unburden the inside from the troublesome stimuli', in an echo of Freud's discussion of the biology of the death drive ('BC' 63).[20] The natural science of borders, however, lacks the suggestion of the agency, or contrived imposition, involved in the political drawing of territories that Green, following Freud's lead, is at once picturing and protesting against. Recall Freud's injunction to his 1933 audience: 'You will not of course have pictured sharp frontiers like the artificial ones drawn in political geography'. In insisting that the borderline is not a sharp frontier but a vacillating territory, Green both obeys Freud's command and resists, again and again in his writing, the kind of splitting – theoretical and psychic, political and historical – that compulsively erects borders where there are only ever, in fact, shadows and contested territories.

Even the language of the borderline itself is shadowed by another territory. In the original French, Green's essay is entitled *Le concept de limite*, although the English word 'borderline' is retained on occasion, bobbing up like a floating archipelago in a sea of French. As Green explains in a footnote to the original French: 'The English term *borderline* makes no distinction between a frontier separating two countries and, more generally, a limit or border' (*Le term anglais borderline signifie indifféremment la frontière séparant deux pays, et, plus généralement, la limite, le bord*).[21] Green is unique in contemporary psychoanalysis for his transformative crossings between the French and the British traditions (between space and sign, affect and drive) and his concept of the borderline vacillates between the two languages just as it shimmers between objects for the patient, between yes and no, the this and not that, always *à la limite, le bord.* As Yasemin Yidliz has argued, the fantasy of a singular mother tongue was a 'vital element in the imagination and production of the homogenous nation state'.[22] In this respect, we might also say that Green is one of the most articulate psychoanalysts today of what Yildiz calls the 'postmonolingual condition'.[23]

In a later essay, 'On the Edge', Green describes psychoanalysis as a 'practice of thinking' that calls for an 'abandonment of sovereignty'.[24] From all I have argued so far, it would be limiting to assume that abandonment is only possible on the couch. As Brown reminds us, political sovereignty is a peculiarly 'borderline concept'.[25] It requires we do at least two things at once: self-govern and submit to being governed. No self-determination, goes the well-worn paradox of nationalised subject-hood, without surrender to the power of the nation state which is why we need the state to so absolutely draw its borders: when it feels threatened so do we. If there is a politics to be derived from Green's concept of the borderline, it might instead begin with his insistence that abandoning sovereignty is not the end, but the beginning of imagining a different way of being. 'The subject already felt deprived of this sovereignty', he writes of the analysand, 'but retained sufficient capacities to have the hope of discovering something of it'.[26] There is an alternative to defensive wall building we might also interpret Green as suggesting here. The borderline patient pointedly refuses the anxious wall building of sovereignty. Instead his symptoms:

> offer a *negative refusal of choice*: neither 'Yes' nor 'No'. One could express the same relation in experiential terms by asking the question: 'Is the object dead (lost) or alive (found)?' Or 'Am I dead or alive?' – to which he may answer: '*Neither Yes nor No*'. ('BC' 82)

Dead or alive, lost or found, but also neither yes nor no, here nor there, then nor now. It is not madness, nor simply indeterminacy Green is evoking here, but a very precise refusal to choose. The borderline maybe without sovereignty, but he or she is not without agency.

This is also where hope begins in Green. Like dreams, states of absence and blankness and affect (the 'essential perplexities' in Green's writing according to Adam Phillips), the borderline's refusal pushes itself into words.[27] At the end of the original French version of the essay, Green concludes (quoting in English) with a poem written by one of Winnicott's patients, Charles, aged 9.

> What's wrong with dying? I said.
> 'Everything', they said,
> 'It's nothing, blackness, evil,' they said.
> 'But it isn't', I said,
> 'I want to die, I've done all I need,'
> 'Here I am a hindrance,
> There, dead, I am gone,
> I have fulfilled my purpose,
> I want to see God', I said.
> 'What is God?' they said. [28]

Charles is a little boy who knows how to work the negative. 'There, dead, I am gone'; his is a syntax that speaks from the space (not here, there) and time (the future, but also 'there' now) of the borderline. Not exactly refusing to live – after all he wants to see God – Charles writes a poem about how to be borderline without disappearing.

Charles' borderline condition, of course, is many miles away from the geopolitical borderlines inhabited by millions. Neither, however, does psychoanalysis exist apart from the history of statelessness, not just because, as in Green's case, so many psychoanalysts have been exiles or refugees since 1933, but also because the theory itself can be described as a struggle to make the stateless mind visible – to 'demonstrate a negative', to recall Carol Batchelor's pithy description of the paradox of legal statelessness. In this context, Green's suggestion that the borderline is not simply lost, not simply either suffering or invisible, but *refusing* to be cast as either inside or outside, sovereign or *apatride,* is a powerful one. With this refusal in mind, I want next to cross from psychoanalysis to the history and writing of modern statelessness.

Poetry of the borderline

'How will I die', ask the first lines of Yousif M. Qasmiyeh's 2008 poem, 'Holes', 'While all/ Can see me?' The dilemma, and also the refusal to resolve it, mirrors that in Charles' poem. Qasmiyeh, however, is not writing therapy poetry, but writes from a contemporary tradition of Arab poetry, and particularly, an engaged free verse modernism that emerged in the mid twentieth century, and that frequently has the experience of statelessness at its very core.[29] Like psychoanalysis, poetry is a practice that calls for the abandonment of sovereignty. The negative experiences of exile, displacement and flight thread through the different geographies and histories of modernist poetry over the past 100 years like a thin fault in the earth's surface. But what we might call, following Green, the poetry of the borderline, has produced different ways of un-belonging: one poet's cosmopolitan leap over the frontier needs to be compared to another's potential disappearance into the no-man's land of the borderline.

Far from being a refugee, when W.H. Auden left England for the United States in 1939, he was wilfully escaping a waning state that for the poet had become more and more cloying as its power diminished. 'Look, stranger, at this island now', runs the first line of the famous 1936 poem that anticipated his departure three years later.[30] Auden well understood the intimate relation between the making and breaking of poetic form and the mass politics of displacement that surrounded him. Looking strangely was something his poetry did a great deal in the 1930s. Frequently viewed from up high, the landscape seen by the hawks and airmen of his poems revealed a geopolitical map of contracting and expanding states. The aerial perspectives of Auden and his contemporaries did more than simply reflect the new technology of air travel and the portable zoom lens; they also gave a poetic form to the decline of the nation as a home for rights and citizenship, and the rise of totalitarian domination (Arendt's famous chapter on statelessness in *The Origins of Totalitarianism* was titled 'The Decline of the Nation-State and the End of the Rights of Man').[31] Just as one can only see both sides of a border from above, so too did the dark masses that moved across the map of Europe appear more starkly when they were viewed at a remove – or looked at strangely. 'The eyes of the departing migrants are fixed on the sea,/To conjure their special fates from the impersonal water', Auden wrote in his 1937 poem 'Dover'. These were not only Auden's about-to-be exiled eyes, but those of a generation of refugees for whom the borderline was fast becoming a lived reality.

In the much-cited epigraph to the collection in which 'Look, Stranger' appeared, Auden aligned the geopolitical contortions of Europe on the brink of war with modernist excess to suggest a timely tactical retreat for his poetry in the age of extremes:

> Since the external disorder, and extravagant lies,
> The baroque frontiers, the surrealist police;
> What can truth treasure, or heart bless,
> But a narrow strictness?

Auden's return to conventional forms in the last collection written in his native country is generally understood as a transitional means of framing what he is about to leave, of giving form – an image – to his nation state so that it might be mourned. To look strangely, in this sense, is to separate at the same time. It is to leave with a remembered image, as the carefully composed closing stanza of 'Look, Stranger' pictures it:

> Far off like floating seeds the ships
> Diverge on urgent voluntary errands;
> And the full view
> Indeed may enter
> And move in memory as now these clouds do.

England, in Jed Esty's fine phrasing of these lines, becomes 'the abandoned thing'.[32]

But what is separated (remember Freud's injunction) must be allowed to merge once more. While, on the one hand, the poem's images contain and enable the experience of separation, they must also navigate the still indistinct territories of the borderline. The chalk walls of the island have not yet moved into full view, only the clouds which at some point they might resemble are visible. The future of a promised remembrance – a thing that will be lost – emphasises only that this separation has not yet been achieved. Auden's border crossing is not yet a departure but what Green, describing the work of the negative, calls a 'passage, a figure, a procession, a moment of transformation'.[33] The transforming figure in this stanza is simile: as clouds now move in memory so too 'may' the full view of the island. In a second move, the clouds themselves are reflected in the 'harbour mirror'; it is (as so often in Auden) the glassy sea that finally offers passage for the image:

> And the full view
> Indeed may enter
> And move in memory as now these clouds do,
> That pass the harbour mirror
> And all the summer through the water saunter.

The late Richard Hoggart once noted that simile was much over-used in 1930s poetry, largely under Auden's influence. Yet to say that something is 'as' or 'like' something else, the abstract and invisible (memory) with a concrete visual image (clouds), is not always to arrive at the allusive 'pungent conciseness' Hoggart values in the best of Auden's similes; it is also to draw attention to a state which is neither quite one thing nor another, neither identical to something else nor discrete from it but 'like' it: simile perhaps is the borderline figure *par excellence*.[34] When I read the final stanza of 'Look, Stranger', I think not of the of the sharp frontiers of political geography that are the poem's historical occasion, but rather of the areas of colour moving through water in Freud's geopolitical analogy of the mind.

Nothing, of course, could be more elegiac (strictly and narrowly speaking) than a last image playing on the light of the sea as one departs. Memory, cloud, mirror, water: as what will be lost processes through the poem it is also distanced or 'attenuated'.[35] And just as the image tapers, so too does the sibilant summer light sauntering on the water whisper a fading song. The first stanza reads:

> Look, stranger, at this island now
> The leaping light for your delight discovers,
> Stand stable here
> And silent be,
> That through the channels of the ear
> May wander like a river
> The swaying sound of the sea.

'Look' asks the poem, but also 'stand stable' and 'silent be', so that the 'swaying sound of the sea' can be heard 'through the channels of the ear'. The speaker is whispering, as if from afar. Nobody writing in English does lyrical pathos better than Auden on his travels in the late 1930s. Form in this poem does not so much shore up the ruins of a waning national sovereignty as offer the lyric poet a passage out: 'the cosmopolitan ego moves off', as Esty puts it.[36]

This reading works well so long as we assume that the 'stranger' the poet is about to become is the one addressed by the poem. Just as the island and its future image are suspended in the repeated 'now' of the poem's moment, however, the identity of Auden's stranger, like the future memory of the island, is not a settled matter. *Look, Stranger!* is also the original title of the 1936 collection as a whole, and is dedicated to the actress and writer Erika Mann (daughter of Thomas) whom Auden had married the year before so that she could be granted the national citizenship that would allow her to leave Nazi Germany. 'To Erika Mann', the dedication reads, just above the epigraph about the baroque frontiers and the surrealist police. There is another stranger in Auden's borderline poems, then, one of the newly stateless, a refugee.[37] The collection that in so many ways announces Auden's cosmopolitan exile is shadowed by the mass politics of statelessness. Thinking about Auden's poems as addressing another kind of stranger does not change their elegiac drift. But it does perhaps pull these poems back into the more equivocal territory of the borderline. Islands look different to people who exist between states than they do to people leaving them: memory, cloud, mirror, water are less, perhaps, similes of departure, than images strung on a pearl necklace without a string.

Or holes, Yousif M. Qasmiyeh might say: 'holes with holes between them on the page' is how he describes (with Bernard O'Donoghue) the 10 episodes that comprise his poem 'Holes', each, as in Auden's poem, enacting an incomplete passage of departure:

> I lean on
> The footsteps of my past
> As I slip towards
> My shadow.

In this poem to turn back is also to risk disappearing into the shadows of the borderline.[38] This is not to claim equivalence between the borderline experiences of the two poems or their writers, but it is to mark their mutually implicated history. At the same moment that the late modernism of the Auden generation turned elegiac, modern Arabic poetry too was responding to modernity, and often directly to Western modernism.[39]

The geopolitical convulsions that made Erika Mann a stranger did not stop with the end of the war, nor at the frontiers of Europe; and neither did their profound effects on poetic form.[40] A Palestinian born in Beddawi refugee camp in Lebanon, Qasmiyeh is a second-generation exile poet whose complex lyricism explicitly echoes that of the late Mahmoud Darwish, and whose intricate re-workings of elegy can be compared to that of the re-known Syrian poet, Adonis (whose writing Qasmiyeh has translated from Arabic into English).[41]

Auden chose to put himself in exile because he wanted to be a stranger. In contrast, for some modern Arab poets exile itself is a primary condition.[42] Abandonment is the beginning: 'The relationship of an Arab poet to his language is like that of a mother who gives away her son after the first stirrings in her body', Adonis has written. Egyptian-born Green, theorist of the emptiness bequeathed to the child by a mother who is dead to his world, might have appreciated the poignancy of the maternal metaphor here. Adonis again: 'For him it can be said: in the beginning was the exile, not the word. In his struggle against the hell of daily life, the Arab poet's only shelter is the hell of exile'.[43]

'Holes' was written as part of the Oxford Poets and Refugees Project, hosted by Oxford Brookes University and the charity Asylum Welcome in 2008. As Rachel Buxton explains in her introduction to the anthology that was produced out of the workshops, the project 'brought together 14 published poets (most of whom were Oxford-based) and 14 exiled writers (most of whom were refugees or asylum seekers). Each established poet worked one-to-one with an exiled writer'.[44] In their co-written comments on their collaboration Qasmiyeh and Bernard O'Donoghue (born in County Cork, arrived in Manchester aged sixteen) remark on the uneasy distinction implied between poetry and exile in the way the project was conceived:

> From our first meeting in November 2008, Yousif expressed concerns that the term 'asylum-seeker/refugee' was featuring so prominently as an overarching heading for this poetry project. Being a refugee should not require foregrounding one's legal condition above all else, overshadowing, for one's personal, professional and writing history beyond and before asylum.[45]

In other words, 'Holes' needs to be understood as a poem that is produced on a troublesome borderline between conceptions of poetry, writing, language and law. The 'refugee writer' category risks consigning Qasmiyeh's distinctive engagement with Islam, Sufism, prophecy and poetic tradition to invisibility, as, of course, does my decision to place the poem alongside Auden's (another 'published Oxford poet' if ever there was one) very different exile. On the other hand, as I also want to suggest, 'Holes' is a poem acutely conscious of its own borderline status: hence its exemplariness for a connective reading of poetic statelessness.

In the workshop all the writers present were asked to 'think of an image that conveys you – the first thing that comes into your mind'.[46] This was also an explicit invitation for the refugee to authenticate himself or herself through a visual image – to produce a kind of testimony ('You can be witness writers', Carole Angier, the workshop leader, urged the participants, 'like the great Italian author Primo Levi').[47] 'Holes' is a brilliantly subtle refusal of this invitation, written very much from the position of the borderline. As Qasmiyeh himself puts it:

> While I was working on the poem, which is in itself composed of fragments of bigger pictures that are marked with all sorts of holes, I was trying to transform a blurry idea, i.e. the blankness that I faced when I was asked (on the spot) to come up with a specific image, into something in Arabic (and English).[48]

Holes, fragments, blankness; the language resonates with Green's 1976 essay.

The largest hole in the poem on the page stretches between the first two stanzas and the rest of the poem:

1
How will I die
While all
Can see me?

2
When is the rain
Going to admit
Its fall?

3
I was born
On the seam of a dress
In the last hour
Of the sixth day,
Between clusters of stars
And the borders of a river.

I was neither
Adam reaching the ground,
Nor was I myself

In cities
Which share their water
With the agents of doom.

This is a linguistic void as profound as the gaps between Green's archipelagos. The Palestinian poet is writing in English; yet his words begin, as they would in Arabic, on the right hand side of the page. Between the movements of the eye – left right and right left at the same time – there is less a lingual barrier to cross than a territory to be traversed.[49] 'Each time a separation occurs between a couple of mental opposites', Green writes, 'two terms, two functions, two processes – at least one of the two split –off elements tends to re-include part of the opposite, excluded element' ('BC' 71). Here the excluded language is experienced as a blank space of white on the page. Holes in this poem are where the negative is kept visible.

Like Auden's, Qasmiyeh's poem speaks of a memory that has yet to settle into a future. Here, however, that suspension is emphatic. Like the rain ('When is the rain/Going to admit/Its fall?'), the poem refuses to make a choice between past and present, here or there. Would the rain admit its falling – images of arrested grief run through the poem – the speaker might proceed to picture the lost home through a series of watery similes, but it will not (or cannot) and instead the recalcitrant rain suspends the promise of elegy: in this poem what is lost cannot yet be mourned through a veil of water. This is a journey to exile not in progress (as in Auden's 'Look, Stranger') but permanently arrested. While the images in each of the poem's ten episodes are often figures of ritual passage – a child dropped from his midwife's hip, 'a wind shaken coffin' moving through a crowd, a descending a caravan, a tunnel out – they do not conjugate, and the holes between holes remain. The refugee ego, in effect, moves nowhere.

'Holes', then, is less the exile's elegy for a home lost that it might at first appear (or, indeed, that it was invited to be) than a verbal picturing of primary statelessness:

I was born
On the seam of a dress
In the last hour
Of the sixth day,
Between clusters of stars
And the borders of a river.

'I was born/On the seam of a dress', writes the poet who was born in a refugee camp. Other poets make memories to mourn out of bits of their mothers (D.H. Lawrence, for example, famously 'pressing the small poised feet of a mother who smiles as she sings' from beneath the piano in the much anthologised 'Piano').[50] This poet's fetish, however, slips into a tongue that is not his mother's and into the seam of another address, another place name. 'I was born/On the seam of a dress'. I was born hidden in the join, tucked in the crevices of another country, in a place that seemed like an address but wasn't quite. This is the newest lost isle in the poetics of statelessness, the permanent refugee camp. Its language is, by necessity, borderline. I was born, we might even say, parsing the vacillating linguistic territories of this poem right down, in the semene of an address, in the minimal unit of meaning of an utterance possible within statelessness.

Yet to be borderline in 'Holes' is not to disappear. Working the negative between languages, places and times, Qasmiyeh performs the 'negative of refusal of choice' that is both the borderline's symptom and his hope: 'Am I dead or alive?' [. . .] '*Neither Yes nor No*', writes Green. 'I was neither [. . .] Nor was I myself', writes Qasmiyeh. Or rather:

I am that dead person
But I don't know
How
He managed to escape

Such enigmatic pronominal shifting is, of course, lyric's prerogative, and elegies have always gone visiting between tenses. What is distinctive about 'Holes', however, is its refusal to move out of its borderline territories. Nothing is ever finally lost in the poem, because the experience it captures is still lived. To an extent, this is part of the poem's explicit historical cause. 'Holes' was begun in the autumn 2008. In the December of that year, Israel launched 'Operation Cast Lead' with the bombardment of Gaza. Qasmiyeh's speaker follows the 'flock of frightened angels [. . .] Roaming at low height'. 'Please stop', he urges, so 'you can return safely/To your dead ones'. If the history of the borderline is, at least in part, produced by the refusal to share land, what emerges as common in its poetry is the sense of a grief arrested by an on-going history of violent displacement.[51]

Auden watched the white border of England saunter on the water with the eyes of the stranger he was to become. Seventy years later, 'Holes' too ends with an image playing on water.

Upside down
And in the middle
Of the yard
His picture was hung.
They did not change
The place of the pail.
He will cry,

And the image
Will float on the
Face of the pail.

No one is more entitled to pathos than the poet in exile from, of all places, a refugee camp. Here, at last, is the image asked of the poet in the Oxford workshop; it is granted, however, not to guarantee the authenticity of the refugee writer – this is no certificate of trauma – but to keep us in the complexity of the borderline. 'He will cry,/And the image/Will float on the/Face of the pail': we neither see the image directly, and nor do we know that he is crying, simply that he 'will'. The suffering of the stateless is not ours to authenticate. Nonetheless, as Auden might have said, in the bucket left in the yard is something for the truth to treasure and the heart to bless.

The poet refuses either to be lost to the past or to give himself up to the present; that is Qasmiyeh's historical piquancy, as I read it, and also his hope. To complete a work of mourning one needs either to have a home (which is why the pilots of the Israeli planes can at least return to mourn their dead) or to be reconciled to homelessness. The borderline can do neither. If Green's endeavour to think what it means to be a borderline is timely, it is surely because there is now no return to a time before the calamity of statelessness reshaped the world. And nor, if we follow the example of the poets of this new condition, is this necessarily something to be mourned; or at least, perhaps, not only to be mourned. Green teaches us that the loss of sovereignty can be the beginning of something as well as the end. 'The subject already felt deprived of this sovereignty but retained sufficient capacities to have the hope of discovering something of it'. Making the complexity of the condition of statelessness visible is a form of hope, a way of discovering something out of the loss of sovereignty. It is to begin to understand how the borderline is not a sharp frontier but a populated territory. To comprehend how that territory is permanent requires a particular type of psychic, but also political courage. One final quote from Green's 'Borderline Concept':

> a tremendous effort is necessary in order to be able to tolerate absence, to differentiate it from loss, and to give the representational world its full role in one's imagination and thought. Only the absence of the object can be the stimulus for imagination and thinking, in other words, for psychic creativeness and aliveness. ('BC' 83)

To be borderline is not only to be lost in the walls, but also, perhaps, stimulated into living through them.

University of East Anglia

Disclosure statement

No potential conflict of interest was reported by the author.

Notes

1 Arthur Koestler, *Scum of the Earth* (London: Eland Publishing Limited, [1941] 2006).
2 Hannah Arendt, 'Bertolt Brecht: 1898–1956', in *Men in Dark Times* (New York: Harcourt Brace & Co., 1983), pp. 226.
3 In autumn 2014, David Cameron announced plans to prevent suspected British Jihadis from re-entering the UK (see: http://www.theguardian.com/uk-news/2014/nov/14/uk-jihadists-citizenship-laws-human-rights [Date accessed: 24 November 2014]). For the use of statelessness in Kuwait, Bahrain and Saudi Arabia, see 'The New Unpeople', *The Economist*, 15 November 2014, http://www.economist.com/news/middle-east-and-africa/21632640-statelessness-punishment-against-political-dissent-gulf-new-unpeople [Date accessed: 24 November 2014]).
4 See Didier Fassin and Richard Rechtman, 'Chapter Nine: The Psychotraumatology of Exile' and 'Chapter Ten: Asylum', in *The Empire of Trauma: An Inquiry into the Condition of Victimhood* (New York: Princeton University Press, 2009), pp. 225–74.
5 This question is indebted to that first posed by Jacqueline Rose in *States of Fantasy*: what does it mean to carry the nation state in one's mind? See *States of Fantasy* (Oxford: Oxford University Press, 1996).
6 Simone Weil, *The Need* for *Roots: Prelude to a Declaration of Duties towards Mankind* (1950), trans. Arthur Wills (London and New York: Routledge, 2002), p. 48.
7 For an insight into what is required of the testimony of current UK asylum seekers, see the recent Home Office guidance, *Asylum Policy Instruction: Assessing Credibility and Refugee Status* (Home Office: January 2015). The guidance is careful to acknowledge 'emotional trauma' and the vulnerability of memory. Nonetheless, the requirements are for a plausible and coherent narrative: 'There should be no significantly or inadequately explored contradictions' (p. 15). This demand for plausibility is uncomfortably twinned with the requirement that asylum seekers demonstrate the exceptional nature of their circumstances. See David Farrier, 'Everyday Exceptions: The Politics of the Quotidian in Asylum Monologues and Asylum Dialogues', *Interventions: International Journal of Postcolonial Studies*, 14.3 (2012), pp. 429–42.
8 Carol Batchelor, UNHCR, Department of International Protection, 'The 1954 Convention relating to the Status of Stateless Persons: Implementation within the European Union Member States and Recommendations for Harmonisation', *Refuge*, 22:2 (summer, 2004), p. 36.
9 André Green, 'La concept de limite', in *La folie priveé: psychanalyse des cas-limites* (Paris: Gaillimard, 1990), p. 126. Translation mine. Translated as

'The Borderline Concept', *On Private Madness* (London: Rebus Press, 1996), p. 64. Henceforth referred to in the text as 'BC'. All future translations from this edition unless otherwise indicated.

10 Étienne Balibar, 'The Borders of Europe', trans. J. Swenson, in Pheng Cheah and Bruce Robbins (eds.), *Cosmopolitics: Thinking and Feeling beyond the Nation* (Minneapolis: University of Minnesota Press, 1998), p. 217.

11 Adolph Stern, 'Psychoanalytic Investigation of and therapy in the Borderline Group of Neuroses', *Psychoanalytic Quarterly*, 7 (1938), pp. 467–89.

12 'The Greening of Psychoanalysis: André Green in dialogue with Gregorio Kohon', in Gregorio Kohon (ed.), *The Dead Mother: The Work of André Green* (London and New York: Routledge, 1999), p. 11.

13 There is no passport proper for the stateless only, at best, temporary documents, such as the notorious Travel Documents ('TDs') carried by Palestine refugees. For the complex (to put it mildly) effects of the vacillation of national, political and legal borders on the Palestinians, the largest refugee population in the world, see Abbas Shiblak, 'Passport for what price? Statelessness among Palestinian refugees', in Are Knusden and Sari Hanafi (eds.), *Palestinian Refugees: Identity, space and place in the Levant* (London and New York: Routledge, 2011), pp. 113–27.

14 Edward Said, 'Reflections on Exile' (1984), in *Reflections on Exile, and Other Literary and Cultural Essays* (London: Granta, 2000), p. 174. Said was writing in the wake of the Sabra and Shatila massacres in 1982 and the routing of the PLO from Lebanon. For a compelling account of his writing in this period see Anna Bernard, *Rhetorics of Belonging: Nation and Narration and Israel/Palestine* (Liverpool: Liverpool University Press, 2013), pp. 42–66. See also Yezid Sayigh, *Armed Struggle and the Search for the State: The Palestinian National Movement 1949–1993* (Oxford: Oxford University Press, 1999), pp. 464–94 and 589–606.

15 Jacqueline Rose, *States of Fantasy*, pp. 6–15.

16 'The Psychical Dissection of the Personality', *New Introductory Lectures on Psychoanalysis*, Pelican Freud Library (London: Penguin, 1988), p. 112.

17 Hannah Arendt, 'The Decline of the Nation-State and the End of the Rights of Man', in *The Origins of Totalitarianism* [1951] (New York: Schocken Books, 2004), pp. 372–73.

18 Wendy Brown, *Walled States, Waning Sovereignty* (New York: Zone Books, 2010), see especially the chapter 'Desiring Walls' for Brown's reading of the psychoanalysis of defences, pp. 107–33.

19 The Israeli wall that loops through the occupied territories is an obvious example of a border that works its power by creating voids between territories. In Ariella Azoulay and Adi Ophir's evocative phrase, the wall is less the impermeable barrier it promises than the snaking tail of a monster: 'A static instrument of spatial separation has turned out be the tail of a crawling monster that devours space and re-territorializes it at the same time, without ever splitting the territory into two'. Creating a borderline space in the territories – a space where 'the Palestinians have been neither annihilated nor assimilated, neither expelled [. . .] in large numbers nor integrated' – is

part of what Azoulay and Ophir describe as the 'suspended violence' that characterizes the conflict (Ariella Azoulay and Adir Ophir, 'The Monster's Tail', in Michael Sorkin (ed.), *Against the Wall: Israel's Barrier to Peace* (New York: The New Press, 2005), reproduced in *Roulotte*, 0.5 (September 2008): http://www.roulottemagazine.com/2011/04/the-monster%E2%80%99s-tail-ariella-azoulay-adi-ophir/ [Date accessed: 2 July 2014].

20 See Chapter V of *Beyond the Pleasure Principle* (1922), *Beyond the Pleasure Principle and Other Writings*, trans. John Reddick (Harmondsworth: Penguin, 2003), pp. 43–101.

21 Green, 'La concept de limite', p. 140.

22 Yasemin Yildiz, *Beyond the Mother Tongue: The Postmonolingual Condition* (New York: Fordham University Press, 2012), p. 2. See also Jacqueline Amati-Mehler, Simona Argentieri and Jorge Canestri, *The Babel of the Unconscious: Mother Tongue and Foreign Languages in the Psychoanalytic Dimension* (Madison, CT: International Universities Press, 1993), which tracks the itinerant affective paths opened up between languages across psychoanalysis.

23 Yildiz, *Beyond the Mother Tongue*, p. 12.

24 André Green, 'On the Edge', in Andrew Weller (trans.), *The Work of the Negative* (London: Free Associations Press, 1999), p. 261.

25 Brown, *Walled States*, p. 52. Carl Schmitt calls sovereignty 'a borderline concept', but what he means, as Brown points out, is the opposite of our current sense of vacillating borders: 'a borderline concept is not a vague concept, but one pertaining to the outermost sphere. This definition of sovereignty [i.e. he who decides the exception], must therefore be associated with a borderline case [i.e. exceptional] and not with routine' (quoted in Brown, *Walled States*, p. 46).

26 Green, 'On the Edge', p. 261.

27 Adam Phillips, 'André Green and the Pragmatics of Passion', in Gregorio Kohon (ed.), *The Dead Mother: The Work of André Green* (London and New York: Routledge, 1999), p. 165.

28 Green, 'La concept de limite', p. 163. The poem, 'I have to live', and Winnicott's commentary on Charles' analysis can be found in D.W. Winnicott, *Therapeutic Consultations in Child Psychiatry* (London: Hogarth and Institute for Psycho-Analysis, 1971), pp. 147–60.

29 Yousif M. Qasmiyeh, 'Holes', in Carole Angier, Rachel Buxton, Stephanie Kitchen and Simon White (eds), *See How I Land: Oxford Poets and Exiled Writers* (Coventry: The Heaven Tree Press, 2009), pp. 47–50. 'Holes' is also published in *Modern Poetry in Translation* 3.12 (2009), see: http://www.mptmagazine.com/feature/see-how-i-land-oxford-poets-and-exiled-writers-31/ [Date accessed: 26 November 2014].

30 W.H. Auden, *Look Stranger!* (London: Faber and Faber, 1936).

31 Arendt, *Origins*, pp. 341–86.

32 Jed Esty, *A Shrinking Island: Modernism and National Culture in England* (Princeton, NJ: Princeton University Press, 2004), p. 217.

33 Green, *The Work of the Negative*, p. 6.

34 Richard Hoggart, *Auden: An Introductory Essay* [1951] (London: Chatto & Windus, 1961), pp. 49–50.
35 Esty, *The Shrinking Island*, p. 219.
36 Ibid., p. 217.
37 Mann and her brother Klaus, along with Heribert Hoven, would later publish an exemplary borderline account of this time entitled *Escape to Life: Deutsche Kultur im Exil.* The bilingual title is deliberate: the German culture in exile stays so linguistically, just as the movement of escape to life (not from death, because otherwise there would be no point in travelling, but from something that is not quite life either) replays the vacillation of the borderline's dilemma according to Green.
38 Qasmiyeh and O'Donoghue, poets' introductory comments, in Angier et al. (eds), *See How I Land*, p. 45.
39 See Mushin Musawi, *Arabic Poetry: Trajectories of Modernity and Tradition* (New York: Routledge, 2006), pp. 30–67, for a fascinating reading of the multi-directional lines of modernism in Arab poetry of this period. See also Bassam K. Frangieh, 'Modern Arabic Poetry: Vision and Reality' for an account of the Nakba in relation to poetry in Hala Khamis Nassar and Najat Rahman(eds), *Mahmoud Darwish: Exile's Poet* (Northampton, MA: Olive Branch Press, 2008), p. 11.
40 As Hannah Arendt (the other woman whom Auden considered marrying, and another Jewish refugee) pointed out in 1951, the founding of State of Israel did not end the calamity of the stateless in the twentieth century, it 'merely produced a new category of refugees, the Arabs, thereby increasing the number of the stateless and rightless by another 700,000 to 800,000 people' (*Origins of Totalitarianism*, p. 368).
41 Yousif M. Qasmiyeh, 'History Riven in a Woman's Body - By Adonis', unpublished manuscript, on file with the author.
42 See Musawi, *Arabic Poetry*, for an account of the different ways in which exile is presented in modern Arabic poetry, pp. 162–217.
43 Adonis, 'Preface', in Samuel Hazo (trans.), *The Pages of Day and Night* (Evanston, IL: The Malboro Press/Northwestern University Press, 1994), p. xiii. Green, 'The dead mother', *On Private Madness*, pp. 142–73.
44 Carole Angier, 'Introduction', in Carole Angier, Rachel Buxton, Stephanie Kitchen and Simon White (eds), *See How I Land: Oxford Poets and Exiled Writers* (Coventry: The Heaven Tree Press, 2009), p. 11.
45 Qasmiyeh and O'Donoghue, poets' introductory comments, p. 45.
46 Angier, 'Introduction', p. 12.
47 Ibid.
48 Private correspondence with the author. Qasmiyeh can also be read as giving a Sufi response to Angier's request. Glossing the work of Egyptian poet and playwright 'Abd Al-Sabūr, Ziad Elmarsafay writes:

> The act of poetic creation involves a separation of the self from the self, both in response to the call of the Other and as a way of accommodating the Other. Writing poetry leaves the self transformed by this encounter.

> Indeed since this encounter is what makes poetry happen, the poet *qua* creator of poetry would not exist without this relationship to and meeting with the Other. Both poet and poem are creations of the Other.

Sufism in the Contemporary Arabic Novel (Edinburgh: Edinburgh University Press, 2012), p. 4. Meeting the self as another well describes the theme of 'Holes'.

49 In this way too, Qasmiyeh splits open the fantasy of the monolingual mother tongue. When I asked him which language he wrote in first, Arabic or English, he responded: 'I think it is a matter of collision between the two languages; the way they compete for the same space in one's memories, that produce what I would call an awkward "third language"'.

50 D.H. Lawrence, 'The Piano', in Keith Sagar (ed.), *Selected Poems* (Harmondsworth: Penguin, 1986), p. 51.

51 Nor is that violence so far from the room where 'Holes' was conceived. In a poem written shortly after he departed for New York, Auden has 'unattended angels' weep over Oxford. They weep because the city's 'Knowledge is conceived in the hot womb of violence'; 'The widow's tears forgotten,/The fatherless unheard', 'Oxford', *Another Time* (1940) (London: Faber, 2007), pp. 10–11.

Hope Wolf

'Paper is patient': tweets from the '#AnneFrank of Palestine'

Farah Baker is a teenager living in Gaza who used Twitter to report the bombings she witnessed over the summer of 2014. She has been controversially named the '#AnneFrank of Palestine'. This article examines how far digital and printed forms of war writing compare, and places particular emphasis on a remark Anne Frank made in, and about, her diary: 'paper is patient'. It discusses the extent to which the expectations of readers, and the limitations of the form of the tweet, shaped what Baker was able to say. It considers how she answered the premium placed upon authenticity and immediacy in war reporting, and also the desire for a medium that would rally support and express solidarity. It also asks how far the digital meme meets the challenge of reconciling the need for expressions of commonality with the recognition of complexity. In comparison with the diary, the ability of users of social media to manipulate form, and to make their own formal choices, is constrained. This article discusses the implications these restrictions might have for both war writers and life writers.

This article is concerned with the life writing of a contemporary witness to war. Her name is Farah Baker, she is a resident of Gaza, and she was 16 years old when this study was conducted in the summer of 2014. During that time, Baker used the social media platform Twitter (her username is @Farah_Gazan and her display name is 'Guess What') to report her experiences of the Israeli–Palestinian conflict.[1] Attacks upon Gaza and Israel were reported in traditional news media, but witnesses also shared their experiences online. Newspapers and television companies took an interest in Baker: interviews and articles about her tweets were broadcast and published in English, Arabic and European languages.[2] Controversially, she began to be referred to as the '#AnneFrank of Palestine' and the 'modern Anne Frank'.[3] Baker at first accepted the association: 'The modern Anne Frank (me) is luckier than the real Anne Frank bc the modern one could survive the war :) #Gaza' (26 August). Yet she soon relinquished it, having received complaints from many of her readers: 'Nothing like Anne Frank. Despicable to even compare' (@awesim123, 7 September). The appropriation of a Jewish icon by a Palestinian Muslim was viewed by some as an act of war, the assumed implication being that ancestors of the persecuted were repeating the actions of their persecutors – an idea propounded in digital posters merging the faces of Adolf Hitler and Israeli Prime Minister Benjamin Netanyahu (see @IsraelWC1, 8 August). This was not necessarily why the link was made, however. Baker's age enabled readers to relate her Twitter feed to a book (or at least an idea of a book) they felt familiar with: a first-person account written by a teenager in captivity (albeit of a different kind) at a time of war (although of a different sort). It lent a kind of authority to her ephemeral posts: Frank as a marker of testimonial merit. Additionally, the link in some respects could be read as a conciliatory gesture: if the opposing sides had something in common, why should they fight? As Judith Butler asked in *Precarious Life* (2004): 'From where might a principle emerge by which we vow to protect others from the kinds of violence we have suffered, if not from an apprehension of a common human vulnerability?'[4]

Frank's diary and Baker's Twitter feed are brought together in this article for different reasons. Frank's reflections on the capacities of the diary as a form of life writing and war writing inspire comparisons with the digital form. I am specifically interested in Frank's musings on the saying 'paper is more patient than man' (20 June 1942), and in the ways in which she cast the diary as a means of coping with the pressures of having to conform to others' expectations.[5] At many points in the diary Frank remarked on differences between the self as it appeared on the page and the self as it appeared in the world. The diary was imagined as a space in which the unruly emotions she was forced to keep at bay in the 'Secret Annexe' (9 July 1942) were given expression:

> Those violent outbursts on paper were only giving vent to anger which in a normal life could have been worked off by stamping my feet a couple of times in a locked room, or calling Mummy names behind her back. (January 2 1944)[6]

Frank also wrote that the diary allowed her to expose a 'deeper' version of herself; in public, by contrast, she could only show her 'lighter superficial side', concerned that if she offered anything more earnest her friends and family would 'laugh', criticising her for being 'ridiculous and sentimental' (1 August 1944).[7] The diary was not imagined as a confidant who would listen unconditionally: it was personified ('Dear Kitty') and imagined to have limited capacity for toleration. Perhaps Frank, desiring a 'real friend' (20 June 1942), sought to humanise the diary, or tried to protect herself, by imposing a limit upon her outpourings.[8] Given that she began to nurture plans of publishing the work, it is also possible that she crafted dialogue with a sensitive character in order to present a sympathetic narrative voice.[9] However, 'Kitty' could not be too sensitive. While Frank always felt compelled to perform for friends and family, 'Kitty' was comparatively accepting of 'unbosomings' (20 June 1942).[10] On 24 December 1943 Frank wrote: 'whatever you think of me, I can't keep everything to myself, so I'll remind you of my opening words – "Paper is patient"'.[11]

This word 'patient' cannot so easily be attributed to readers of Twitter feeds. Writers, causes and events compete for recognition. Where there is a plethora of voices to choose from, that which fails to charm or interest can be cast aside. This might also be said of the published diarist, but one important difference is that the author of the Twitter feed can adapt her writing to the responses of readers as she writes – hence Baker defending herself against criticisms for adopting the Anne Frank analogy: 'ppl who support me named me Modern Anne Frank not me' (7 September). This possibility of readers acting as co-editors is important to the central theme of this journal edition: authenticity. Here I am not figuring authenticity straightforwardly as a synonym for adherence to factual truth. It also has, to borrow Geoffrey Hartman's description, 'moral overtones': 'Like "integrity," it suggests an earthly quintessence, firmly local, and with a constancy that, in Shakespeare's words, will not "bend with the remover to remove"'.[12] It need not be assumed that Baker has an integral self that she bends to the will of her readers. Frank's construction of a divided self may have helped her to manage her emotions and retain a sense of privacy (there was an aspect of her personality that belonged to her alone). However, it is still worth considering the extent to which the close relationship between Twitter readers/'followers' and writers, and the manufactured form of the tweet, might impact upon what the digital witness is able to say. In comparison with printed ('paper') forms of life writing and war writing, is the digital form more likely to be inauthentic?

Frank experimented with using different forms in her diary: confession, ode, reportage, romance, reflection, adventure story and anecdote, to name a few. Over the summer of 2014, Baker used different rhetorical techniques in her feed. However, in comparison with the diary, the ability of users of social media to manipulate form, and to make their own formal choices, is constrained. In the concluding section of this article I will think about how formal limitations might impact upon the efficacy of digital war writing for protest, and not only for the specific Palestinian protest, but for injustices that the taxonomy of 'war' excludes (that is, expressed in life writing as well as war writing). A blending of formal analysis with politics was advocated by W.J.T. Mitchell in his 2003 article 'The Commitment to Form; Or, Still Crazy After All These Years': 'a commitment to form is also finally a commitment to emancipatory, progressive political practices united with a scrupulous attention to ethical means'.[13] He praised *After the Last Sky: Palestinian Lives* (1986), a book Edward W. Said composed with photographer Jean Mohr, and quoted the following line from it: 'Most literary critics ... focus on what is said in Palestinian writing ... its sociological and political meaning ... But it is the form that should be looked at'.[14] In this book Said also wrote: 'Especially in the West, particularly in the United States, Palestinians are not so much a people as a pretext for a call to arms'.[15] Opposing this polemical mode of representation, he and Mohr sought 'to show Palestinians through Palestinian eyes without minimising the extent to which even to themselves they feel different, or "other"'.[16] Said's book was published almost 30 years ago. Palestinians can now represent themselves to the world without the mediation of professional writers and photographers. However, the extent to which they are able to use social media to show themselves through their own eyes remains to be tested. This is not only an important issue for Palestinian writers, but for life writers and war writers more generally.

Immediacy

Part of the rhetorical force of digital war writing stems from perceptions about the proximity of the witness to the incidents she reports. Proximity is of course important to the ways in which non-digital forms of war writing are valued and hierarchised: this is one of the reasons James Campbell has given for the canonicity of the First World War trench poets.[17] Yet digital technologies enable further foreshortening of the period between event and narration. Baker 'manages to tweet through her smartphone amongst the bloody chaos of war that surrounds her', wrote Pankti Dalal, reporter for *Daily News and Analysis* (*DNA*), a newspaper published in India.[18] It is also the case that the capacity of tweets to narrow the temporal gap between writers' experiences and readers' knowledge of them considerably contributes to their affective power. Seeing there are further pages to come, we know Frank survived the bombing she witnessed on 26 July 1943: 'Each moment I thought: "One's falling now. Here it comes"'.[19] Baker's readers encouraged her to keep tweeting, viewing her brief posts as 'evidence' that she survived (see @sunnysingh_nw3, 30 July). 'Patience', then, is a virtue neither digital war reporter nor reader is expected to have. Newspaper articles remarked upon the 'live' or 'real-time' quality of Baker's tweets.[20] The use of these terms highlighted their perceived immediacy and value as sources of 'information'. As Bernard Stiegler wrote in *Technics and Time* (1996): 'information's value is tied to its time of diffusion, and it is all the more a piece of information if it is *less* known'.[21] Walter Benjamin made a similar point in his 1936 essay 'The Storyteller', published when newspapers were compromising stories, rather than social media overtaking newspapers: 'The value of information does not survive the moment in which it was new. It lives only at that moment; it has to surrender to it completely and explain itself to it without losing any time'.[22] Reporting her feed, newspapers were perhaps assimilating the power of a potential competitor. It seemed that Baker's responses could be published more quickly than accounts of professionals that were likely to be vetted for accuracy.

Immediacy and authenticity are related concepts. Descriptions of diaries have often included the assumption that the less time there is to edit, the less likely the author is to manipulate the information presented.[23] New technologies, making it possible for anyone who has access to them to publish their work, might also be seen to reduce a kind of distancing that is sometimes said to arise from literary self-consciousness. Baker was described as 'just an ordinary girl in extraordinary circumstances' (@presdl, 27 August). The writings of 'ordinary' people have often been linked with a kind of authenticity, possibly because they are thought to retain a more immediate impression of situations and events. Reviewing a recently published anthology of First World War life writing, Libby Purves distinguished materials found in archives from the writings of published authors: 'simplicity scores higher than writerly rhetoric . . . The detail of small lives needs no adorning'.[24] Desire to be thought of as 'eloquent', to be esteemed as a 'good writer', is imagined to get in the way of raw expression. Two perceived antidotes to this assumed artificiality are lack of knowledge of formal conventions and, alarmingly, trauma. With regard to the latter, the idea is that if the event is fully apprehended then it will brutally strip away older frames of reference; the violence the writer experiences is imagined to render prior training defunct.[25] When texts and experiences is valued and viewed in this way, no one wins: the professional is criticised for being too 'writerly', the amateur is depicted as stylistically callous, and the ideal writer is reduced to inarticulacy by suffering. Insufficient attention is paid to how far the professional writer has internalised his stylistic proclivities. A blind eye is turned to the many discourses 'ordinary' people participate in. One of these is the discourse of war reporting itself.

Looking now to Baker's tweets, we can see that she used several rhetorical strategies for signifying how far she was able to transcend delay. First of all, she eschewed the rules of formal writing, marking her prioritisation of responding quickly over accuracy: 'Massive bombs toooo close to the area I can see the smoke clearyy omg :'(i'm uploading the video it took it while i was crying #Gaza' (12 July). This is not a technique exclusive to digital war writing. On 11 July 1943 Frank drew attention to her privileging of documentation (and health) over style: 'I have decided to let my shorthand go a bit, firstly to give me more time for my other subjects and secondly because of my eyes'.[26] On 28 November 1942 she highlighted her decision not to edit her work: 'Oh, heavens above, now I'm getting you in a muddle too. Forgive me, but I don't like crossing things out, and in these days of paper shortage we are not allowed to throw paper away'.[27] However, there are also differences in the extent to which immediacy was permitted to shape the writers' published compositions. Frank, or Frank's editor, did not tolerate a spelling mistake: grammar matters, and apologies for her muddled style are themselves stylish. Baker flouted formalities more thoroughly, showing rather than telling. This may be simply because she, unlike Frank, was not writing in her native language. However, her deviations from the conventions of writing also had a performative function. While Frank's writing is often conversational, Baker added a kind of intimacy to her posts by more explicitly mimicking the variable intonation and volume of speech. The multiple 'o's in the tweet quoted earlier show how she would give it emphasis and convey a sense of how the event is bearing upon her emotions. She also made use of capital letters, signifiers of shouting and a means of attaining attention: 'HUGE 3 BOMBS CLOSE TO MY AREA NOW #GazaUnderAttack' (23 August). The reference to speech plays into a preconception that spoken words are more 'immediate' than written ones.[28] Were Baker speaking to us directly we would share in her experiences; simulating speech, she foreshortened perceptions of distance between reader, writer and event.

Baker placed much greater emphasis on the speed of her response than Frank. Published as a whole, the diary is not competitively involved in publishing information first. There are points in Frank's diary where her shorthand bears some resemblance to a Twitter feed: 'Turkey is in the war. Great excitement. Waiting in suspense for the news' (18 March 1943).[29] However, in general, she seemed aware that her work would be valued more for how well, than how quickly, it was written. Baker, by contrast, used the word 'NOW' frequently, and, having reported the falling of the 'HUGE 3 BOMBS' (see above), proceeded to count those that followed:

> 6th massive shell #GazaUnderAttack
>
> 5th bomb #GazaUnderAttack
>
> @juuu_becker yes
>
> 4th shell #GazaUnderAttack

Baker, laconically counting, spent no time evocatively describing the bombs – a rhetorical move in itself, suggestive of confidence that their mere existence should outrage her readers: no further persuasion was required. When interrupted by a reader, she replied with as little inflection as possible, and more briefly than the already brief form required: 'yes'. Abruptly concise tweets such as these drew attention to her dedication to the act of reporting: now she had to concentrate on giving as accurate an account of what was happening as she could. It was necessary to limit delay, as a temporal lag would devalue her writing as 'information'. If Baker was to be heard, she needed to publicise her observations before anyone else did, before they ceased to be news. She had to do so, despite other demands made of her. So, on 25 July, she wrote: 'The window fell over my 6yrs old sis and she got injured slightly but she's shaking and unable to breathe #Gaza'. The tweet evokes the ethical dilemma faced by the war photographer: should the time taken to represent the victimised person be instead used to help them? In Baker's case, the moment, for that moment, became omnipotent; to use Benjamin's terminology, she surrendered to it.

There were moments, however, when Baker permitted a delay between event and report: 'I'v been sitting n th balcony 4 more than 2hrs trying 2 record a bomb sound but th problem is when i hear th rocket falling I freeze! #Gaza' (11 July). That she did not apologise for the lack of non-textual evidence here may partly be because she was aware of its limitations. Soldiers' writing has historically emphasised that those who were not 'there' do not have the authority to represent war.[30] Baker had a new competitor: the machines of professionals. Compared with the equipment used by television crews, hers was comparatively cheap. She could not get a quality sound. On 9 July she wrote: 'The sound of drones. It's not clear enough but this us what I could record while i'm on the rooftop #Gaza'. A photograph uploaded on the same day showed a puff of smoke in the distance: 'the last bomb which was close to my home'. To those used to seeing explosions up-close in blockbuster movies, the photographs Baker took might not seem particularly shocking. The bombs were close enough for Baker to feel terrified, but were they close enough for her readers to be shocked into action? Often, her writings expressed frustration at the ineffectiveness of spectacle: 'Make protests and revolution against what is happening in #Gaza, don't keep watching. Bring humanity back.MOVE MOVE MOVE #GazaUnderAttack' (25 August). Reluctance to give viewers a show, and the problems of presenting sounds and images that sufficiently conveyed her subjective experience, might then have deterred Baker from directly uploading recordings. But she may also have been seeking to preserve the authenticity of events intact. In 'The Work of Art in the Age of Mechanical Reproduction' (1936) Benjamin characterised 'authenticity' as 'not reproducible'.[31] He suggested that replication contributes to the loss of the 'mystery' or 'aura' of the work of art.[32] Might the same be said of the violent event?

Resisting replication, Baker alluded not only to what she had been unable to record, but also to what she had been unable to write: 'I wannn thank all of u 4 supporting me, and I'm really sorry 4 not answering but I was really so nervous and unable 2 talk 2 anybody. #Gaza' (29 July). Such remarks pose the paradoxical question of whether truly authentic testimony is the reserve of the witness who has experienced events so proximately that she is unable to testify.[33] That is, if Baker was able to count the bombs then surely she cannot have been close enough to them? Readers who privilege this kind of authenticity are asking the witness to do the impossible. Yet, as the second part of this article will now show, authenticity is not the only criterion by which war writing is valued. The quickness of response enabled by digital media has uses other than that of reportage: the tweet can also be used to rally support. Authenticity has a role to play here too, as revelations that an account has been doctored can damage reputations. Yet 'story' (drawing again on Benjamin's terminology), as opposed to 'information', is also important. Baker seemed aware of the limited rhetorical power of representations that included too much of the latter. Editing was needed lest the barrage of information numbed the senses. She wrote: 'I dnt keep tweeting about bombs bc they dot stop 4 a moment, so it would be kinda boring to keep tweeting th same thing all the time #Gaza' (30 July). While this comment might be interpreted as another means of sustaining the capacity of the event to shock and awe, it is also suggestive of a wish to sustain readers' interests, and the writer's own, through the construction of a compelling narrative. Frank also drew attention to her omissions: 'You don't know anything about all these things, and I would need to keep on writing the whole day if I were to tell you everything in detail' (29 March 1944).[34] However, Baker's posts were generally more reactive given that she was not only imagining readers, but conversing with them.

Slogans and memes

For the dependency of writers upon readers, the tweet is very like a letter: 'All good letter writers feel the drag of the face on the other side of the page and obey it – they take as much as they give'.[35] However, with social media different posts can be directed at different readers (different faces). One of the difficulties of interpreting Baker's feed lies in determining how far she presents a coherent identity, and how homogenous she imagines her readers' expectations to be. Self-representations and readerships can change over time. However, it is hard not to see the paratexts framing her tweets, some of which remained consistent over the summer, as expressive of a projected persona and audience. Comparisons can be drawn here to the way in which Frank's diary has been marketed. Photographs on the cover of the diary and at the top of the summer 2014 feed present the writers as vulnerable and direct. Baker, taking a self-portrait, had greater control over her image. The focalisation of the picture made her appear small: the viewer looked down at her from above, in a position of power, perhaps, to help her. Framed thus, it was easier to view her as a victim: her littleness set against the bigness of war. Her age contributed to this impression. As well as having associations with innocence, it may have impacted upon the presumed authenticity of her writing, fueling the assumption that she had not developed substantive tools for rhetorical manipulation. Her gaze added to the impression of guilelessness: looking straight at the viewer, wearing a non-belligerent expression, she, like Frank in her photograph, offered readers an open, honest and frank image of a war writer. Baker later criticised how people used her age. She appears older in the picture displayed at the time of the submission of this article (25 January 2015), and underneath it is the caption: 'I'm senior 2015, I hate the fact I'm a teenager. Future lawyer inshallah'. However, earlier tweets show her drawing on the rhetorical power of her age: she called herself a 'Gazan girl' (22 August 2014). This label is of course gendered too, and her identity as a female war reporter may have compounded the non-aggressive image she presented. While the writing of combat has traditionally been viewed as the dominion of men, the writing of grief has more often been delegated to women.[36]

In some respects Baker's curation of her feed might be viewed as an attempt to construct, to use Judith Butler's expression, a 'grievable life'. In *Precarious Life*, Butler critiqued the 'hierarchy of grief' apparent in public mourning practices in the USA (she was writing after the September 11 bombings), whereby some lives were treated as more 'grievable' than others.[37] Although she has more extensively written about the Israeli–Palestinian conflict elsewhere, she made reference to unmourned Palestinian lives in this book: 'we seldom, if ever, hear the names of the thousands of Palestinians who have died by the Israeli military with United States support'.[38] Giving suffering a human face, Twitter has the capacity to redress under-representation. However, the above reading of Baker's photograph begs the question of whether, in order for 'common human vulnerability' to be recognised, witnesses need to conform to a particular version of what the 'human' looks like. The camera angle in Baker's 2014 portrait drew attention to her eyes, the colour of which was remarked upon by her readers: 'the young palestine blue eyes girl' (@NereaZaballos, 11 August). A reader of an *NBC News* article questioned whether the broadcasting network was raising support for Hamas by publicising the tweets of a civilian with light coloured skin and blue eyes.[39] The comment suggests that despite the emancipatory possibilities of digital technologies, traditional powers are still able to direct readers towards the few. It could be argued that Baker's feed as a whole included just enough familiarity and just enough exoticism to be compelling to cosmopolitan readers in comparatively powerful and wealthy countries (who might then put pressure on their governments).[40] Baker's chosen background picture showed lights spelling out, in Arabic, 'Gaza'; she sometimes wrote in Arabic and retweeted Arabic posts. This article, focusing on Baker's tweets in English, may contribute to the familiarisation of her image to Western readers. However, it is also the case that she directed the majority of her tweets posted between July and August to an English-speaking audience. In August the caption under her profile picture included the memorable analogy ('I'm the modern Anne Frank Gaza-Palestine') and was accompanied by a two-finger peace sign.

There were moments, however, when 'exoticism' tipped into something more dangerously 'other'. While Frank used the diary as an outlet for violent emotion, Baker was disciplined for treating her Twitter feed thus. On 10 July she wrote: 'Qassam resistance just thrown a rocket to Israel. Allahu Akbar :D pray for them'. It received such comments as: '@Farah_Gazan So you are ok with Israeli civillians to get killed but when it comes to you its not legitamate? #FreeGazaFromHamas' (@shiranofir, 29 July). Anna Bernard writes that the authors she focuses on in her recent book *Rhetorics of Belonging: Nation, Narration, and Israel Palestine* (2013) use 'their status as "world" writers to authorise, in the most literal sense of the word, their accounts of the region's history and their visions of its political future'.[41] Baker might be considered a '"world" writer' given the reach of her representations, but is she compelled to a greater extent to use conciliatory language? Over the summer, her more belligerent remarks were counterbalanced by pacifist contributions. On 11 August she posted the Official 2014 FIFA World Cup song, 'Dar um Jeito (We Will Find a Way)', which included the lyric, 'We are united even though we're different flags'. Twitter users can attain a sense of what kinds of posts readers most want to see and hear because rhetorical effectiveness on the Internet is crudely quantifiable. In general, Baker's pacifistic comments seem to have trumped not only aggressive comments but also documentary descriptions. Two examples of the latter, posted on 19 August, received comparable responses: 'MANY HUGE BOMBS ARE LIGHTENING UP THE AREA #GazaUnderAttack' (retweeted 585 times, and nominated as a 'favourite' 190 times); 'HUGEEE EXPLOSIONS CLOSE TO MY AREA, THEY JUST LIT UP THE SKY #GazaUnderAttack' (597 retweets, 167 favourites). On 18 August, Baker posted tweets that read like slogans, including rhetorical questions and general statements. They proved to be much more popular: 'What if peace get spread all around the world? a wish of a Gazan teenager! #GazaUnderAttack' (978 retweets, 831 favourites); 'It's the last day of the cease fire, the only thing I dream of hearing today is that I will live in peace for ever #Gaza' (1214 retweets, 1021 favourites).[42]

It might be argued that if change is sought there is a need to compromise on authenticity: one needs to tell readers what they want to hear to avoid estranging them in the first instance. One might also want to use other people's words. War writers and life writers often indicate community membership through the use of shared vocabularies: jargon, clichés and conventions. However, digital technologies make direct repetition quick and easy (so, for instance, the retweet). Using the hashtag, taxonomies can also be shared. Baker often connected her tweets with those posted by other Twitter users by including a hashtag followed by the phrase 'GazaUnderAttack'. Slogans like this can be used to express solidarity. Yet they may also exacerbate the problems users are protesting by inciting further violence. Baker's feed attracted extremely aggressive reactions as well as supportive ones. Perhaps a less polemical approach, together with a more complex self-image, would be less likely to prompt the former kind of response. Said presented a multifaceted Palestinian portrait in *After the Last Sky*: 'acting, acted upon, proud, tender, miserable, funny, indomitable, ironic, paranoid, defensive, assertive, attractive, compelling'.[43] His descriptions are balanced and carefully nuanced, resisting polarisation: 'Yes, we have been victimized and our identity has been threatened, but no, we have been neither passive nor innocent'.[44] Baker's popular tweets do not share the complexity of his descriptions; his list of adjectives can more easily be applied to her feed as a whole, but a feed is rarely read as a continuous narrative.

Is it possible to make clear collective demands while at the same time allowing for complexity? The final part of this section will consider whether the new digital form of the meme, allowing individuals to show that a connection has been made through their mutual use of a form, facilitates a kind of compromise. The term 'meme', when coined by Richard Dawkins in *The Selfish Gene* (1976), was described as 'a noun that conveys the idea of a unit of cultural transmission, or unit of *imitation*'.[45] The 'meme' concept is now popularly used to describe digital modes of simultaneous self and collective representation. The Israeli–Palestinian conflict has generated memes. On 9 August Baker retweeted a picture of an English banknote with 'FREE PALESTINE' inscribed upon it. It was posted by @clgascoigne, who added the caption: 'Just got out the taxi and this is the change I got'. 'Change' spread the message of 'change' to people who might not otherwise have received it. The currency of others drew attention to the lack of Palestinian currency (in 2011 Facebook was used to promote the idea of Palestinians writing 'Free Palestine' on Israeli bank notes).[46] The meme disseminated online blended the affective qualities of non-digital media (the handwritten note acted as a counter to the way in which typeface effaces individuation) with the capacity of technology to connect and proliferate. Because individual pictures of banknotes could be connected by hashtags (for instance, '#themoneymovement'), it was possible to attain a quick impression of the global reach of the campaign. The digital meme also offered a means of protesting that did not exclude those who would not want to repeat someone else's words verbatim. The different photographs and captions distinguished participants, and enabled them to show others that they had participated.

In some respects the meme constitutes an important intervention in how war is represented. The best-known war photography has tended to capture a single, un-reproducible moment: Nick Ut's 1972 image of a naked Vietnamese girl running from a napalm bombing or Eddie Adams' 1968 photograph of a Viet Cong prisoner being executed. The meme-making/developing photographer need not adhere to the imperative that she is in the right place at the right time. Indeed, with the 'FREE PALESTINE' bank note, the photograph is posed and there is no 'right place': the aim is to encourage people from all places to take a similar photograph. The aptitude of the meme to bring together dispersed peoples has been harnessed in representations of Palestinians ('no right place' has here particular poignancy). Baker's older sister (user name:

@LayanBaker) posted photographs of Palestinians holding keys to their houses from which they were displaced in 1948. A portrait posted on 3 September included the caption: 'A Palestinian refugee holding his home key in which was forced to abandon 66 years ago'. On 16 September she posted a set of four small photographs, captioned: 'Palestinians still have keys and identification papers to the homes and properties in the stolen land of Palestine'. The photographs individuate the people affected, and refute the tendency of statistics to homogenise and flatten. So, for example, a man in one of the 16 September pictures peers through the handles of his two keys, indicating, perhaps, how his whole perspective has been shaped by his experience of displacement.

While memes most often comprise images, or have a large visual component, forms of writing have also developed that encourage adaptation. On 30 July Baker posted the following:

> When some1 shuts the door firmly, the first thing comes to my mind is that it's a bomb #GazaUnderAttack
>
> When I hear a car passing quickly, the first thing comes to my mind is that it's a rocket falling #GazaUnderAttack
>
> When I see a heavy cloud, the first thing comes to my mind is that it's heavy smoke #GazaUnderAttack

On the same day AngelRobinFox (username, @WildFTracks), signified a connection between her experiences and Baker's through mirroring the form that she used:

> @Farah_Gazan when I pass by a cemetery the 1st thing that comes 2mind r all the graves improvised in #Gaza bc there's neither place nor time
>
> @Farah_Gazan when I see a building standing the first thing that comes to my mind r mountains of rubble which were once Shijaia

Baker's tweets suggest that living in a war zone has forced the writer into self-protective anxiety. The display name of her Twitter feed is 'Guess What'. Where sounds and sights are benign and not war-related, she will guess wrong. She has learned to assume the worst. Other tweets show that her younger sister too has lost her innocence: 'My 6yrs old sis is crying and shouting! We're telling her that that was a balloon but she doesn't believe us #Gaza #GazaUnderAttack' (21 July). Did Baker imagine readers to share her frame of reference? On 28 July she educated them by retweeting a photograph accompanied by a caption: 'This is not the sunlight ... this light of bombs'. On 25 August she retweeted a picture of a boy holding a plastic and metal object with the description: 'It's not a toy. it's Prosthesis'. In both instances she polarised readers' experiences and assumptions with her own. Where they await good surprises, she could expect only bad ones. AngelRobinFox's responses challenge these depictions of readers at ease. The representations of conflict Baker has presented are shown to have altered her perspective. Exposed to representations of the bombing of Gaza, order cannot be seen without thinking of disorder. AngelRobinFox's tweets give volume to Baker's lament that ordinariness can be neither recognised nor appreciated while war is ongoing.

The meme, then, is able to simultaneously show commonality and difference. Yet it remains to be shown how much difference can be introduced if the form remains consistent. While the meme would seem to allow for individual adaptation, it does not readily lend itself to the expression of complex identities and situations. The miniature form seems to encourage dichotomising. Baker retweeted images sharply juxtaposed pictures of Gaza before and after the bombing (8 August). Similar distinctions were made in her textual entries, interweaving life writing with war writing: 'Be4 war, I used 2 take photos of nature, sea, ppl having fun. Nw, I take photos of targeted buildings #Gaza #AJAGAZA' (30 July). She also polarised friends and enemies. On 21 August she retweeted a poster comparing the results of Google searches for 'Gaza Children' (dead) and 'Israeli Children' (writing on bombs). While the construction of oppositions is not only a characteristic of war memes (see, for instance, the trend of comparing 'what people think I do' with 'what I really do'),[47] they are perhaps particularly liable to it. Scholars of earlier conflicts have described the propensity of witnesses to represent war using oppositional terms.[48] On this point, it is interesting to consider Baker's responses to memes relating to issues exterior to the Israeli–Palestinian conflict. On 21 August, for instance, she took part in the 'icebucket challenge': volunteers, from different parts of the globe, poured a bucket of iced-water over themselves on camera in order to raise awareness of the disease Amyotrophic Lateral Sclerosis. On 23 August she retweeted an adaptation of the meme, introducing a friend-enemy distinction: Netanyahu taking the 'blood bucket challenge'.

Binary structures can of course be found in non-digital forms of war writing too. Frank, like Baker, sometimes conveyed the impression that she had acclimatised to war, opposing her situation to her pre-war life: 'We are quite used to the idea of going into hiding, or "underground," as in bygone days one was used to Daddy's bedroom slippers warming in front of the fire' (28 January 1944).[49] However, once she gave herself a little more space to describe how war had transformed her expectations, the narrative complicated. As with memes, anecdotes can replicate formal structures and new content can be inserted. Anecdotes also tend to be short and pithy. But it matters how short. On 1 October 1942 Frank wrote:

> I got a terrible shock yesterday. Suddenly at eight o'clock the bell rang loudly. Of course, I thought that someone had come: you'll guess who I mean. But I calmed down a bit when everyone said it must be some urchins or perhaps the postman.
>
> The days are becoming very quiet here.[50]

Given its inclusion of different perspectives, and because it does not present each day as unswervingly anxiety provoking, it is difficult to read this anecdote as a symbol or synecdoche for the impact of war. The tweet, by contrast, has a greater leaning towards generalisations that communicate a clear message: that can be understood and replicated quickly. While memes can express the beginning of complex ideas, their implications tend not to be drawn out. Speed would again seem to be privileged – but this time it is the speed of the reader's rather than the writer's response that is prioritised.

Fragmentation

While the discussion above has explored how the close relationship between readers and writers of tweets might effect what is published, this concluding section will raise questions about the limitations of the fragmented form. To begin with, it would not seem to lend itself to sustained reflective work, raising the question of who has control over the metanarrative. Representations focusing on isolated events (immediacy), and dividing those implicated into two narrowly defined sides (slogans and memes), tend to confine 'war' to military conflict. Attention to the 'there' and 'now' can be seen to preclude more radical analyses. As Benjamin wrote: 'War and war only can set a goal for mass movements on the largest scale while respecting the traditional property system'.[51] Conversely, fragmentation may detract from the specificity of the Palestinian situation. One might say that the Twitter form is appropriate for a group of people who are grappling with, to quote from Bernard's book, 'geographic, political, and experiential "fragmentation"'.[52] Said described the 'characteristic mode' of Palestinian writing as: 'broken narratives, fragmentary compositions, and self-consciously staged testimonials, in which the narrative voice keeps stumbling over itself, its obligations, and its limitations'.[53] The metonymic expressiveness of analogies between form and experience, and the possibility of reading form as evidence of the impact of events on the construction of life writing, is lost with the imposed fragmentation of Twitter. It is hard to determine whether hybridity is indicative of a fragmented identity or results from an attempt to appeal to multiple audiences. The normalisation of fragmentation may also compound the difficulties of forging sufficiently complex narratives by which groups and individuals might represent themselves.

With regard to this later point, it is significant that Baker tended neither to reference her earlier tweets, nor reflect on tensions between conciliatory and aggressive gestures. Frank, by contrast, looked back over what she had written in order to examine how much she had changed: 'This diary is of great value to me, because it has become a book of memoirs in many places, but on a good many pages I could certainly put "past and done with"' (2 January 1944).[54] With fewer distractions than Baker, she made her own self her principal object of investigation. The implications these differences have, given that social media would seem to be displacing the diary as a means of documenting daily life, are not yet clear. However, it is apparent that writing was emancipatory for Frank, helping her to forge a space for herself, and to develop awareness of how others influenced her behaviour. Digital writing may be emancipatory in the sense that it can facilitate collective challenges to authority. Yet it can also give over power. That information is added as events are happening may encourage writers to allow machines to remember for them: why make efforts to remember when one can keyword-search a digital archive? This might encourage the forgetting of injustices and abuses – 'now' is pushed to the foreground; the Twitter feed displays the most recent tweet first. It might also discourage the work of self-reflection, an activity that can provoke consideration of the causes of one's actions and the limitations of one's agency. On the final pages of her published diary Frank described how she would stand a better chance of bringing the 'good' to the 'outside', of 'becoming' what she 'would so like to be', if 'there weren't any other people living in the world' (1 August 1944).[55]

Baker, as this article has shown, recognised many of the limitations of the Twitter feed as a form of life writing and war writing. On 22 August she decided another medium would be more appropriate for the 'Introduction about Farah Baker' she wanted to share. She attached to a tweet an image of an inscription on a digital notepad:

> I am Farah Baker, 16 years old Gazan girl, I have witnessed three wars and an Intifada. I am going to enter grade 12 in the school and I want to study Law in the university, and after I graduate I want to focus on the Palestinian situation and try to bring some of

> our _Palestinians_rights which have been stolen from us by Zionists since 1948, and also I want to defy Human Rights Institutes which claim that they care about human rights but they don't and the biggest evidence is seeing innocent people getting killed in the world but they do not care and keep watching, my hobbies are walking, dancing, singing, fixing electronics, photographing, browsing, and I have a lot of dreams and my best ones are traveling to Spain and learning guitar. I seek for being a good person and make a good change in the world.

It is striking how fragmentation persists here, despite the choice of a medium that allows more space for reflection. One explanation for its disjointed form, linking with this article's discussion of authenticity, could be that different remarks had different rhetorical functions – i.e. narrative is beside the point. While the list of 'hobbies' could incite sympathy or identification, Baker's legal aspirations might inspire or rally. A desire to engage as many readers as possible may also explain her hobbies' lack of cultural specificity, and also the way in which religion is not emphasised (hence also, the unelaborated idea of 'good'). Because it has not been obviously externally imposed, fragmentation could also be read as an expression of the difficulties of identity-construction. Indications that Baker belongs to a Palestinian collective, unified by a narrative of shared loss (what has been 'stolen from us'), are juxtaposed, but not integrated, with markers that she participates in contemporary global networks (she dreams of 'traveling to Spain and learning guitar'). Why did Baker not labour to meld the two? Perhaps she still felt compelled by imperatives that shaped so much of her writing: Surrender to the moment! Don't delay! It is also possible, given that she was accustomed to writing in fragments, that habit hurried her. Or perhaps haste was imposed by circumstances. Hartman, as mentioned earlier, used Shakespeare's Sonnet 116 to gloss authenticity as steadfast and unshakeable (as that which will not 'bend with the remover to remove'); in the context of thinking about Gazan experiences, 'the remover' takes on violent physical and spatial resonances. Given that Baker's life could change dramatically at any moment, she may have felt it necessary to capture a self-portrait before it was too late. These final reflections draw attention to difficulties, beyond the peculiarities of Twitter, of writing authentically online and about war. Whether hastened by readers, habit or transient circumstances, Baker could not be as 'patient' as the imitation paper notepad she selected as an alternative.

University of Sussex

Disclosure statement

No potential conflict of interest was reported by the author.

Notes

1 Farah Baker's Twitter feed can be found at http://twitter.com/Farah_Gazan. Websites referenced in this article were last accessed 25 January 2015. All tweets quoted, unless otherwise specified, were posted in 2014. Their spelling and grammar have not been corrected. A limited number of tweets can be viewed by scrolling through the user's feed, but earlier posts can currently be accessed through the 'Advanced Search' function https://twitter.com/search-advanced.

2 Baker draws readers' attention to her interviews for *Al Arabiya* (in a tweet dated 12 August), *Al Falastinia* (13 August), *Al Jazeera* (12 and 14 August), *El programa de Ana Rosa* (31 August) and *Sky News* (8 August). She was also interviewed for *CNN*, 31 July 2014 http://newsroom.blogs.cnn.com/2014/07/31/palestinian-teen-describes-life-under-attack/. British newspapers reported on her tweets too: e.g. Radhika Sanghani, 'Teen Girl "live tweets Gaza bomb attack"', *The Telegraph*, 29 July 2014 http://www.telegraph.co.uk/women/womens-politics/10997610/Teen-Palestinian-girl-on-Twitter-live-tweets-Gaza-bomb-attack.html and Sarah Dean, '"I have survived three wars and I think this is enough": Gazan Girl, 16, Sends Desperate Plea as Rockets Trap Her in Her Home', *Daily Mail Online*, 29 July 2014 http://www.dailymail.co.uk/news/article-2709143/The-Gaza-teens-desperate-plea-twitter-I-survived-3-wars-I-think-enough.html. Baker has a Wikipedia page: https://en.wikipedia.org/wiki/Farah_Baker. Various other newspaper articles are referenced throughout this article.

3 For '#AnneFrank of Palestine' see @WorldHijabDayUK, 5 August; for 'modern Anne Frank' see @Farah_Gazan, 26 August.

4 Judith Butler, *Precarious Life: The Powers of Mourning and Violence* (London and New York: Verso, 2006 [2004]), p. 30.

5 Anne Frank, *The Diary of Anne Frank*, trans. B.M. Mooyaart-Doubleday, with a foreword by Storm Jameson (London: Pan, 1954 [1947]), p. 14.

6 Ibid., pp. 26, 112.

7 Ibid., pp. 220, 221.

8 Ibid., p. 14.

9 See Ibid., p. 162 (29 March 1944).

10 Ibid., p. 14.

11 Ibid., p. 109.

12 Geoffrey Hartman, *Scars of the Spirit: The Struggle Against Inauthenticity* (New York: Palgrave Macmillan, 2002), pp. 93, 3.

13 W.J.T. Mitchell, 'The Commitment to Form; or, Still Crazy after All These Years', *PMLA*, 118.2 (2003), 321–5, p. 324.

14 Ibid. See also Edward W. Said, *After the Last Sky: Palestinian Lives*, with photographs by Jean Mohr (New York: Columbia University Press, 1999 [1986]), p. 38.
15 Said, *After the Last Sky*, p. 4.
16 Ibid., p. 6.
17 James Campbell, 'Combat Gnosticism: The Ideology of First World War Poetry Criticism', *New Literary History*, 30.1 (1999), pp. 203–15.
18 Pankti Dalal, 'Images from the War-zone: 16-Year Old Girl Live-tweets Israel–Palestine Conflict', *DNA India*, 11 August 2014. http://www.dnaindia.com/world/report-images-from-the-war-zone-16-year-old-girl-live-tweets-israel-palestine-conflict-2009802.
19 Frank, *The Diary of Anne Frank*, p. 85.
20 See Ludovica Iaccino, '"I might die tonight": Gaza Teen Farah Baker Live-tweets Terrifying Israeli Missile Attack', *International Business Times*, 29 July 2014. http://www.ibtimes.co.uk/i-might-die-tonight-palestinian-farah-baker-tweets-harrowing-messages-during-israeli-attacks-1458814.
21 Bernard Stiegler, *Technics and Time, Disorientation*, trans. Stephen Barker (Stanford: Stanford University Press, 2009 [1996]), Vol. 2, p. 112.
22 Walter Benjamin, 'The Storyteller' (1936), in *Illuminations*, trans. Harry Zorn, introduced by Hannah Arendt (London: Pimlico, 1999), 83–107, pp. 89–90.
23 See Hope Wolf, 'Mediating War: Hot Diaries, Liquid Letters and Vivid Remembrances', *Life Writing*, 9.3 (2012), pp. 327–36, 327.
24 Libby Purves, 'All Disquiet on the Home Front', a review of Sebastian Faulks and Hope Wolf (eds.), *A Broken World: Letters, Diaries and Memories of the Great War* (London: Hutchinson, 2014), *The Times*, 28 June 2014, p. 12.
25 'Mr Sassoon's verses – they are not poetry', wrote John Middleton Murry in 1918; he likened them to a 'cry'; 'Mr Sassoon's War Verses' in *The Penguin Book of First World War Prose*, edited and with an introduction by Jon Glover and Jon Silkin (London: Penguin, 1990 [1989]), pp. 344–8, 344.
26 Frank, *The Diary of Anne Frank*, p. 79.
27 Ibid., p. 57.
28 See Wolf, 'Mediating War', p. 331.
29 Frank, *The Diary of Anne Frank*, p. 68.
30 See Campbell, 'Combat Gnosticism'.
31 Walter Benjamin, 'The Work of Art in the Age of Mechanical Reproduction' (1936), in *Illuminations*, trans. Harry Zohn, introduced by Hannah Arendt (London: Pimlico, 1999), pp. 211–44, 236.
32 Ibid., pp. 212, 215.
33 See Giorgio Agamben, *Remnants of Auschwitz: The Witness and the Archive*, trans. Daniel Heller-Roazen (New York: Zone Books, 2002), p. 39.
34 Frank, *The Diary of Anne Frank*, p. 163.
35 Virginia Woolf, 'The Humane Art' (1940), in Leonard Woolf (ed.), *The Death of the Moth and Other Essays* (London: The Hogarth Press, 1942), pp. 41–4, 42.
36 Carol Acton discusses 'gender binaries' in *Grief in Wartime: Private Pain, Public Discourse* (Basingstoke: Palgrave Macmillan, 2007): 'the woman's sacrifice takes place in the home and the man's in the action of combat', p. 20.

37 Butler, *Precarious Life*, p. 32.
38 Ibid. For more on Butler and the Israeli–Palestinian conflict, see *Parting Ways: Jewishness and the Critique of Zionism* (New York: Columbia University Press, 2012).
39 See the comment of 1980 U.S. hockey, *NBC News*, 29 July 2014 http://worldnews.nbcnews.com/_news/2014/07/29/25056294-palestinian-teen-farah-baker-live-tweets-nighttime-bombardment-in-gaza?lite.
40 Gillian Whitlock made a similar point about Salam Pax's blog written during the invasion of Iraq in 2003: 'We know just enough about Pax's tastes and preferences for this avatar to be recognizable and feasible as a secular cosmopolitan intellectual'; *Soft Weapons: Autobiography in Transit* (Chicago, IL and London: Chicago University Press, 2007), p. 34.
41 Anna Bernard, *Rhetorics of Belonging: Nation, Narration and Israel/Palestine* (Liverpool: Liverpool University Press, 2013), p. 5. Grateful thanks also to Anna Bernard for her insightful comments upon reading an earlier draft of this article.
42 These statistics were last checked 25 January 2015.
43 Said, *After the Last Sky*, p. 6.
44 Ibid., p. 5.
45 Richard Dawkins, *The Selfish Gene* (Oxford: Oxford University Press, 2006 [1976]), p. 192.
46 See Elior Levy, 'Facebook Protest: "Free Palestine" on NIS', *ynetnews*, 3 July 2011 http://www.ynetnews.com/articles/0,7340,L-4038561,00.html.
47 See http://knowyourmeme.com/memes/what-people-think-i-do-what-i-really-do.
48 See Paul Fussell, *The Great War and Modern Memory* (Oxford: Oxford University Press, 2000 [1975]), Chapter 3.
49 Frank, *The Diary of Anne Frank*, p. 126.
50 Ibid., p. 41.
51 Benjamin, 'The Work of Art', p. 234.
52 Bernard, *Rhetorics of Belonging*, p. 70.
53 Said, *After the Last Sky*, p. 38.
54 Frank, *The Diary of Anne Frank*, p. 112.
55 Ibid., p. 222.

Sue Vice

Inventing the eyewitness: Araki Yasusada and Jiri Kajanë

In this article, I analyse the work of two writers who have been presented as if they were the eyewitnesses to war and historical calamity, namely the poetry of Araki Yasusada, about the atomic bombing of Hiroshima, and the short stories of the Albanian writer Jiri Kajanë, about the last years of Enver Hoxha's Cold-War-era dictatorship. Neither writer actually exists: their work was composed by those named as their translators. In each case, the eagerness with which the work was received under its false attribution lays bare the high literary value accorded to testimonial works, and the incorporation of life-writing, here in the form of elaborately invented biographies and the insistence on a link between author and text, into war-writing. In this way, satire is directed at current literary priorities in the same act that enabled the work of little-known American writers to be published under pseudonyms. For good measure, each implies criticism of US foreign policy through the representation of past atrocities.

The presence of eyewitness testimony in histories of war and traumatic historical events has been viewed with ambivalence, due to the likelihood of individuals not only misunderstanding extreme events in the moment of their occurrence, but misremembering the details afterwards.[1] On the other hand, some psychologists and historians have defended accounts of this kind precisely by reason of testifiers' errors, since slippages and mistakes offer insights into the psychic significance of extreme occurrences, as can be seen for instance in such cases as witnesses' imperfect recall of the Sonderkommando revolt in Auschwitz, or of survival on the run in Nazi-occupied Europe.[2]

Both kinds of critical response to testimony, whether suspicious or adulatory, emphasise the value given to documentary evidence where the history of war is concerned, a view that surprisingly also characterises the reception of literary works in which war is represented. Thus, even in the case of poetry and fiction, a biographical link between the text's author and speaker or narrator can generate acclaim which arises from the value given to 'social representation', when this is viewed as 'more important – and more real – than aesthetic considerations'.[3] In relation to such events as those at stake here, that is, the bombing of Hiroshima represented in Araki Yasusada's poetry, and the end of the Cold War era in Albania as it appears in Jiri Kajanë's short stories, literary writing is itself seen as a 'trace' or as 'evidence',[4] and the fictive or poetic narrator taken not just to be enacting a testimonial 'performance', in Antony Rowland's phrase,[5] but offering unmediated access to their traumatic experience. My focus here is on literary work by two writers which was put forward in terms of a biographical link of just this kind, so that the author was constructed as eyewitness, in the context of extreme historical events that seemed both to demand and support such authenticity. Yet this link turned out to be unreliable in a much more comprehensive way than that suggested by forgetful or deluded testifiers. Despite the claims of their respective author biographies and the subject of their writing, Araki Yasusada was not a Hiroshima survivor, nor was the nameless Albanian narrator of Jiri Kajanë's Cold-War-era short stories a fictive version of the author. In each case, those American writers who were named as the texts' translators, and whose own published work had met with only minor success, turned out to be the real authors.

Araki Yasusada was presented as a *hibakusha*, or survivor of the atomic bombing of Hiroshima in August 1945, and a poet whose work consists of first-person lyrics about the attack and its effects. Jiri Kajanë's short stories, set in the last years of Enver Hoxha's Albanian rule and the aftermath of the dictator's death in 1985, were said to be by a writer whose work was never published in his native language and appeared only in English translation.[6] However, despite their extensive literary production, and the elaborate biographical detail provided for each, in neither case does the named author actually exist. Yasusada's identity was revealed as fictive after extracts from his 'Notebooks' appeared in *American Poetry Review* in 1996, while Kajanë was discovered to be an impostor in 2008 just before a collection of his stories was to be contracted by Granta Books. Yasusada's poetry is usually ascribed to Kent Johnson, a writer who teaches Spanish at an Illinois community college, although Johnson has never admitted his role in the poems' composition; while authorship of Kajanë's stories has been claimed by Kevin Phelan and Bill U'Ren, writers who are fellow alumni of a creative writing course at Johns Hopkins University. Analysis of these cases reveals the aesthetic and political implications of such deception, as well as contemporary expectations on the part of publishers and readers in relation to the 'autobiographical pact' identified by Philippe Lejeune,[7] one that applies most inflexibly to the literature of atrocity and war.

Araki Yasusada

Araki Yasusada's writing has appeared in a variety of different settings, including contemporary poetry journals of varying renown, an anthology of nuclear-war poetry, and *Doubled Flowering*, an edited volume of material from Yasusada's notebooks.[8] These varied publication contexts differ not only in terms of format, literary profile and likely readership; they also represent a gradual unfolding, or perhaps flowering, over time of a project relating to the construction of authorship. Such a construction alters with each new appearance, as determined by the specific authorial ascription in each case as well as the particular selection of poems. The identification of Yasusada not simply as a Japanese poet but as one concerned with the legacy of the bombing of Hiroshima, to which he was said to be an eyewitness, also takes shape and solidifies over time. Yasusada's poetry is striking for its combination of Japanese and western literary influences, evident in the direct approach to grief in such poems as 'Trolley Fare and Blossom', where a distraught father describes carrying the urnful of cremated remains of his daughter on a tram, and 'Telescope with Urn', another first-person address also about bereavement, in which a man visiting an observatory looks at the stars and recalls his daughter's babyhood. The poems' speakers are not identified, but their paratextual apparatus of biographical note and footnotes detailing Yasusada's loss of his wife and younger daughter in the atomic blast, the older daughter four years later to radiation poisoning, ensures that they are read as testimonial.

In 1987, Kent Johnson, the purported Yasusada author, published as his own work in the literary journal *Ironwood* four poems entitled 'From the Daybook of Ogiwara Miyamora'.[9] As its title suggests, the 'Daybook' collection presents less of an explicit emphasis on the poems' speaker's personal losses in the bombing of Hiroshima than is to be found elsewhere, for instance in a selection of seven poems published in *Stand* nearly a decade later, which is entitled 'Poems from Hiroshima' and authorship ascribed simply to Araki Yasusada.[10] The 'Daybook' title is ironic in making Hiroshima seem simply to be part of an everyday record, a blending of life- and war-writing that migrates to the poetry's paratexts in later versions. In the four 'Daybook' poems, a narrative of the whole span of the fictive Ogiwara's adult life is implied, ranging from the prelude to the atomic attack in 'High Altitude Photograph of Hiroshima (circa 1944)', to the late effects of the attack in 'Trilobytes', the poet's recovery from an operation in 'Convalescence', and concluding with 'Because I Live', a meditation on mortality, which is said to have been written in the last year of his life.

It is the clear gap between Ogiwara Miyamora, the Japanese persona, and Kent Johnson, the American author, which is the most significant element of the 'Daybook' poetry, forming a contrast to the later appearance of the same poems in instances where authorship is attributed simply to Araki Yasusada. In her essay on the implications of the 'Yasusada hoax', Marjorie Perloff argues that in the poems which appeared in *American Poetry Review* in 1996 under Yasusada's name, Johnson took what she calls 'the Ossian route rather than the route of Pound'.[11] Perloff invokes here the distinction between Ezra Pound's *Homage to Sextus Propertius* (1919), which was published under his own name since it was clearly his own work and not a 'real' Latin translation, while James Macpherson claimed in 1760 to be the translator of a Gaelic epic by the third-century bard Ossian, when he had in fact written it himself. Yet the development of a deceptive Ossianic rather than a masked Poundian aesthetic itself took place gradually in Yasusada's case, since the version of Johnson's poetic practice to be found in the 'Daybook' poems does follow Pound's technique, while the Ossian methodology only appears later when a persona is suppressed in favour of a pseudonym.

It might seem to contradict current notions of the irrelevance and inaccessibility of writers' biographies to argue that it is precisely the detail of authorship in the various appearances of Yasusada's writing that transforms the experience of reading. Yet the Yasusada project is an instance that simultaneously exemplifies Roland Barthes' and Michel Foucault's theories of this kind,[12] and offers a challenge to them, not least because of the apparently documentary nature of the poetry. It is tempting to see the different settings in which Yasuada's work has been received in the terms suggested by Jorge Luis Borges' story 'Pierre Menard, Author of the *Quixote*' (1939), in which the editor of Menard's project, which involves transcribing *Don Quixote* verbatim three centuries on, argues the case for just such a change in reception where context alters.[13] In Yasusada's case, we see an equivalent experiment in action in relation to the poem 'Trilobytes', as I argue below, which has appeared in the same form in three different contexts: in *Ironwood* in the 'Daybook' poems, under Johnson's own name while using the Poundian persona of Ogiwara Miyamora; under Johnson's name but without the Miyamora persona in the poetry anthology *Atomic Ghost*; and in a state of suspended authorship in *Doubled Flowering*, as the work of Araki Yasusada, who was, by the time of the book's publication in 1997, known not to exist. Yasusada's fictional nature is acknowledged in the paratexts of the blurb and critical appendices to *Doubled Flowering*, although the actual author's identity remains undeclared and is subject to debate. David Wojahn sees the trajectory of these poems as one that starts out as conventional 'dramatic monologue' in the 'Daybook', and asks rhetorically whether 'Trilobytes', when presented in the persona of Miyamora, is 'a less successful or empathic poem than the identical poem which later appears as Yasusada's?'[14] Although it may seem that the implied answer here is no, Wojahn goes on to argue, in terms similar to those of Borges' Menard, that 'Yasusada is a better poet than Johnson'.[15] This implies that, regardless of fictionality, the construction of a poetic persona is crucial to war poetry. In the anthology *Atomic Ghost*, a transitional point between the 'Daybook' and *Doubled Flowering*, 'Trilobytes' appears under Kent Johnson's name without the attribution of either persona or pseudonym. The context of the anthology, and its subtitle, *Poets Respond to the Nuclear Age*, accounts for the absence of such mediation in the explicit focus on 'the nuclear'. It also explains the impulse for the development of the Yasusada figure as a way of grounding historically a concern with the threat of atomic warfare, as suggested by the appearance of his *hibakusha* writings in *American Poetry Review* only a year later.

In *Doubled Flowering*, the poems from the 'Daybook', including 'Trilobytes', are reproduced alongside many others, under the name of Yasusada which is now overtly acknowledged to be a false attribution. Wojahn's higher regard for Yasusada's poetry than Johnson's refers in part to a literal comparison between the writing published under the two names. Johnson's failure to make as much impact with collections such as his *Homage to the Last Avant-Garde* (2008) has given rise to assertions that the motivation for the imposture must lie in his 'white male rage', or a species of poetic backlash against the perceived benefits of a non-mainstream identity.[16] More conceptually, Wojahn's comment implies the specifically literary benefit of the Yasusada persona and its history, which, he suggests, both enabled Johnson to write at all,[17] and enhanced the quality of that writing. The very existence of a gap between poet and voice, in an amplification of the Ogiwara mask, adds to the poetry's significance. Johnson has not reproduced an earlier canonical text, as Menard did, but his construction of a witness utterance read in the knowledge of its inauthenticity shares the 'new technique' Borges' narrator identifies, 'that of the deliberate anachronism and the erroneous attribution', with similarly 'astounding' effects.[18] For instance, the details of Yasusada's education in the mid-1920s at the University of Hiroshima, before it was founded, and impossibly early familiarity with Roland Barthes and Paul Celan, appear in the biographical material prefacing the poetry in both *Stand* and *American Poetry Review*, while the project's fictive nature is signalled in such instances in the latter as the anachronistic line from a haiku included in a letter from '30 March 1925':

> iris moon sheaves
> scubadivers chrysanthemums also

As Perloff points out, scubadiving technology was not developed until two decades after this date.[19] So significant to the Yasusada project is the nature and the clear presence of this 'deliberate anachronism', with its combination of contemporary American and classical Japanese tropes, that an anthology of essays on Yasusada, *Scubadivers and Chrysanthemums*, is titled after it. These 'melodramatically apparent' solecisms, as Johnson himself puts it, have their fullest expression in *Doubled Flowering*, where they are not unmarked, as they were in *American Poetry Review*, but foregrounded.[20]

The experience of reading 'Trilobytes' in the three different contexts of the 'Daybook', *Atomic Ghost* anthology and Yasusada collection *Doubled Flowering*, testifies to the profound effect of apparently small changes in framing. Indeed, the idiosyncratic spelling of the fossil's name in the poem's title, which is more usually 'trilobite', changes from seeming to be the representation of a translator's error in 'The Daybook', to its appearance in *Doubled Flowering* as a self-conscious combination in the same word of ancient and modern, the name of the extinct marine arthropod having as a suffix a unit of digital information.[21] The poem 'Trilobytes' relies on a juxtaposition of natural and human, of a kind that underlies much of Yasusada's writing. It is often cosmology, in the form of the imagery of ancient or explosive stars and constellations, which is set against that of the atomic blast, most strikingly in the poem 'Mad Daughter and Big-Bang' of 1945. The title's yoking together of the personal with the collective relies on a second juxtaposition, since 'Big-Bang' here refers at once to the atomic bomb – perhaps as a translation of the Japanese term 'pika-don', meaning 'bright light followed by great noise', as Hosea Hirata speculates[22] – and to the origin of the universe, although the phrase 'big bang' in this sense was not used until Fred Hoyle's coinage of it in 1949. It is even possible to read the phrase as a sly hint at the poem's own creation *ex nihilo*, from an explosive clash of discourses rather than real-life experience. In 'Trilobytes' it is not cosmology but the traces of prehistoric animal life that are contrasted with the personal, evident in the dedication to the poet's friend, 'the potter Sakutaro Ishihara (1897–1949)'.[23] The poem is an elegy, dated 1949 for the last year of the fictive Ishihara's life, and is once more placed within the context of the atomic bomb. Although it is not stated, it appears that Sakutaro, like the poem's author, is a *hibakusha*, and that the symptoms the poem alludes to are those of radiation cancer. We learn that Sakutaro is coming from his 'treatment' when he brings 'the fossils of trilobytes' to a rendezvous with the poem's speaker; the latter is fleetingly aware of the 'beautiful face of [Sakutaro's] youth' beneath the 'scarred flesh' of the present, and registers his friend's mortality:

> I gazed at him, gazing at the fossil:
> The clumps of hair on his skull, the hands
> curled into claws. Was he thinking
> of his pottery, all of it, scattered into atoms?

The ambiguous syntax of the first line, in which it could seem that the speaker is the subject of both acts of gazing, transforms Sakutaro himself into a 'fossil'. Although the trilobyte is, like the 'skull' and the fragile, 'scattered' pottery, an image of extinction and death, it also implies persistence through time and preservation in a different form. The 'archetypal' trilobyte fossil is implicitly likened to Sakutaro, since both are symbols of 'an archaic world',[24] respectively, one that flourished almost half a billion years ago before the 'great extinction', and the pre-atomic bomb world of Japan. Sakutaro has, it emerges, stolen the fossil which he presents to the narrator from the 'fossil collection donated by the Americans' at the 'Central Museum'. References in Yasusada's work to Japanese museums and public buildings often turn out to be invented locations with North American origins, a trope that is thematised here.[25] If the poem's setting is Hiroshima, there is no likely candidate for this 'museum': the only such institution extant in 1949 was the Museum of Meteorology, while the city's famous Peace Museum was not established until 1955, and, in an instance of proleptic anachronism, the Hiroshima Fossil Museum only opened in 1995, almost a decade after 'Trilobytes' was first published. Thus, settings are invented for symbolic purposes, an effect that has a metatextual significance. Such inventions, like the anachronistic uses of words and literary forebears, appear to be authenticating but, read in the knowledge of Yasusada's non-existence, are themselves the signifiers of deception.

It is this self-consciousness about the rift between author and text which makes the poetry continue to offer reflection on Hiroshima, but implicitly from an American rather than a Japanese perspective. The American donation of fossils is presented as an ironically apt gesture of restitution, since it involved the gift of fossilised remains to a people whose own obliteration had been threatened. Sakutaro's pride in his theft of the trilobyte – 'A challenge to get past the guards!', as he puts it – itself alludes to the snatching back of memory from those, conceived of as 'guards', who threaten its existence. This is emphasised in the poem's concluding stanza, which takes place after Sakutaro's death and in which the creation of fossils and the destruction of human life in the bomb are brought together in the speaker's words:

> This morning I cradled the stone
> through the ruins, past the shadows of bodies,
> and bowing to his memory
> placed it
> soundlessly
> at the epicenter

Just as Sakutaro's pottery had been smashed to 'atoms' by the atomic bomb, here the memory of the bomb is almost indistinguishable from the moment of its blast. Although bodies are now 'shadows' and the sound of detonation has become 'soundless', the poem's speaker's gesture of placing the trilobyte 'at the epicenter' makes the moment of the bomb's explosion continuously present, an effect supported by the absence of a concluding full stop. The location's identity is described in the same way now as it was then. Indeed, referring to the fossil as a 'stone' enacts a transformation seen in other poems, as Eric Hayot argues is the case in 'Mad Daughter and Big-Bang', where, in the surreal mise-en-scène, the speaker mistakes a turnip in his garden, first for the head of his dead daughter, then for a 'stone', an object which constitutes a 'fragment of personal, individual histories *and* geologic, collective ones'.[26]

Although these poetic effects might appear to be stable, there are significant shifts in meaning arising from the three different contexts in which 'Trilobytes' has been published. These include most obvious changes in the reader's view of the poem's speaker, and the effect of its symbolism. Had the poem appeared in one of the locations in which Yasusada was described as the author with no reference to his non-existence, in the collections of poems that featured in *Stand*, *Grand Street* or *Conjunctions*, the presence of the poet's biography would have made 'Trilobytes' appear to be a work of witness or confession, and its first-person speaker, by association with Yasusada, who is said to have died in 1972 'after a long struggle with cancer', destined to share Sakutaro's fate. As written by Yasusada, the poem itself could be seen as a memorial object for its narrator, just as the trilobyte 'stone' is for Sakutaro. The poem thus enacts what it describes. In *Ironwood*'s 'Daybook' poems, with the clearly marked poetic persona of Ogiwara Miyamora, the poem is read at more of an aesthetic distance as part of the construction of an imagined Japanese life. While its poetic strategies might spring into relief in the 'Daybook', the status of 'Trilobytes' as testimony vanishes. In *Atomic Ghost*, where it is published straightforwardly under Kent Johnson's name with no mention of the Ogiwara persona, 'Trilobytes' has a specifically American implied author and reader. Its effect is thus more relevant to national politics and might be associated with the satirical representation of US foreign policy in Johnson's other poetry. It could then be considered, in Paisley Rekdal's term, an 'American elegy' for Hiroshima,[27] on the part of the perpetrating nation in its quest for absolution.

The fossil itself seems in this context to be less an object associated with the poet's memory of his friend, and more of a literary symbol, in the tradition for instance of Thomas Hardy's *A Pair of Blue Eyes* of 1873, in which Henry Knight slides down a cliff and comes face-to-face with an 'imbedded fossil'; or John Fowles' 1969 novel *The French Lieutenant's Woman*, where the paleontologist Charles Smithson's fossil-hunting on the beach at Lyme Regis also stands for his personal interest in 'the accretions of the past', in particular those of Sarah Woodruff's history, as they affect the present.[28] The fossils in these texts signify contemporary concerns in each case, including contemporary and neo-Victorian views of evolution in Hardy's and Fowles' novels and the Cold War in Yasusada's.[29] Indeed, the trilobyte embodies not only the persistence of the past in the present, but the literary figure of anachronism itself. The other examples of anachronism in Yasusada's work, including references to scubadivers and the Big Bang, are more precisely *prochronisms*, since they do not simply involve the appearance of past or old-fashioned entities in the present, but, in the opposite formation, the existence of phenomena in contexts that are too early for them. It is these elements that come into clearest focus in *Doubled Flowering*, where it is advertised that 'Yasusada' is a pseudonym and the work is in effect anonymous. Thus, in *Doubled Flowering* the prochronisms are no longer metatextual clues to Yasusada's non-existence, which has already been exposed, but imply a poetic and political interest in temporal as well as linguistic layering, by means of which clashing elements come into unexpected or abrasive contact. Thus, in 'Trilobytes', a poem first published during the Cold War, such a layering might imply that the danger of atomic attack is not limited to the wartime bombing of Japan. Indeed, seen in such a light, Yasusada's work turns out to be committed and politicised poetry presented in the guise of life-writing.

Doubled Flowering consists of extracts from Yasusada's notebooks, including English exercises, letters, a shopping list, draft poems, haiku and renga. In the knowledge that this is not a documentary collection of papers found after his death by the poet's son, as the biographical note originally claimed, the cumulative effect of this material on the reader is more than simply that of the creation of a persona with an elaborately imagined oeuvre. Instead, Yasusada comes to constitute a fictional character in something akin to an unconventional, mixed-media novel, who is constructed polyphonically through his own distinctively articulated words, alongside the utterances of others in the form of replies to his letters and comments on his language exercises. The Yasusada project, or deception, and its incarnation in *Doubled Flowering* have been taken to embody other kinds of cultural and literary significance than the simply fictive, the ethics of which have been widely debated. These range from its amounting to a backlash against multicultural and witness writing, to parodic engagement with contemporary theories of authorship. Yet it seems that the varied and extensive 15-year-long aesthetic effort represented by the project and its associated publications, which also includes an anthology of haiku and one consisting of further extracts from Yasusada's notebooks,[30] must surpass some of these more specific concerns, or at least that these concerns have been subsumed by the act of writing itself. The extremity of war and suffering might seem in this case to be subsumed by the extremity of the urge to publish, but the persona of Yasusada in fact enables a critique of US foreign policy both in 1945 and in the present from a poeticised perspective, one directed by means of the imposture at a specifically Anglophone, if not North American, readership.

Jiri Kajanë

The construction of Kajanë as an authorial figure was, like that of Yasusada, a gradual process. From the mid-1990s onwards, stories under his name, about the life of a hapless and lovelorn government official in communist Albania, appeared in North American literary journals, while the story 'The Same, Only Different!' was published in an anthology of short stories about assassins, *The Killing Spirit*,[31] alongside writing by Graham Greene and Patricia Highsmith. According to the biographical details given in the *Chicago Review* in 2001, Kajanë grew up in Krujë, Albania, and trained as an engineer at Tiranë University in the 1960s, a description that allows for, but does not insist upon, identification between author and narrator. The implication that Kajanë is an important but marginalised historical witness is borne out by the biographical note's observation that his 'satirical drama' was 'banned by the Albanian Ministry of Culture' after a single acclaimed performance, as well as the fact that his fiction has never been published in his own language. Once more, an Anglophone readership is not just implied but demanded from the outset.

As with Yasusada, the moment of Kajanë's greatest publishing success – for the latter, the appearance of his work in *American Poetry Review*, for Kajanë, interest in a collection of his stories on the part of Granta Books – was also the moment of the revelation of inauthenticity. Ian Jack, the editor of the literary periodical *Granta*, became suspicious when only Kevin Phelan, Kajanë's 'translator', was available to attend a meeting, and although Jack's article on Kajanë's non-existence is rhetorically subtitled, 'But Does It Really Matter?', it seems that the answer is yes: the collected stories were never published by Granta. Thus, by the time the collection *Winter in Tiranë* appeared, issued by the online imprint Fiction Attic, Kajanë's invented nature was no longer secret, and the blurb presents a description of the book that makes metafiction out of the overlap between extra-textual and diegetic concerns, while also making clear the stories' origin in the contemporary politics of witnessing the overthrow of tyranny:

> Set against the final days of the Albanian empire . . . *Winter in Tiranë* is an exploration of the meaning of identity, the power of suggestion, and the complex relationship between a story and its creator.[32]

Such categories as 'identity', 'power of suggestion' and 'creator' refer at once to the pressures of life in a totalitarian regime, and to the relationship between constructed author and implied reader. The metafictional effect here is akin to that of revealing Yasusada's non-existence: the political meaning of the writing becomes broader both geographically and historically. Throughout *Winter in Tiranë*, the narrator's graduation from his job as Deputy Minister of Symbols to that of Slogans, although a promised promotion to Information never takes place, has a clearly symbolic force, acting not just to a metafictional but also to a meta-deceptive effect in the wake of Kajanë's exposure. Jack describes his high regard for the Kajanë stories that were submitted to the literary journal *Granta* in terms of their 'laconic strangeness', a phrase which acknowledges the overlap of form and content in its combination of geographical distance with literary 'estrangement'. Jack's description of the 'new and mysterious' nature of the narrator's 'voice' conflates the mystery of 'remote' Albania with that of the work's construction.[33] However, the text's background of Albanian life and history exists, paradoxically, to domesticate its narrator, once more, it could be argued, to political effect: distance does not necessarily entail difference. The narrator is presented as irreducibly foreign, living in a former eastern bloc country complete with 'dingy' apartments and 'faded concrete buildings' (31), shadowy threats, travel restrictions, nepotistic appointments, poor television reception, inhospitable weather, in order that he can be shown to be surprisingly familiar, undergoing marital regret, social embarrassment, schemes for betterment which never work out, and a 'daily dread' (177) of the office.

By contrast with Kajanë's, Phelan and U'Ren's writing has had less than modest success on its own account, just as the poetry Kent Johnson published under his own name has been overlooked in comparison to Yasusada's. As Jack puts it, for Kajanë's creators, 'Albania changed everything',[34] giving a more overtly politicised new element to their own stories, in which North American protagonists undergo social mishaps at home, or travel in order to encounter other cultures. In opposition to this perspective on foreign destinations from the limited viewpoint of tourists, events are represented from the inside in Kajanë's stories. Yet, in the wake of the revelation of Kajanë's non-existence, the political significance lies, by a kind of double bluff, in the fact that the perspective remained a North American construction. Such a shift inwards is apparent in the movement between focalisers: in the story 'Turn-Down Service', published under Phelan's own name,[35] the narrator travels to an unnamed country in the throes of civil unrest and journeys by bus to the sniper-beset 'Boulevard of Heroes', perhaps an equivalent to Tiranë's Boulevard of National Martyrs. He views the nameless country from the distance of a bus window and does not reach his destination within the story. In *Winter in Tiranë*, a small change in perspective from that of an American to an Albanian focaliser makes a crucial difference. In 'Believe Me!', the narrator sees the reflection of his friend Altin Leka, a former party official, in the 'tinted window' of one of the locked and empty buses parked on Skanderbeg Square, whose drivers are taking part in the 'celebrations' (124–5): being situated outside the bus on this occasion reveals the narrator's insider status. Later, the narrator travels to Vlorë, 'famous for being the first city to riot, the first to reject Berisha and the pyramid schemes' (208), the bus journey again suggesting not the remoteness of a tourist perspective, but a citizen's view from within of the events of 1997, a time when protests at corrupt investment brought Sali Berisha's presidency to an end. Yet such an impression of an insider viewpoint is of course only that. The narrator of *Winter in Tiranë* is diegetically and metafictionally at a distance from the events he recounts, in mediating them for an equally distant readership. The fact that he does not take part in the riots or 'celebrations' himself may be best accounted for in terms of his construction by the American alumni of a creative writing course, as much as in relation to the fictive factors of his cautious temperament and government job.

Winter in Tiranë's Albanian setting was crucial, as Jack argues, in offering something 'darker' to Phelan and U'Ren's penchant for a 'playful' style out of step with the late-1990s interest in 'trailer-park realism'. Indeed, elements of setting and style are blended in Kajanë's writing in a way that lends it an impression of truthful immediacy. The nameless, naïve protagonist relates his stories in the present tense and begins them *in media res*, as in the opening to 'Wake Up, It's Time to Go to Sleep!': 'Sometime after the power returned and the water began rumbling through the pipes, my young friend Leni arrived, still dressed in his cook's uniform' (36). This conjunction of direct address with the representation of communist privation offers an aura of authenticity. Such an impression is replaced, however, in the three final stories of *Winter in Tiranë* which have not been published elsewhere. These late stories, written in the wake of Kajanë's exposure as a non-existent author, are notable for their metafictional and meta-deceptive leanings; as a corollary, they are the most surreal and impish of the collection, showing that not having to maintain a convincing façade released the authors from the constraint of representing Albania naturalistically, and Kajanë's fictional nature could be made a part of the plot. Yet that plot implies a questioning of an outsider view of apparently distant cataclysmic events. In earlier stories, totalitarian parody and metafiction share the same details, for instance in 'Believe Me!', where the narrator's obliviousness to the planning of a contract murder also operates to warn the reader of a different kind of concealed reality, that of the story's non-existent author.[36] In the three previously unpublished stories, the creation of fictions takes the form of a plot device. The most extreme example of such self-reflexiveness occurs in the story 'Weights and Measures', in which reference to its own fraudulence provides the grounds for a fictional narrative of Ian Jack's real-life encounter with Kevin Phelan. In this overdetermined, surreal version, the British publisher Ian James visits Tiranë in order to meet the non-existent Bhanuprasad Armritraj, professor of Indian literature at the University of Tiranë and editor of a bestselling anthology of Indian writing, as well as to collect Albanian stories for another anthology.[37] James, unflatteringly described as looking as if he is a slave to 'ale and heavy desserts' (151), is the editor of the 'intellectual quarterly' *Der Trüben Fluss*, the 'foggy river', a version of the equally fluvially named *Granta*. While the narrator pretends to be Armritraj, succeeding in his role 'because [James] wants to be fooled', according to Leni (152), the man who calls himself 'Ian James' is in fact his younger brother Roderick Newton James, to whom Leni presents a collection of Albanian stories allegedly by various hands but all composed by him.

Leni's first attempt at creating this collection meets with James' disapproval:

> they're not very Albanian, if you know what I mean. Love and relationships and family concerns, these are all fine, but where is the political strife, the tales of the zealous underground resistance, the humanity in the face of the oppressive dictatorship? (159)

In a species of *mise-en-abîme*, this is an apt characterisation of the very collection in which this estimate occurs. *Winter in Tiranë* not only satirises but enacts the notion that, despite James' remark, war-writing must also be life-writing in order to be successful. The very setting of this Cold War dictatorship makes the reader wish to know more about the fiction's protagonist, as if public concerns inevitably provoke private interest. Yet the satire itself unexpectedly arises from a real-life misrecognition of these historical events, making the reader look both ways: at the apparently ludicrous errors on the part of Ian James, and back at their own fictive and historical interpretive agency.

In 'Weights and Measures', Leni rewrites all the stories that had disappointed Ian James, and weighs the result on the scales that the narrator is repairing on his behalf:

> 'I have assembled nearly three hundred grams of Albanian fiction!' he shouts towards the kitchen.
>
> 'That's quite impressive', I say. 'You have nearly doubled the entire canon!' (161)

As part of a strategy of including verdicts on the text as part of the fiction, this exchange presents both a literal commodification, since the stories are weighed rather than weighed up, and the narrator's apparent awareness of the fictional form in which he appears. His claim that Leni has 'doubled' the Albanian canon paraphrases a widely quoted *Time Out* review of Kajanë's contribution to *The Killing Spirit* that described the author as 'Albania's second greatest living writer', that is, after the prize-winning Ismail Kadare.[38] The narrator's remark also casts a sideways glance at negative comments on the Kajanë fraud in relation to 'Anglo-American literary provincialism', lack of genuine translations from Albanian, and western ignorance of Albania's 'ancient [literary] tradition'.[39] Like his and the narrator's impersonation of respondents to hotel customer questionnaires, Leni's rewritten stories attempt to pre-empt their reception, as he explains:

> I merely took the information that Ian had given me, and I mixed it up and gave it back to him. I asked him to describe Albania, and these stories are what he said. (164)

Winter in Tiranë both satirises and draws upon such a sentiment, one that provoked dismay in Jack's critics for its suggestion that only the 'stimulant' of 'other people's oppression' can make native literatures interesting to an English-speaking readership.[40] In 'Weights and Measures', Ian James recalls the final collapse of Albania's ruling communist regime when he looks out at Skanderbeg Square from the steps of the Palace of Culture, and pronounces:

> It is all so familiar: the statue, the palace, the mosque. I recognize it all. Positively CNN, 1991 . . . Of course I could be wrong. Perhaps I am thinking of Prague and the Velvet Rebellion. Another city, another square. (156)

The reaction of the narrator, in his guise as Professor Amritraj, is to 'nod and stroke my false beard for effect'. Such comic undercutting has a complex effect as part of the stories' response to their own gradual revelation as deceptions, implying that post-Cold War confusions on the part of critics and readers, in which different cities' 'signifiers fade into one another',[41] may blind them to such obvious falsity as that of the narrator's glued-on beard. James' elision of the difference between medium and message – 'Positively CNN, 1991' – is a detail that resounds self-consciously with the discourse of Jean Baudrillard's notion of simulation, itself first introduced in 1991 in an article on the Gulf War. Baudrillard's comment that 'we are no longer in a logic of the passage from virtual to actual but in a hyperrealist logic of the deterrence of the real by the virtual' describes modes of knowing about war, which include CNN's 'invention' of the event by placing 'information' and 'artificial commentary' above it,[42] leading to the kind of substitution of one event for another that Ian James' remark betrays. Baudrillard's argument also offers a way of viewing the construction of *Winter in Tiranë* itself, drawing historical and literary meaning intricately together. The collection is a 'virtual' work which offers a linguistic simulacrum of an Albanian translation, conceived to benefit from its readership's receptiveness to such a mediated representation. There is no Albanian original in relation to the text or its author, nor in terms of experience or research conducted by those responsible. It might seem that the Albanian backdrop provokes interest in the narrator's life and his ways of responding to Hoxha's dictatorship, but in fact it is the other way round: the ironic effect of such a naïve and limited voice gains by means of its extreme setting. The authors produced an effective simulacrum of Albania in the main by drawing on proper names and oblique historical references in the service of scenes from the life of an unremarkable man, the recognisability of which substituted for a specific narrative of 'political strife', but allows the reader to reflect on such circumstances more widely. While Phelan had visited Albania twice in the 1980s, U'Ren had never been there; the narrator in 'Weights and Measures' is reassured to think that Ian James 'didn't have a tourist-oriented guidebook that would contradict' his and Leni's construction of the invented Albanian stories, 'because none exist' (153). Thus, we learn from the fictional text that falsification is likely to go undetected, and gain insight into the reasons why.

Conclusion

In both the cases of authorial invention explored in this article, an invented, exotic biography of wartime and post-war experience represents not just the construction of an imaginary writer, but the context in which that writer's work is received. While Yasusada's poems have provoked literary controversy, this has been less apparent in the reception of Kajanë's imposture, in part because his work falls within a prose fiction genre that is 'licensed to impersonate'.[43] In both instances, what seemed to be the newly discovered and translated writing by marginal, historically victimised figures, turned out instead to cast an uncomfortably ironic light back on the reader. In each case, being caught out in a literary sense entails a realisation on the reader's part of the danger of not being equally attentive to historical enormity.

When they are reread in the knowledge of their authors' non-existence, many elements of both *Doubled Flowering* and *Winter in Tiranë* are transformed from constituting the tropes of witness into self-consciously literary devices. Such a transformation provokes the reader to question where their attention to the real should be directed. While this transformation takes place in Kajanë's *Winter in Tiranë* in the parodic manner of incorporating the drama of exposure into the stories' plots, in Yasusada's *Doubled Flowering* the process occurs the other way round: what appeared to be the details of historical tragedy turns out to be signifiers of 'the death of the author'. This is the case, for instance, in relation to the frequent references to Yasusada's papers existing in the form of carbon copies, a detail which is a necessary fiction to account for the preservation of letters that he wrote to others. Furthermore, 'carbon paper' itself may appear to be a material figure for writing that draws on the carbonised remains of the atomic bomb's firestorms, a detail that comes uneasily into metaphorical being only when 'Yasusada' is known not to be survivor of Hiroshima and the carbons themselves revealed as inventions. The carbon signature – visible for instance in the copy of Yasusada's letter to Ogiwara Seisensui that is reproduced in *Doubled Flowering*[44] – invokes Derrida's argument, quoted by Kent Johnson,[45] that the very presence of a signature substitutes for the author who is necessarily absent. Both cases have multiple literary as well as political effects, through satirising the marketing and reception of life-writing as war-writing while benefiting from this very confusion. Yet this is not just a cynical or self-serving stunt, since the very accessibility of the viewpoint in Yasusada's and Kajanë's writing reveals the proximity of the events themselves to current affairs.

While Johnson has taken refuge in the heteronymic defence of ascribing the actual authorship of Yasusada's writing to someone else, the recently deceased Tosa Motokiyu, itself allegedly a pseudonym for an unnamed American author, Phelan and U'Ren have included their own names with that of Jiri Kajanë's on the front page of *Winter in Tiranë*, implying that less is at stake in this invention historically and aesthetically. The latter collection seems to be more of a recontextualising of its real authors' 'playful' aesthetic than the exploration of identity, nationality or ethical witness that characterises *Doubled Flowering*. Yet both texts are concerned with the apprehension of other cultures and the contemporary reception of extreme historical events such as the fall of communism in Albania and the bombing of Hiroshima, and, precisely in order to enable such an apprehension, of that reception's aesthetic construction.

University of Sheffield

Disclosure statement

No potential conflict of interest was reported by the author.

Notes

1 See for instance Lucy Dawidowicz's view that testimony may be 'more hazard than help' to the historian, quoted in Annette Wieviorka, *The Era of the Witness* (Ithaca, NY: Cornell University Press, 2006), p. xiii.

2 See respectively Dori Laub, 'Bearing Witness, or the Vicissitudes of Listening', in Dori Laub and Shoshana Felman (eds.), *Testimony: Crises of Witnessing in Literature, Psychoanalysis, and History* (London: Routledge, 1992), pp. 59–63, and Mark Roseman, 'Surviving Memory: Truth and Inaccuracy in Holocaust Memory', *Holocaust Studies*, 8.1 (1999), pp. 1–20.

3 Greg Glazner and Jon Davis, 'Bring Back Excellence', *Boston Review*, 22. 3–4 (1997), pp. 35–6: 35.

4 See for instance Carolyn Forché and Duncan Wu, eds., *Poetry of Witness: The Tradition in English, 1500–2001* (New York: Norton, 2014).

5 Antony Rowland, *Poetry as Testimony: Witnessing and Memory in Twentieth-Century Poems* (London: Routledge, 2014), p. 1.

6 Araki Yasusada, 'Doubled Flowering: From the Notebooks of Araki Yasusada', *American Poetry Review*, 25.4 (1996), pp. 23–6; Jiri Kajanë, Kevin Phelan, and Bill U'Ren, *Winter in Tiranë: The Stories of Jiri Kajanë* (Burlingame, CA: Fiction Attic Press, 2010), online publication, unnumbered pages (ii). All page references in the text, following my numbering.

7 Philippe Lejeune, *On Autobiography* (Minneapolis: University of Minnesota Press, 1989).

8 John Bradley, ed., *Atomic Ghost: Poets Respond to the Nuclear Age* (Minneapolis: Coffee House Press, 1995); Araki Yasusada, *Doubled Flowering: From the Notebooks of Araki Yasusada*, ed. and trans. Tosa Motokiyu, Ojiu Norinaga, and Okura Kyojin (New York: Roof, 1997), all page references in the text.

9 Kent Johnson, 'From the Daybook of Ogiwara Miyamora', *Ironwood*, 10 (1987), pp. 187–91.

10 Araki Yasusada, 'Hiroshima Poems', *Stand*, 37.3 (1996), pp. 4–11.

11 Marjorie Perloff, 'In Search of the Authentic Other: The Poetry of Araki Yasusada', in Bill Freind (ed.), *Scubadivers and Chrysanthemums: Essays on the Poetry of Araki Yasusada* (Exeter: Shearsman, 2012 [1997]), p. 166.

12 See Roland Barthes, 'The Death of the Author', in *Image-Music-Text*, trans. Stephen Heath (London: HarperCollins, 1977 [1967]), pp. 142–8; Michel Foucault, 'What is an Author?', trans. Donald F. Bouchard and Sherry Simon, in Donald F. Bouchard (ed.), *Language, Counter-Memory, Practice: Selected Essays and Interviews* (Ithaca, NY: Cornell University Press, 1977), pp. 113–38.

13 Jorge Luis Borges, 'Pierre Menard, Author of *Don Quixote*', trans. Anthony Bonner, *Ficciones* (New York: Grove Press, 1962), pp. 45–56.

14 David Wojahn, 'Illegible Due to Blotching: Poetic Authenticity and Its Discontents', in Bill Freind (ed.), *Scubadivers and Chrysanthemums: Essays on the Poetry of Araki Yasusada* (Exeter: Shearsman, 2012 [1997]), p. 300.

15 Ibid., pp. 306, 301.

16 Kent Johnson, 'Some Thoughts on Araki Yasusada the Author', in Bill Freind (ed.), *Scubadivers and Chrysanthemums: Essays on the Poetry of Araki Yasusada* (Exeter: Shearsman, 2012 [1997]), p. 80. The impulse behind other instances of constructed authorship, including that of John Bayley and Leon Carmen's invention of the Aboriginal novelist Wanda Koolmatrie, and Tim Barrus' of the Native American writer Nasdijj, was stated by the perpetrators to be just such a sense of lost entitlement and even, in the former case, a wish to expose its operations.

17 The necessity of a fictional persona for the real author to write at all has been cited in defence of other examples of authorial deception, including Laura Albert's creation of the novelist J. T. LeRoy.

18 Borges, 'Pierre Menard', pp. 50, 53.
19 Perloff, 'In Search of the Authentic Other', p. 28.
20 Johnson, 'Some Thoughts on Araki Yasusada the Author', p. 81.
21 Such a pun is evident in the name of the computer games company 'Trilobyte', whose logo consists of the familiar exoskeletal shape of the trilobite, and whose advertising tagline is 'Quality since 600,000,000 BC': the era of the eponymous arthropod's flourishing. http://www.trilobytegames.com/index.html [Date accessed: 1 July 2015].
22 Hosea Hirata, 'Letter to Araki Yasusada', in Bill Freind (ed.), *Scubadivers and Chrysanthemums: Essays on the Poetry of Araki Yasusada* (Exeter: Shearsman, 2012 [1997]), p. 314.
23 This fictive figure's name seems to be drawn from that of two Japanese poets, both influenced by western culture, including the pre-war writer Sakutarō Hagiwara who had interests in western philosophy, but died young of pneumonia in 1942; and Yoshiro Ishihara, a Christian convert and student of German and Russian whose poetry was inspired by his experiences as a prisoner-of-war in Siberia.
24 Natalie Angier, 'Once They Ruled the World', *New York Times* (7 March 2014), p. D1.
25 For instance, 'Loon and Dome' features the poem's speaker and his wife Nomura strolling through the 'plaster chambers/of the giant Model of the Heart' in Hiroshima's Industrial Promotion Hall, an image which Wojahn identifies as drawn from the model heart in Chicago's Museum of Science and Industry ('Illegible Due to Blotching', p. 303).
26 Eric Hayot, 'The Strange Case of Araki Yasusada: Author, Object', in Bill Freind (ed.), *Scubadivers and Chrysanthemums: Essays on the Poetry of Araki Yasusada* (Exeter: Shearsman, 2012 [1997]), p. 192.
27 Paisley Rekdal, 'Doubled Flowering: Charles Yu, Araki Yasusada and the Politics of Faking Race', in Bill Freind (ed.), *Scubadivers and Chrysanthemums: Essays on the Poetry of Araki Yasusada* (Exeter: Shearsman, 2012 [1997]), p. 113.
28 Karel Reisz in interview with Harlan Kennedy, referring to the film version of *The French Lieutenant's Woman* (dir. Karel Reisz 1981), 'The Czech Director's Woman', *Film Comment* (September/October 1981), pp. 26–31.
29 See Adelene Buckland, 'Thomas Hardy, Provincial Geology and the Material Imagination', *Interdisciplinary Studies in the Long Nineteenth Century*, 6 (2008). http://www.19.bbk.ac.uk/index.php/19/article/view/469 [Date accessed: 11 July 2015].
30 Araki Yasusada, *Joyous Young Pines: Haiku by Araki Yasusada* (LaCrosse: Juniper Press, 1995); Tosa Motokiyu, *Also, With My Throat, I Shall Swallow Ten Thousand Swords: Araki Yasusada's Letters in English* (New York: Combo Books, 2005).
31 Jiri Kajanë, 'The Same, Only Different!', in Jay Hopler (ed.), *The Killing Spirit: An Anthology of Assassins* (Edinburgh: Canongate, 1996; New York: Overlook Press, 1998), pp. 104–25. The story had previously appeared in the *Minnesota Review*, 44/45 (1995). Hopler is an alumnus of the same

Johns Hopkins creative writing course as Phelan and U'Ren, and it is likely he knew that they were the story's authors.

32 Fiction Attic Press. http://fictionattic.com/our-titles [Date accessed: 7 December 2014].

33 Ian Jack, 'Albania's "Second-Greatest Living Writer" Was a Hoax, But Does it Really Matter?', *Guardian* (17 June 2011). http://www.theguardian.com/commentisfree/2011/jun/17/ian-jack-jiri-kajane-albanian-hoax [Date accessed: 7 July 2015].

34 Ibid.

35 Kevin Phelan, 'Turn-Down Service', *Fiction Attic Press* (8 May 2005).

36 This is a renamed version of the story 'The Same, Only Different!' *The Killing Spirit*, ed. Hopler; some clear hints to the reader about the scenario that the narrator is failing to understand have been removed from the later version in *Winter in Tiranë.*

37 The choice of Indian literature appears to be motivated not only by its relevance to orientalizing impulses, but also by Ian Jack's journalistic writings on India, collected in his book *Mofussil Junction: Indian Encounters 1977–2011* (London: Penguin, 2013).

38 Jack, 'Albania's "Second Greatest Living Writer" Was a Hoax'.

39 Literalab, 'The Non-Assassination of Jiri Kajanë', *Central European Literary Life*. http://literalab.com/2011/06/21/6758394115 [Date accessed: 5 July 2015].

40 Ibid. See also an interview with Ismail Kadare in which he rejects the legitimacy of likening the Czech to the Albanian communist regime: Shusha Guppy, 'The Art of Fiction no. 153', *Paris Review* 147 (Summer 1998).

41 Paul Patton, 'Introduction', in Jean Baudrillard (ed.), *The Gulf War Did Not Take Place*, trans. Paul Patton (Bloomington: Indiana University Press, 1995 [1991]), p. 2.

42 Baudrillard, *The Gulf War Did Not Take Place*, pp. 27, 48.

43 Brian McHale, 'A Poet May Not Exist', p. 235. Linda Swanson-Davies of *Glimmer Train* claims that 'It was a surprise – though somehow not a shock – to find out, years later, that there was no such person' as Kajanë, and adds that, 'We didn't regret the publication' (personal communication).

44 Yasusada, *Doubled Flowering*, p. 50.

45 Interview between Thomas Swan and Kent Johnson, in Martin Corless-Smith, 'Three Dialogues Between Real and Imaginary Poets', in Bill Freind (ed.), *Scubadivers and Chrysanthemums: Essays on the Poetry of Araki Yasusada* (Exeter: Shearsman, 2012 [1997]), pp. 226–7.

Index

Note: Boldface page numbers refer to figures.